Garfield
Brings Home the Bacon

BY JIM DAVIS

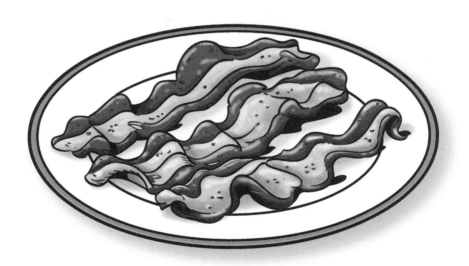

Ballantine Books • **New York**

A Ballantine Books Trade Paperback Original

Published in the United States by Ballantine Books, an imprint of The Random House Publishing Group, a division of Random House, Inc., New York.

BALLANTINE and colophon are registered trademarks of Random House, Inc.

ISBN 978-0-345-52586-4

Printed in the United States of America

www.ballantinebooks.com

9 8 7 6 5 4 3 2 1

NUTS ABOUT WORK

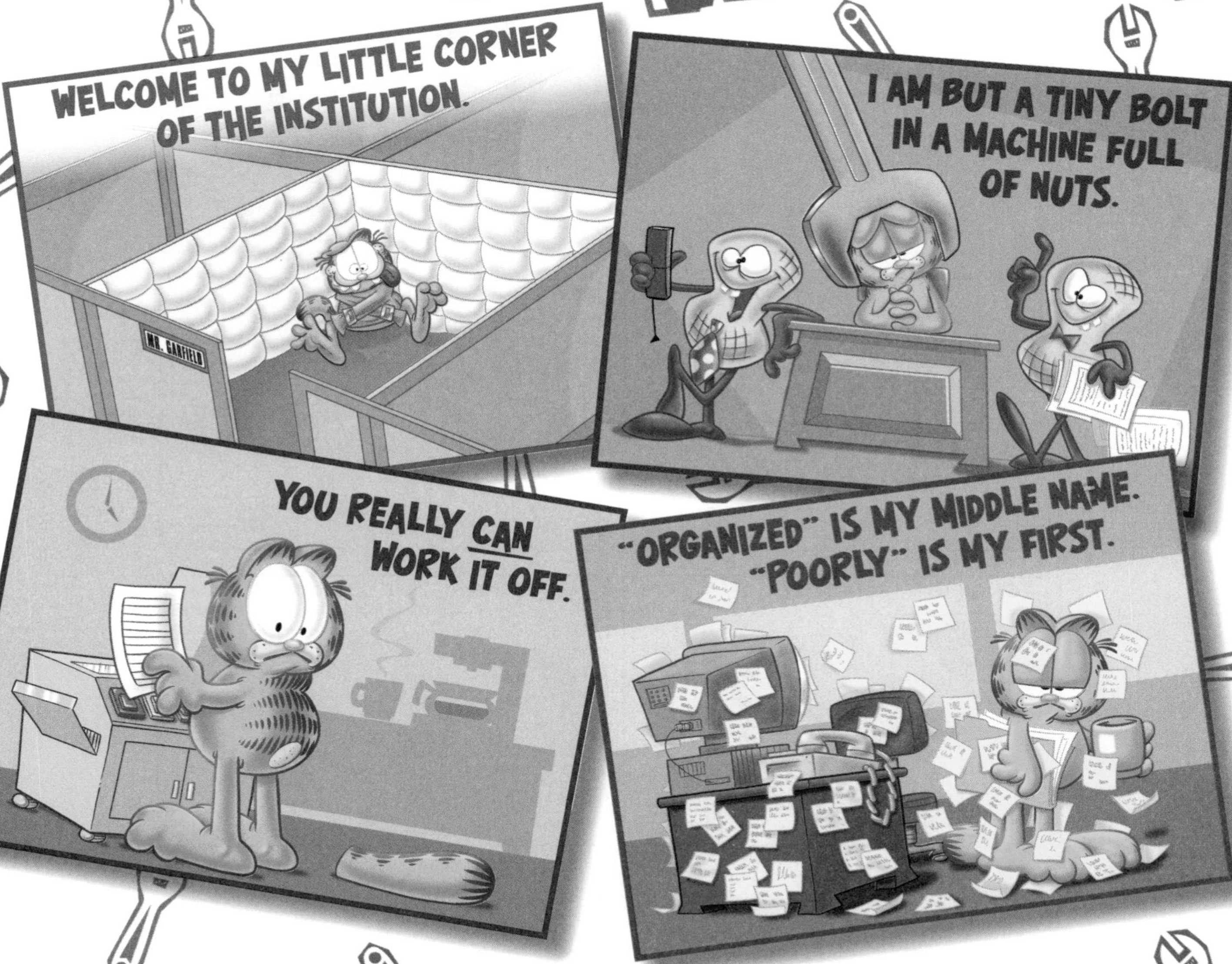

WELCOME TO MY LITTLE CORNER OF THE INSTITUTION.
MR. GARFIELD
I AM BUT A TINY BOLT IN A MACHINE FULL OF NUTS.
YOU REALLY CAN WORK IT OFF.
"ORGANIZED" IS MY MIDDLE NAME. "POORLY" IS MY FIRST.

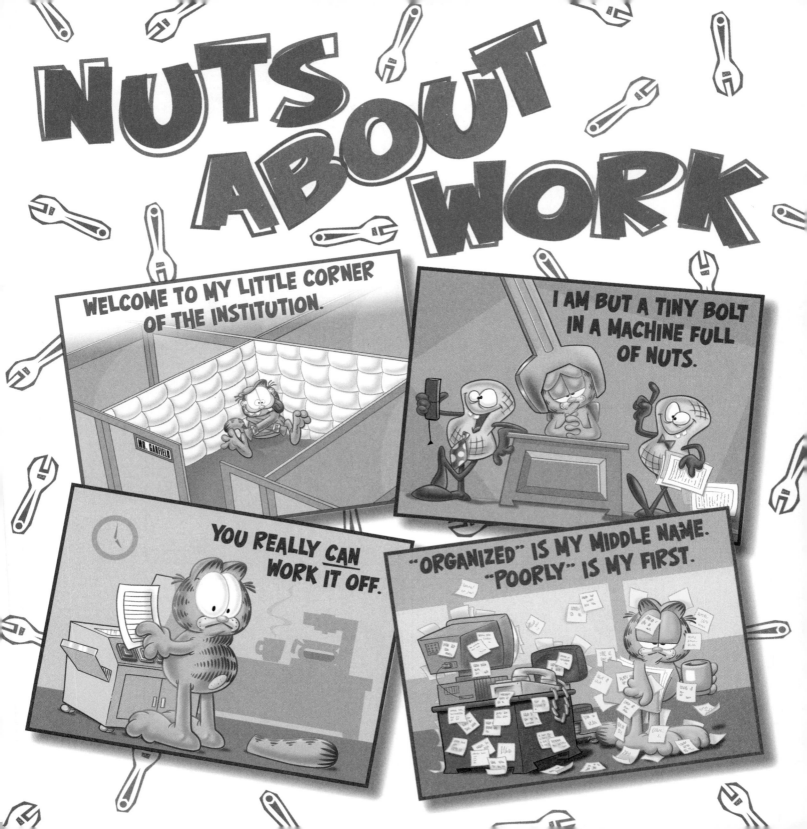

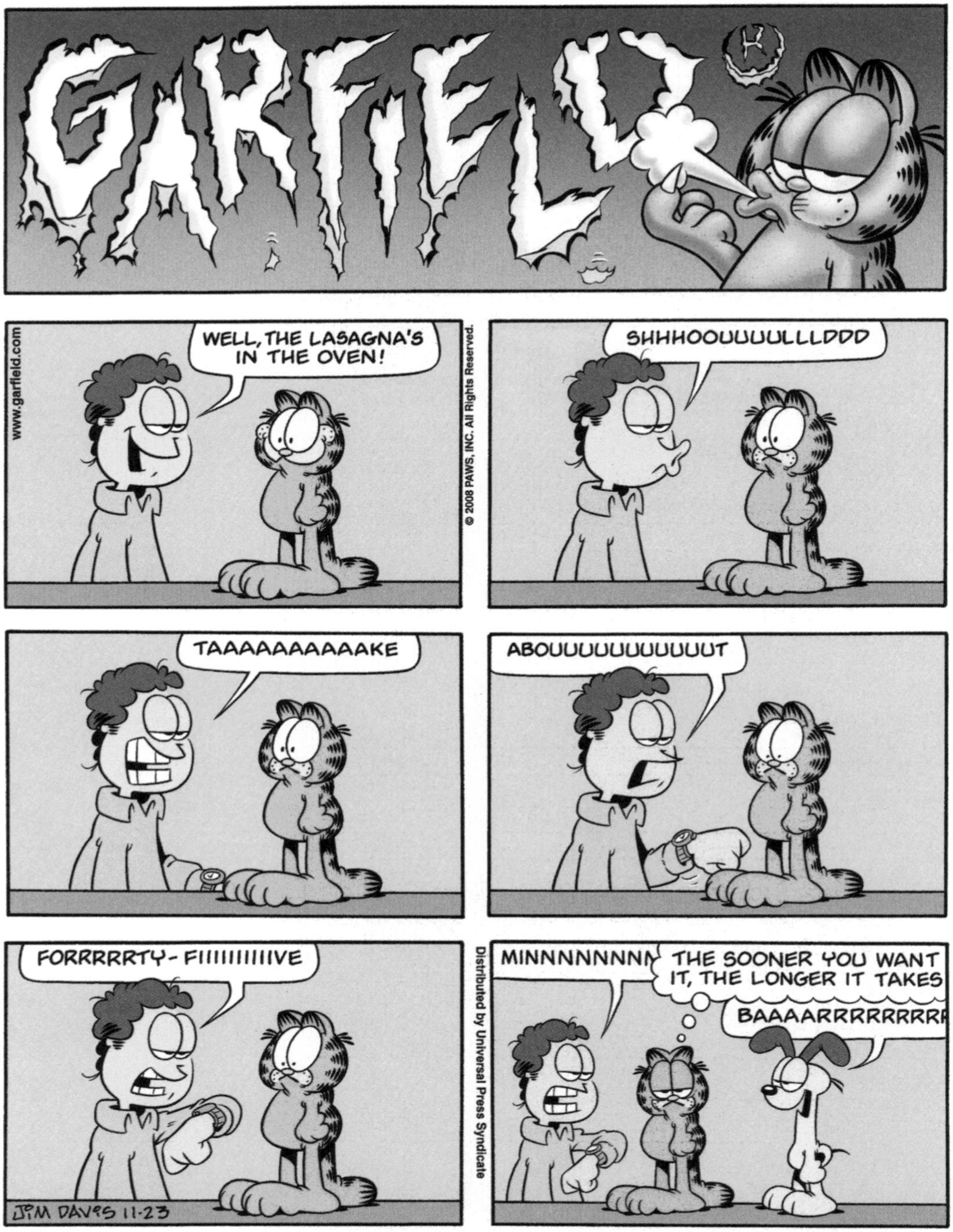

GARFIELD
www.garfield.com
WELL, THE LASAGNA'S IN THE OVEN!
© 2008 PAWS, INC. All Rights Reserved.
SHHHOOUUUUULLLDDD
TAAAAAAAAAAKE
ABOUUUUUUUUUUUT
FORRRRRTY- FIIIIIIIIIIVE
JIM DAVIS 11-23
Distributed by Universal Press Syndicate
MINNNNNNNN
THE SOONER YOU WANT IT, THE LONGER IT TAKES
BAAAARRRRRRRR

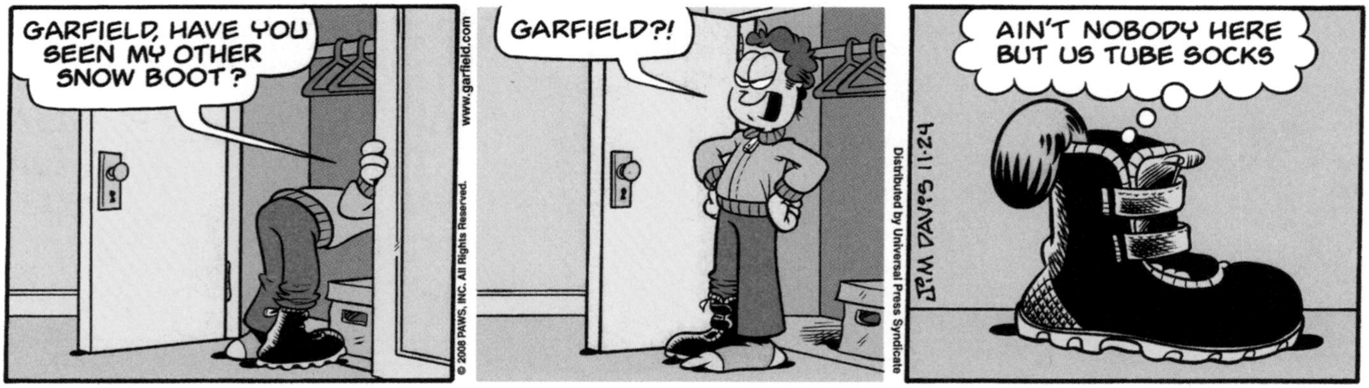
GARFIELD, HAVE YOU SEEN MY OTHER SNOW BOOT?
© 2008 PAWS, INC. All Rights Reserved.
www.garfield.com
GARFIELD?!
Distributed by Universal Press Syndicate
AIN'T NOBODY HERE BUT US TUBE SOCKS
JIM DAVIS 11-24

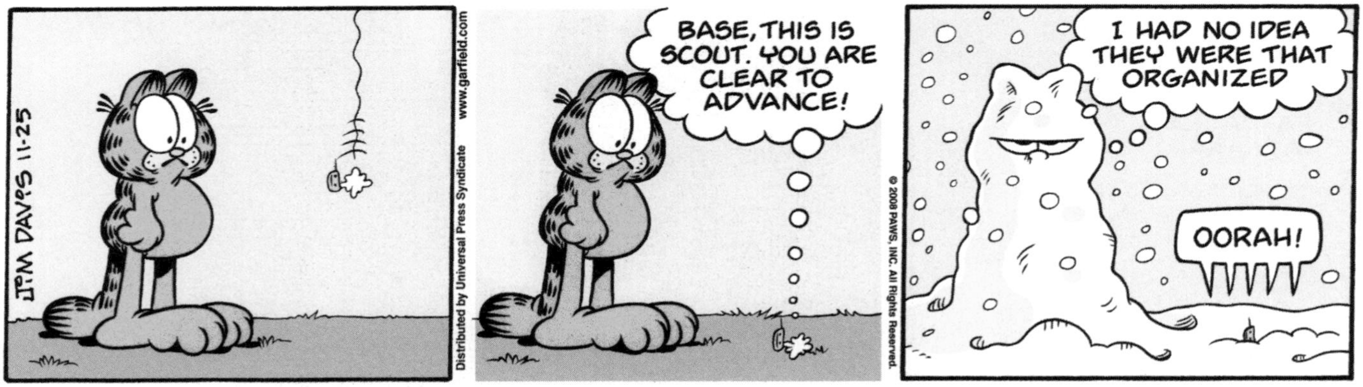
JIM DAVIS 11-25
Distributed by Universal Press Syndicate
www.garfield.com
BASE, THIS IS SCOUT. YOU ARE CLEAR TO ADVANCE!
© 2008 PAWS, INC. All Rights Reserved.
I HAD NO IDEA THEY WERE THAT ORGANIZED
OORAH!

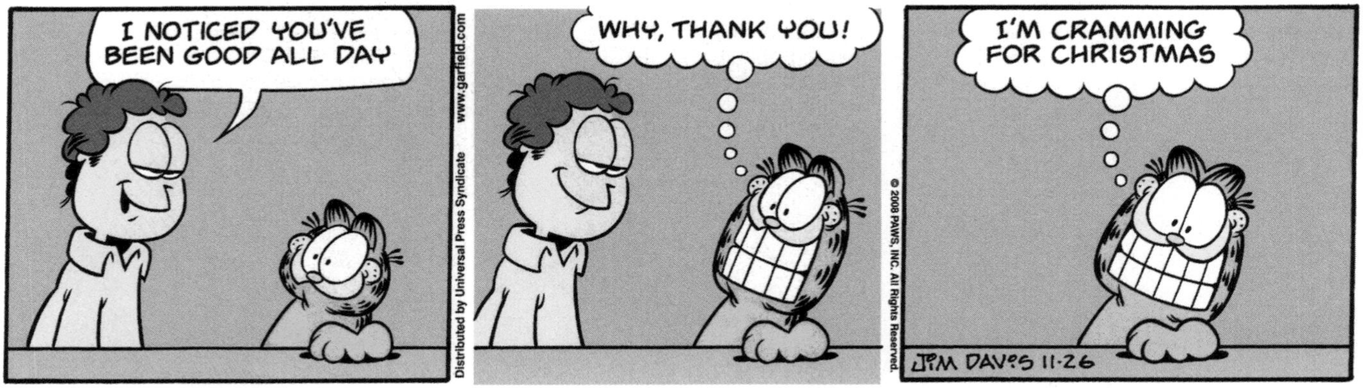
I NOTICED YOU'VE BEEN GOOD ALL DAY
Distributed by Universal Press Syndicate
www.garfield.com
WHY, THANK YOU!
© 2008 PAWS, INC. All Rights Reserved.
I'M CRAMMING FOR CHRISTMAS
JIM DAVIS 11-26

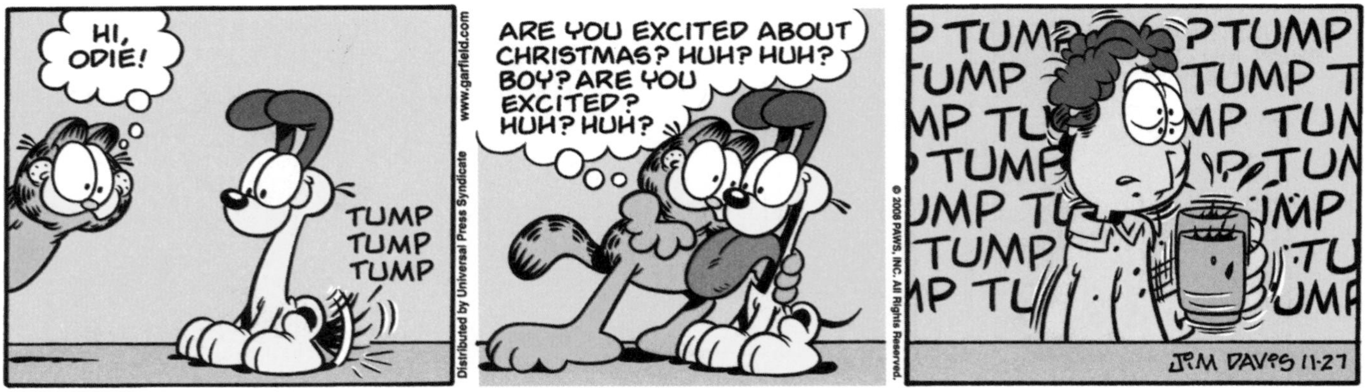
HI, ODIE!
TUMP TUMP TUMP
ARE YOU EXCITED ABOUT CHRISTMAS? HUH? HUH? BOY? ARE YOU EXCITED? HUH? HUH?
TUMP TUMP TUMP TUMP
JIM DAVIS 11-27
www.garfield.com Distributed by Universal Press Syndicate
© 2008 PAWS, INC. All Rights Reserved.

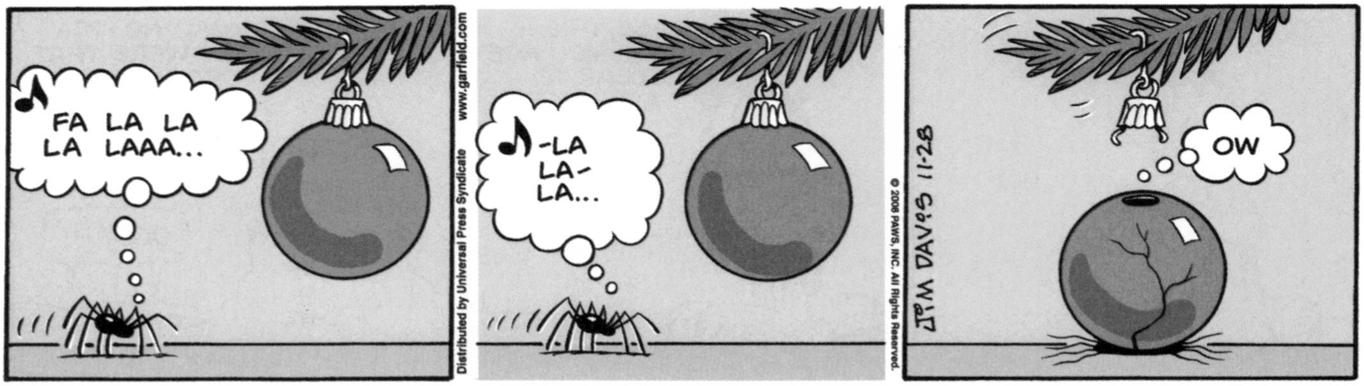
FA LA LA LA LAAA...
-LA LA- LA...
OW
JIM DAVIS 11-28
www.garfield.com Distributed by Universal Press Syndicate
© 2008 PAWS, INC. All Rights Reserved.

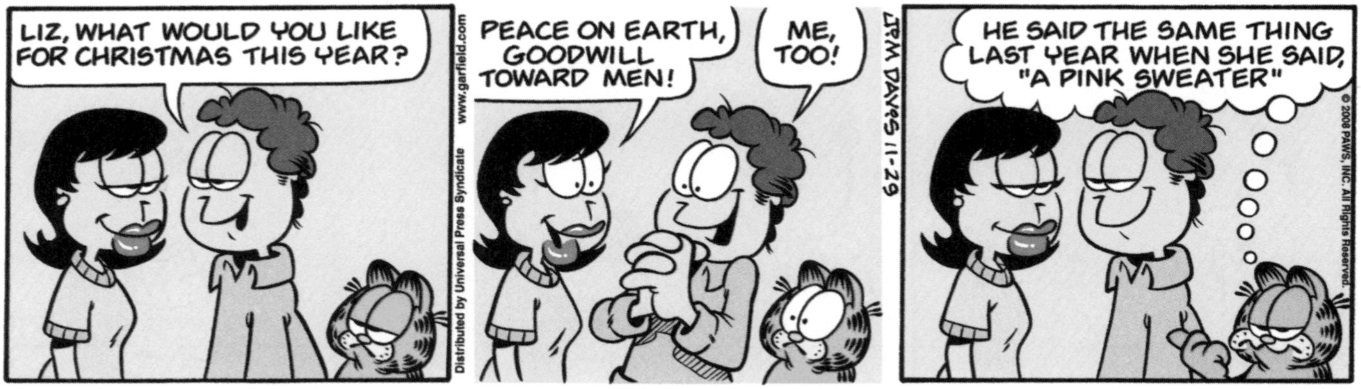
LIZ, WHAT WOULD YOU LIKE FOR CHRISTMAS THIS YEAR?
PEACE ON EARTH, GOODWILL TOWARD MEN!
ME, TOO!
HE SAID THE SAME THING LAST YEAR WHEN SHE SAID, "A PINK SWEATER"
JIM DAVIS 11-29
www.garfield.com Distributed by Universal Press Syndicate
© 2008 PAWS, INC. All Rights Reserved.

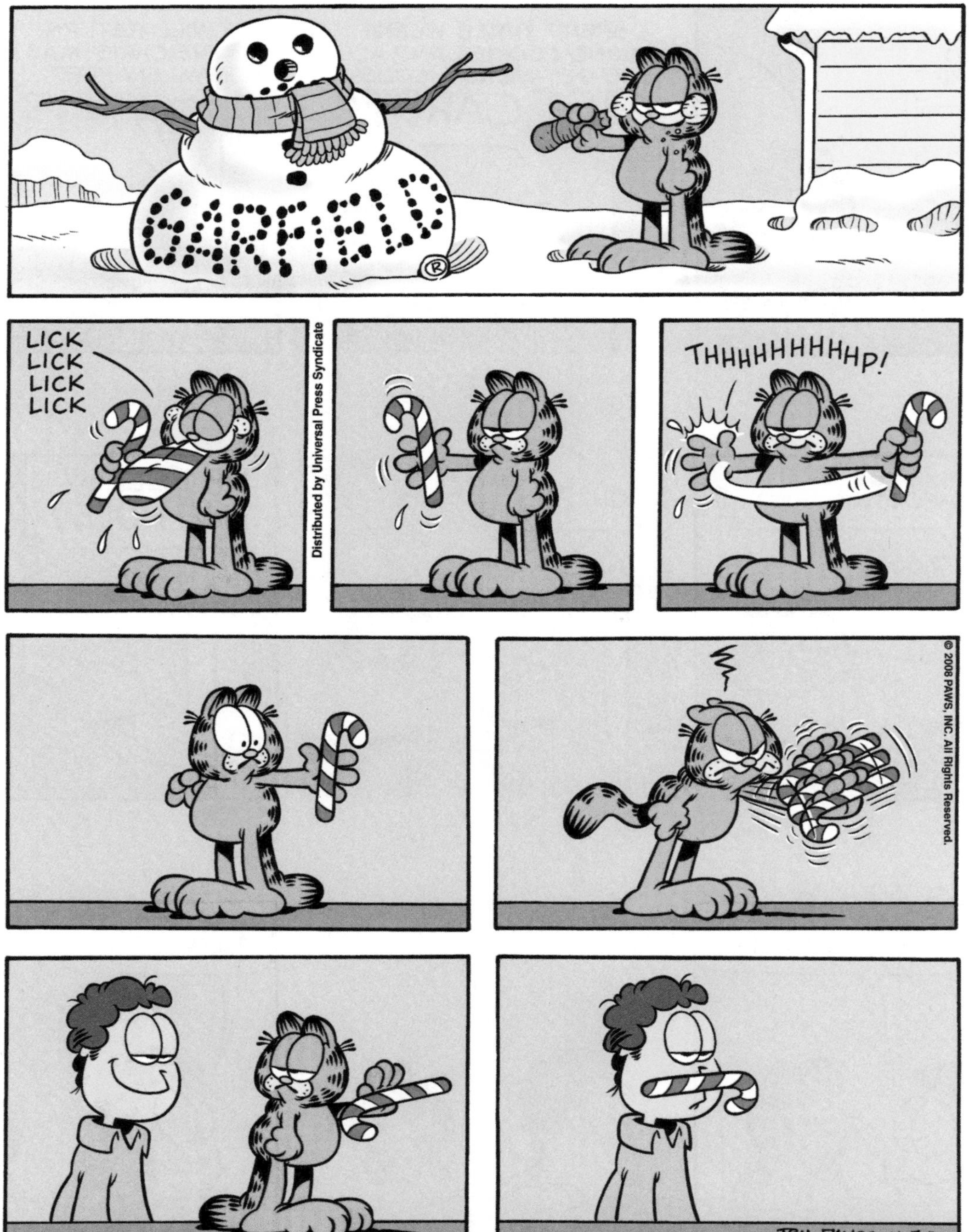
GARFIELD
LICK
LICK
LICK
LICK
Distributed by Universal Press Syndicate
THHHHHHHHHP!
© 2008 PAWS, INC. All Rights Reserved.
JIM DAVIS 11-30

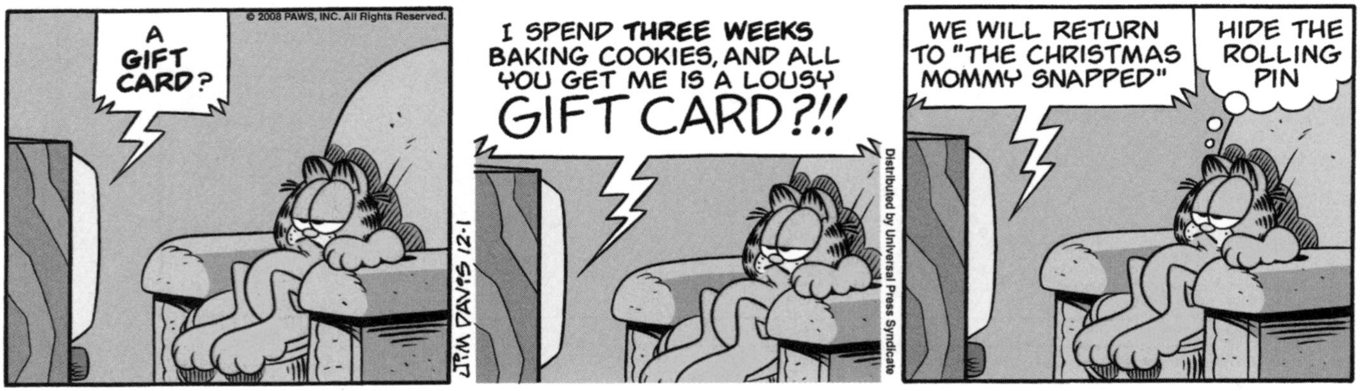
© 2008 PAWS, INC. All Rights Reserved.
A GIFT CARD?
JIM DAVIS 12-1
I SPEND THREE WEEKS BAKING COOKIES, AND ALL YOU GET ME IS A LOUSY GIFT CARD?!!
Distributed by Universal Press Syndicate
WE WILL RETURN TO "THE CHRISTMAS MOMMY SNAPPED"
HIDE THE ROLLING PIN

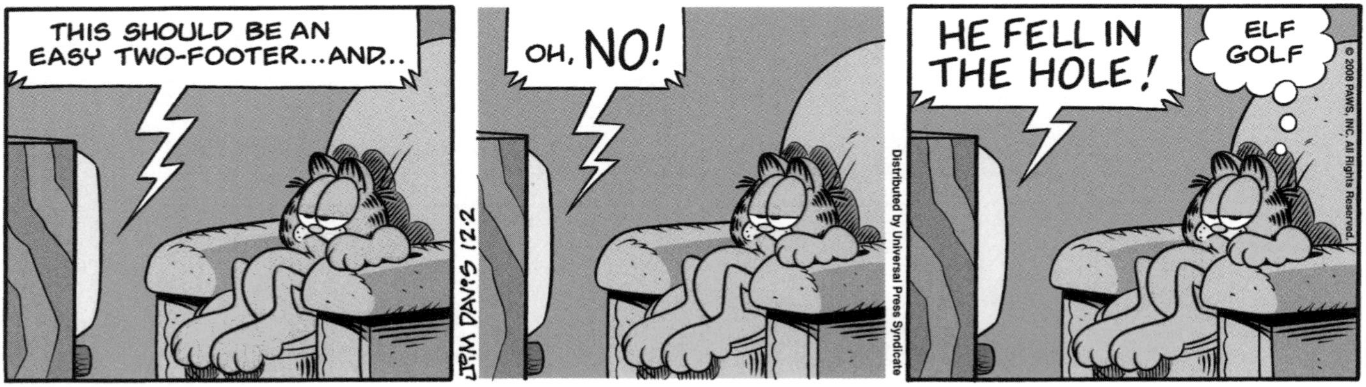
THIS SHOULD BE AN EASY TWO-FOOTER...AND...
JIM DAVIS 12-2
OH, NO!
Distributed by Universal Press Syndicate
HE FELL IN THE HOLE!
ELF GOLF
© 2008 PAWS, INC. All Rights Reserved.

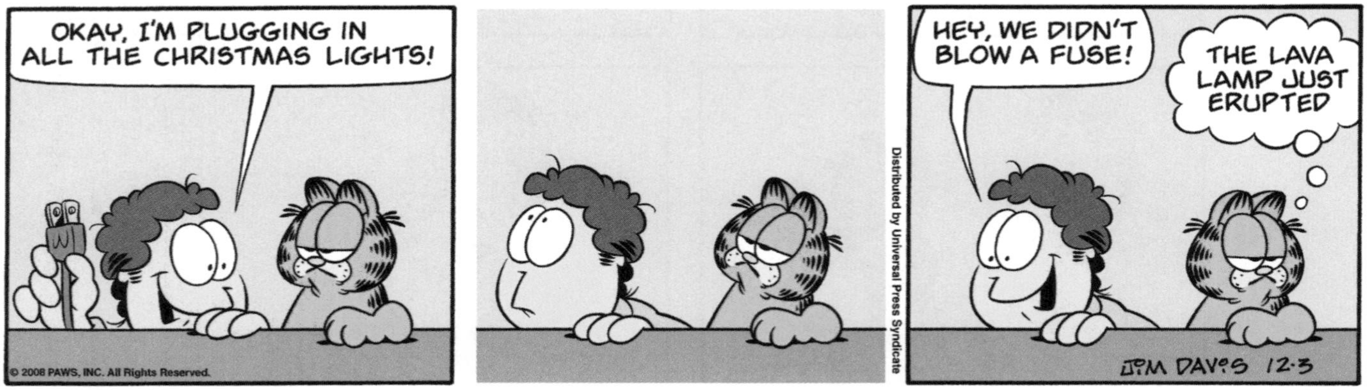
OKAY, I'M PLUGGING IN ALL THE CHRISTMAS LIGHTS!
© 2008 PAWS, INC. All Rights Reserved.
Distributed by Universal Press Syndicate
HEY, WE DIDN'T BLOW A FUSE!
THE LAVA LAMP JUST ERUPTED
JIM DAVIS 12-3

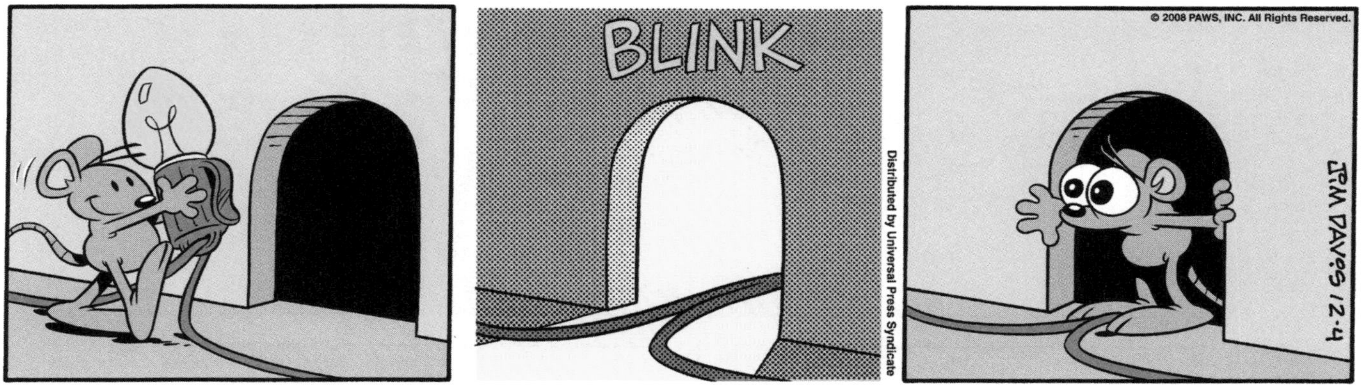
BLINK
Distributed by Universal Press Syndicate
© 2008 PAWS, INC. All Rights Reserved.
JIM DAVIS 12-4

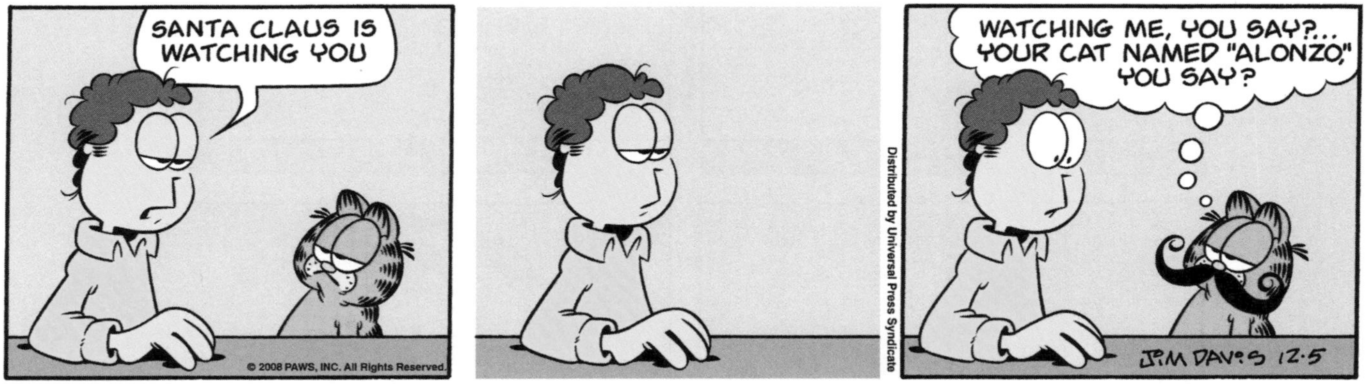
SANTA CLAUS IS WATCHING YOU
© 2008 PAWS, INC. All Rights Reserved.
Distributed by Universal Press Syndicate
WATCHING ME, YOU SAY?... YOUR CAT NAMED "ALONZO," YOU SAY?
JIM DAVIS 12-5

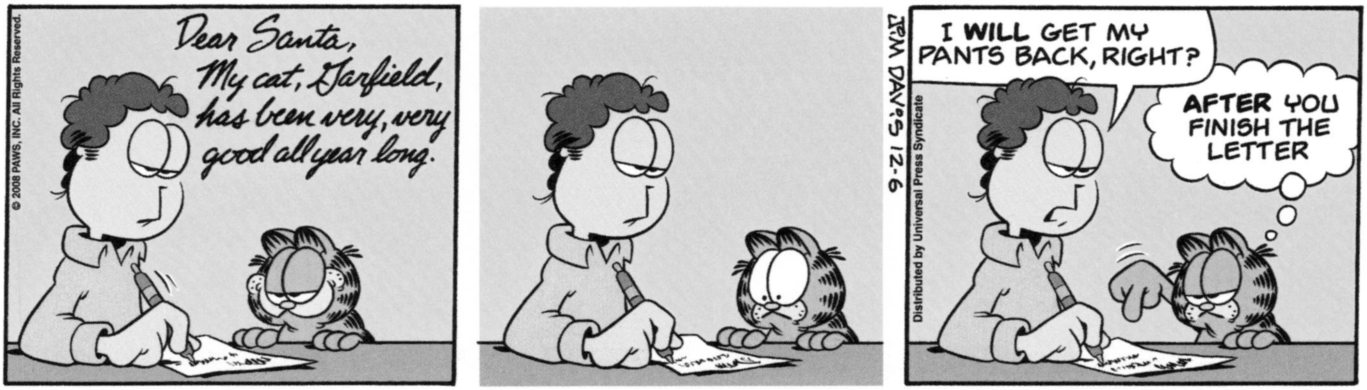
© 2008 PAWS, INC. All Rights Reserved.
Dear Santa,
My cat, Garfield, has been very, very good all year long.
JIM DAVIS 12-6
Distributed by Universal Press Syndicate
I **WILL** GET MY PANTS BACK, RIGHT?
AFTER YOU FINISH THE LETTER

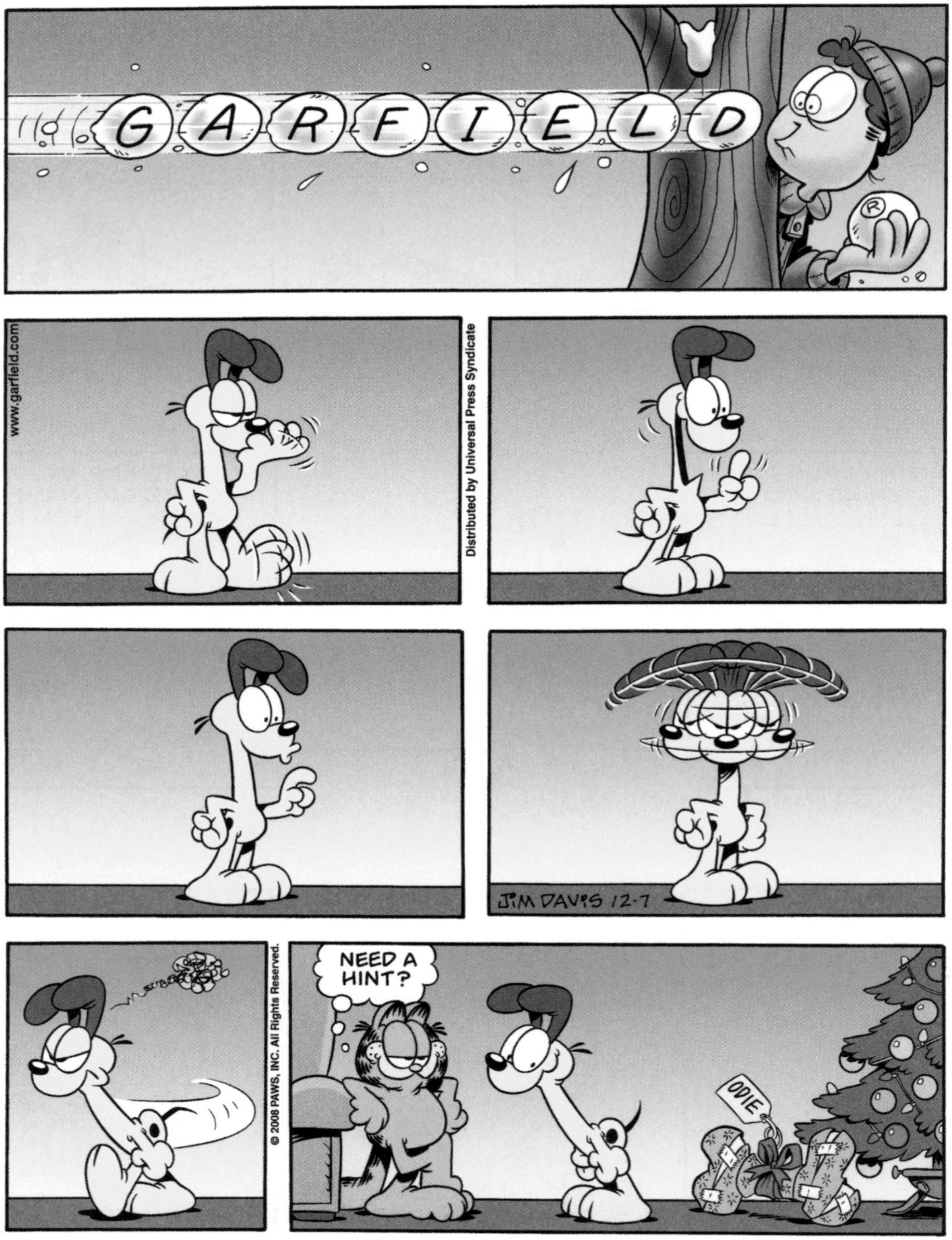
GARFIELD
www.garfield.com
Distributed by Universal Press Syndicate
JIM DAVIS 12-7
© 2008 PAWS, INC. All Rights Reserved.
NEED A HINT?
ODIE

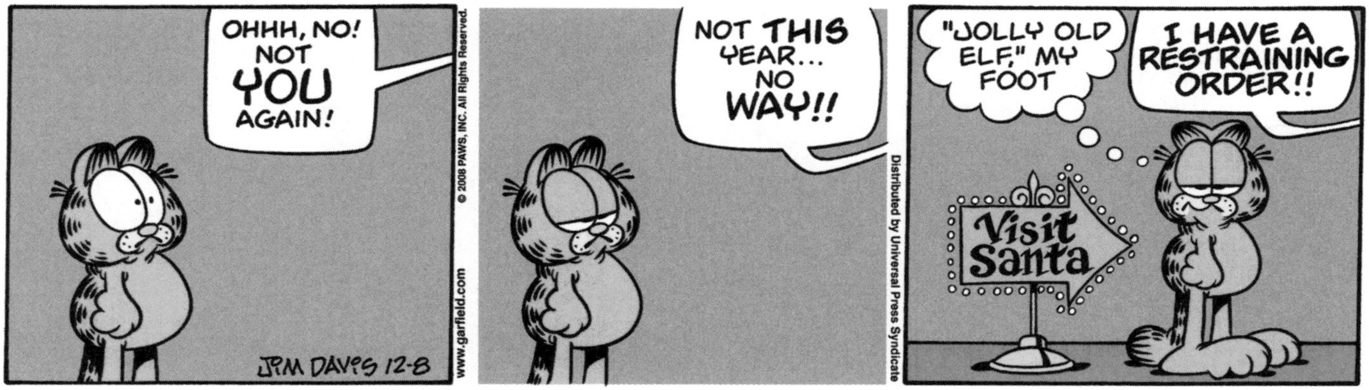
OHHH, NO! NOT YOU AGAIN!
JIM DAVIS 12-8
© 2008 PAWS, INC. All Rights Reserved.
www.garfield.com
NOT THIS YEAR... NO WAY!!
Distributed by Universal Press Syndicate
"JOLLY OLD ELF," MY FOOT
I HAVE A RESTRAINING ORDER!!
Visit Santa

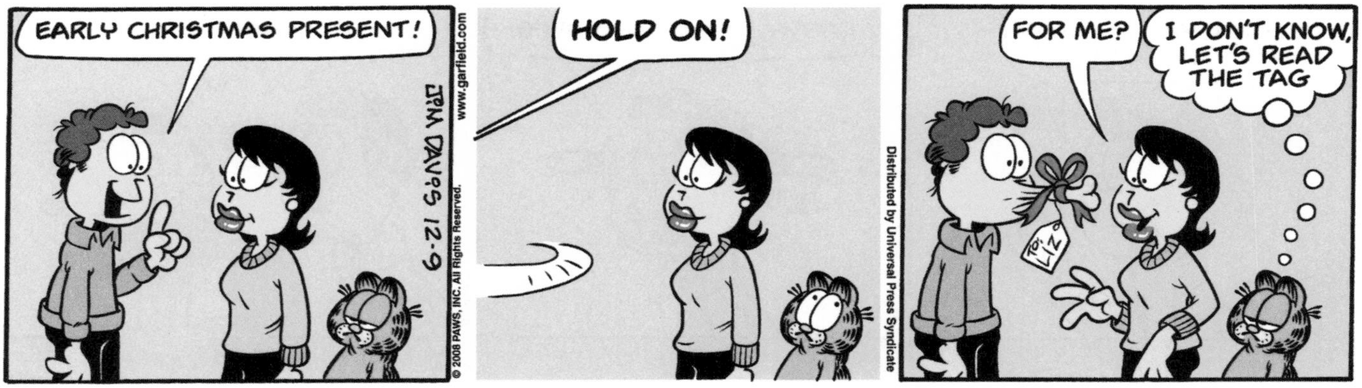
EARLY CHRISTMAS PRESENT!
JIM DAVIS 12-9
www.garfield.com
© 2008 PAWS, INC. All Rights Reserved.
HOLD ON!
Distributed by Universal Press Syndicate
FOR ME?
I DON'T KNOW, LET'S READ THE TAG
TO: LIZ

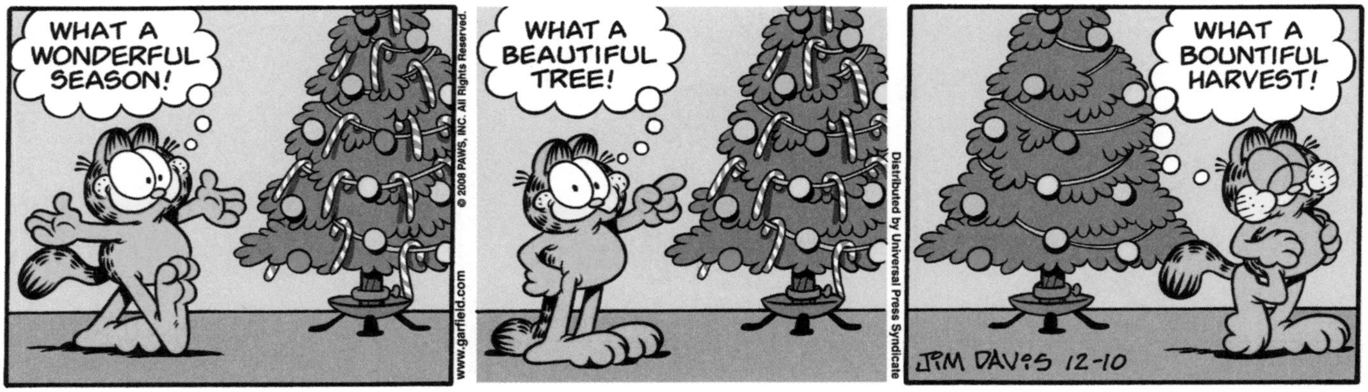
WHAT A WONDERFUL SEASON!
© 2008 PAWS, INC. All Rights Reserved.
www.garfield.com
WHAT A BEAUTIFUL TREE!
Distributed by Universal Press Syndicate
WHAT A BOUNTIFUL HARVEST!
JIM DAVIS 12-10

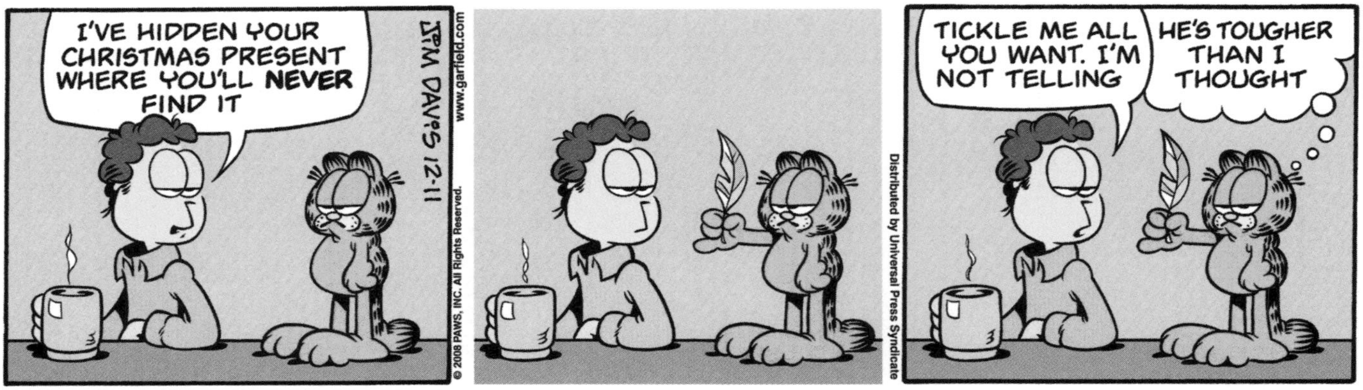
I'VE HIDDEN YOUR CHRISTMAS PRESENT WHERE YOU'LL **NEVER** FIND IT
JIM DAVIS 12-11
www.garfield.com
© 2008 PAWS, INC. All Rights Reserved.
TICKLE ME ALL YOU WANT. I'M NOT TELLING
HE'S TOUGHER THAN I THOUGHT
Distributed by Universal Press Syndicate

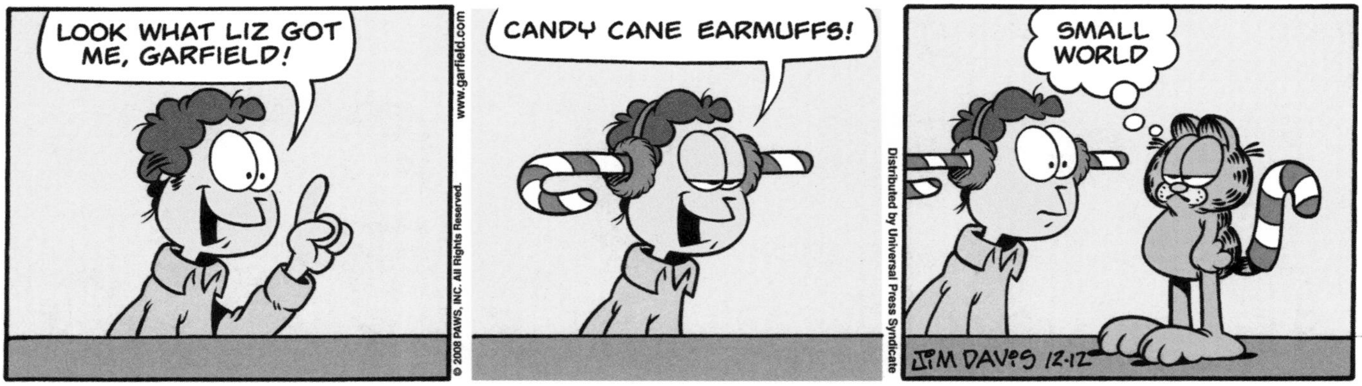
LOOK WHAT LIZ GOT ME, GARFIELD!
www.garfield.com
© 2008 PAWS, INC. All Rights Reserved.
CANDY CANE EARMUFFS!
Distributed by Universal Press Syndicate
SMALL WORLD
JIM DAVIS 12-12

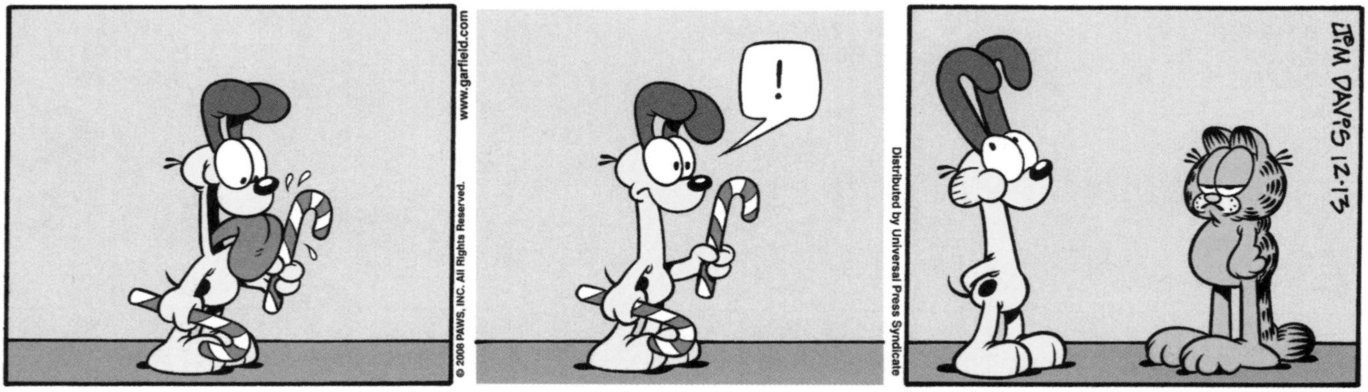
www.garfield.com
© 2008 PAWS, INC. All Rights Reserved.
!
Distributed by Universal Press Syndicate
JIM DAVIS 12-13

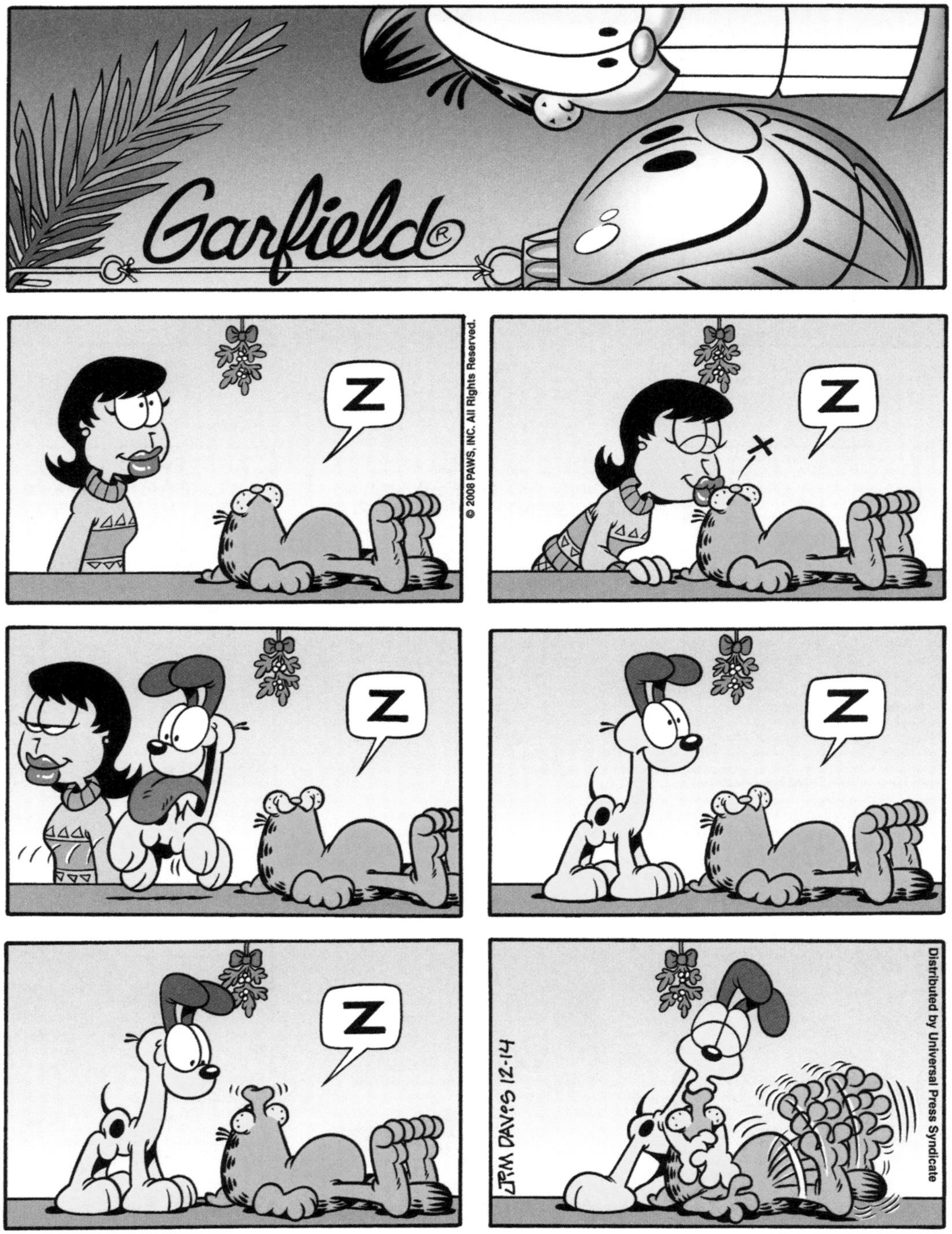
Garfield®
© 2008 PAWS, INC. All Rights Reserved.
Z
Z
Z
Z
Z
JPM DAVPS 12-14
Distributed by Universal Press Syndicate

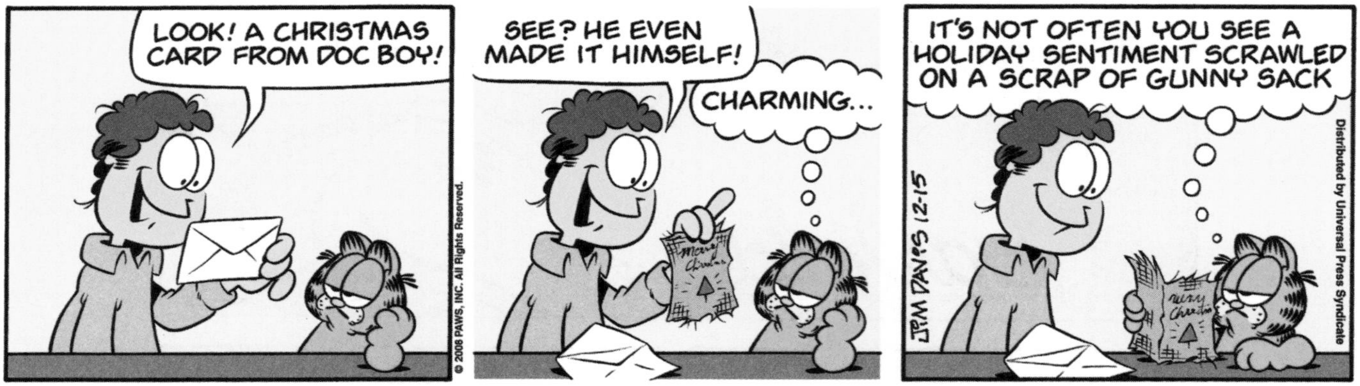
LOOK! A CHRISTMAS CARD FROM DOC BOY!
© 2008 PAWS, INC. All Rights Reserved.
SEE? HE EVEN MADE IT HIMSELF!
CHARMING...
IT'S NOT OFTEN YOU SEE A HOLIDAY SENTIMENT SCRAWLED ON A SCRAP OF GUNNY SACK
JIM DAVIS 12-15
Distributed by Universal Press Syndicate

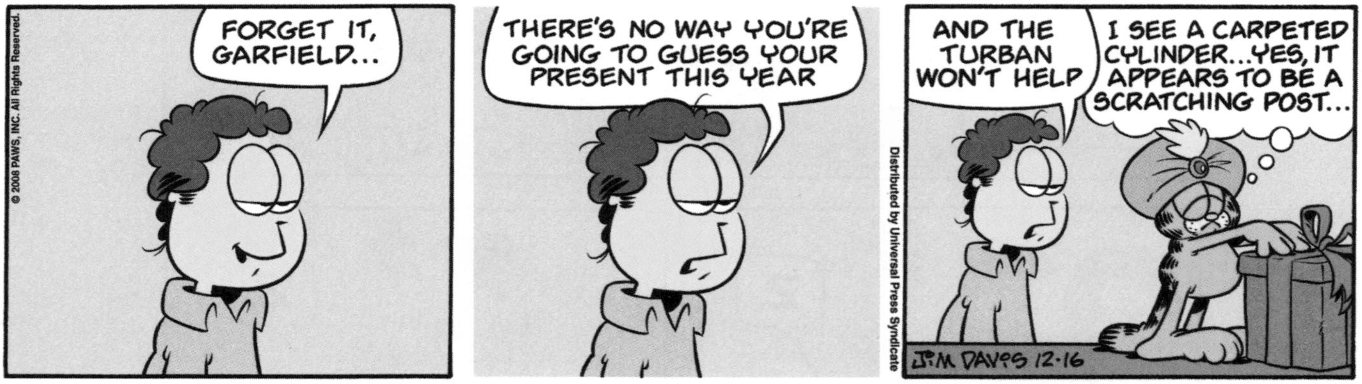
© 2008 PAWS, INC. All Rights Reserved.
FORGET IT, GARFIELD...
THERE'S NO WAY YOU'RE GOING TO GUESS YOUR PRESENT THIS YEAR
Distributed by Universal Press Syndicate
AND THE TURBAN WON'T HELP
I SEE A CARPETED CYLINDER...YES, IT APPEARS TO BE A SCRATCHING POST...
JIM DAVIS 12-16

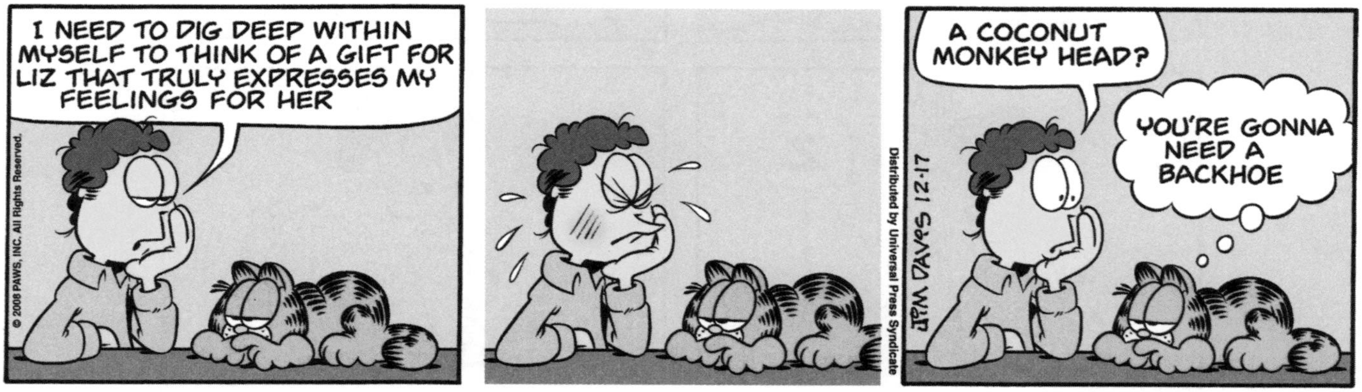
I NEED TO DIG DEEP WITHIN MYSELF TO THINK OF A GIFT FOR LIZ THAT TRULY EXPRESSES MY FEELINGS FOR HER
© 2008 PAWS, INC. All Rights Reserved.
Distributed by Universal Press Syndicate
JIM DAVIS 12-17
A COCONUT MONKEY HEAD?
YOU'RE GONNA NEED A BACKHOE

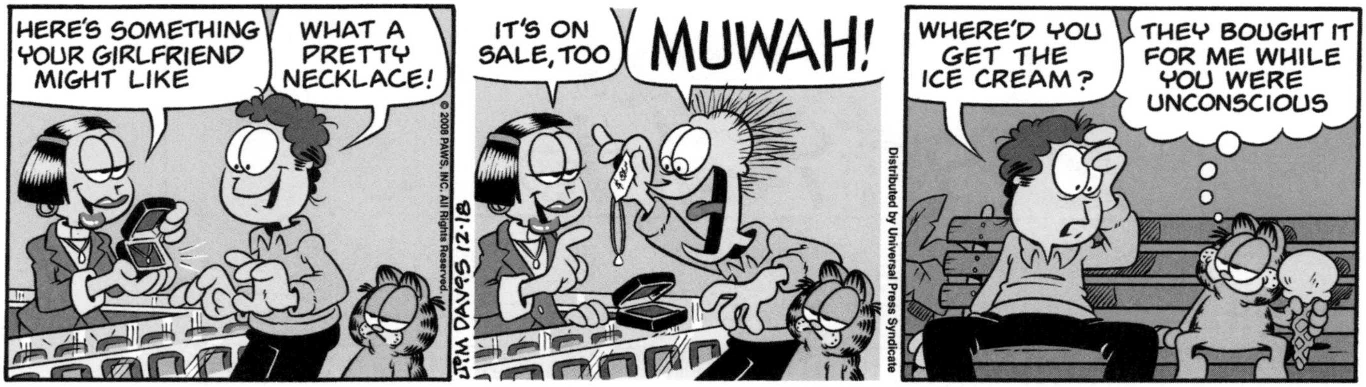
HERE'S SOMETHING YOUR GIRLFRIEND MIGHT LIKE
WHAT A PRETTY NECKLACE!
© 2008 PAWS, INC. All Rights Reserved.
JIM DAVIS 12·18
IT'S ON SALE, TOO
MUWAH!
Distributed by Universal Press Syndicate
WHERE'D YOU GET THE ICE CREAM?
THEY BOUGHT IT FOR ME WHILE YOU WERE UNCONSCIOUS

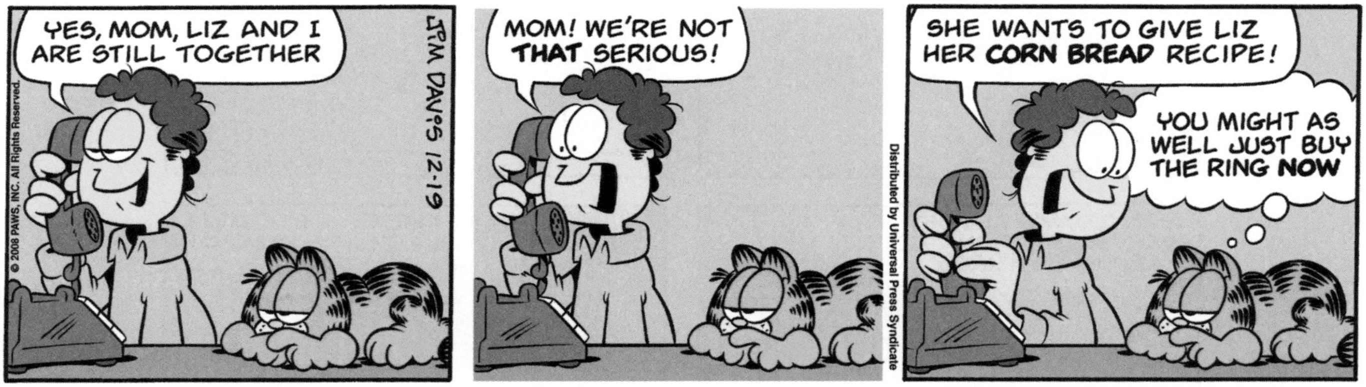
YES, MOM, LIZ AND I ARE STILL TOGETHER
© 2008 PAWS, INC. All Rights Reserved.
JIM DAVIS 12·19
MOM! WE'RE NOT **THAT** SERIOUS!
Distributed by Universal Press Syndicate
SHE WANTS TO GIVE LIZ HER **CORN BREAD** RECIPE!
YOU MIGHT AS WELL JUST BUY THE RING **NOW**

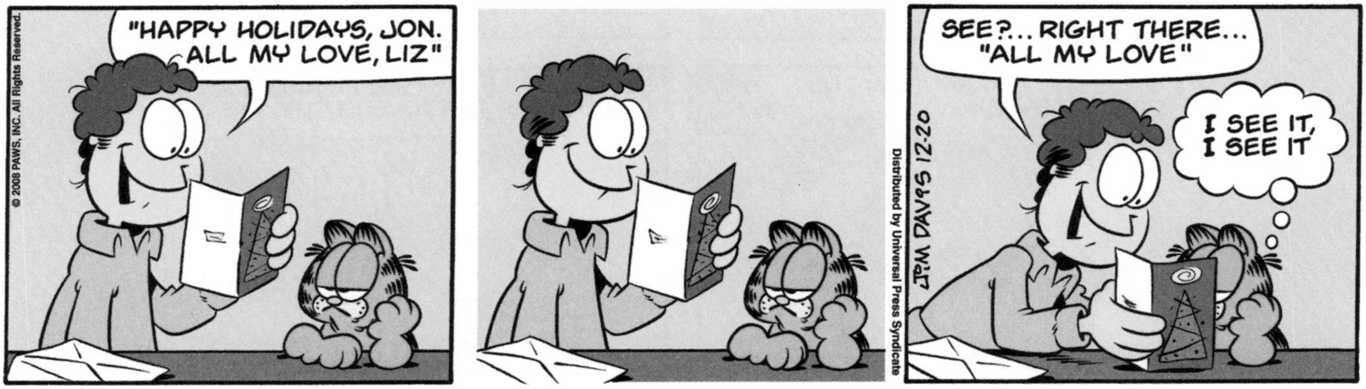
© 2008 PAWS, INC. All Rights Reserved.
"HAPPY HOLIDAYS, JON. ALL MY LOVE, LIZ"
Distributed by Universal Press Syndicate
JIM DAVIS 12·20
SEE?... RIGHT THERE... "ALL MY LOVE"
I SEE IT, **I** SEE IT

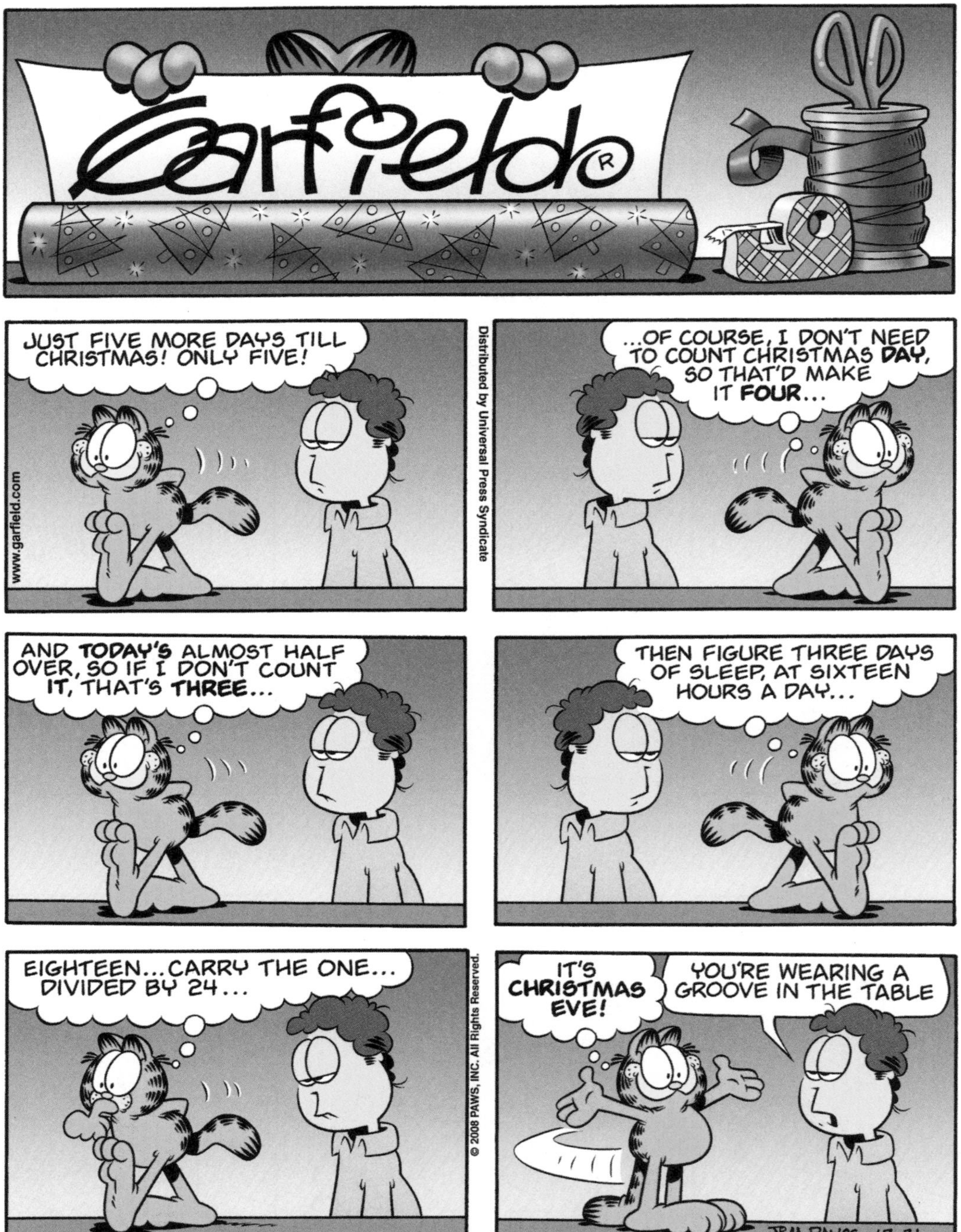
GARFIELD®
JUST FIVE MORE DAYS TILL CHRISTMAS! ONLY FIVE!
www.garfield.com
Distributed by Universal Press Syndicate
...OF COURSE, I DON'T NEED TO COUNT CHRISTMAS DAY, SO THAT'D MAKE IT FOUR...
AND TODAY'S ALMOST HALF OVER, SO IF I DON'T COUNT IT, THAT'S THREE...
THEN FIGURE THREE DAYS OF SLEEP, AT SIXTEEN HOURS A DAY...
EIGHTEEN...CARRY THE ONE... DIVIDED BY 24...
© 2008 PAWS, INC. All Rights Reserved.
IT'S CHRISTMAS EVE!
YOU'RE WEARING A GROOVE IN THE TABLE
JIM DAVIS 12-21

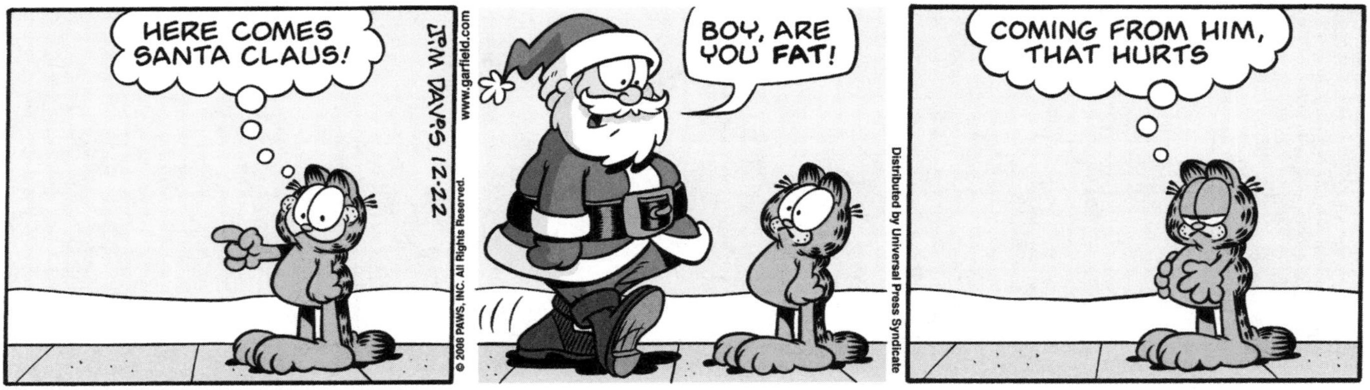
HERE COMES SANTA CLAUS!
JIM DAVIS 12-22
www.garfield.com
© 2008 PAWS, INC. All Rights Reserved.
BOY, ARE YOU **FAT**!
Distributed by Universal Press Syndicate
COMING FROM HIM, THAT HURTS

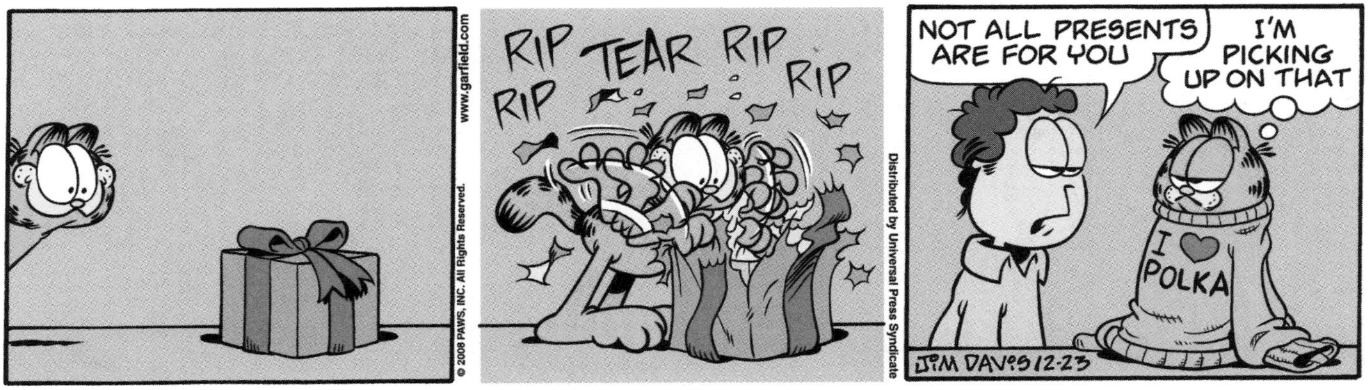
www.garfield.com
© 2008 PAWS, INC. All Rights Reserved.
RIP TEAR RIP
RIP RIP
Distributed by Universal Press Syndicate
NOT ALL PRESENTS ARE FOR YOU
I'M PICKING UP ON THAT
I ♥ POLKA
JIM DAVIS 12-23

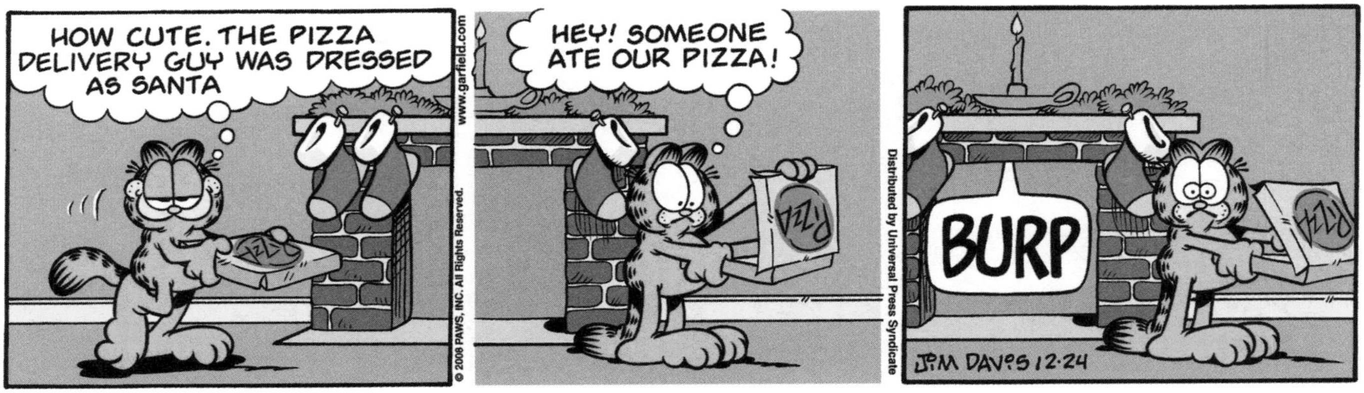
HOW CUTE. THE PIZZA DELIVERY GUY WAS DRESSED AS SANTA
www.garfield.com
© 2008 PAWS, INC. All Rights Reserved.
HEY! SOMEONE ATE OUR PIZZA!
PIZZA
Distributed by Universal Press Syndicate
BURP
JIM DAVIS 12-24

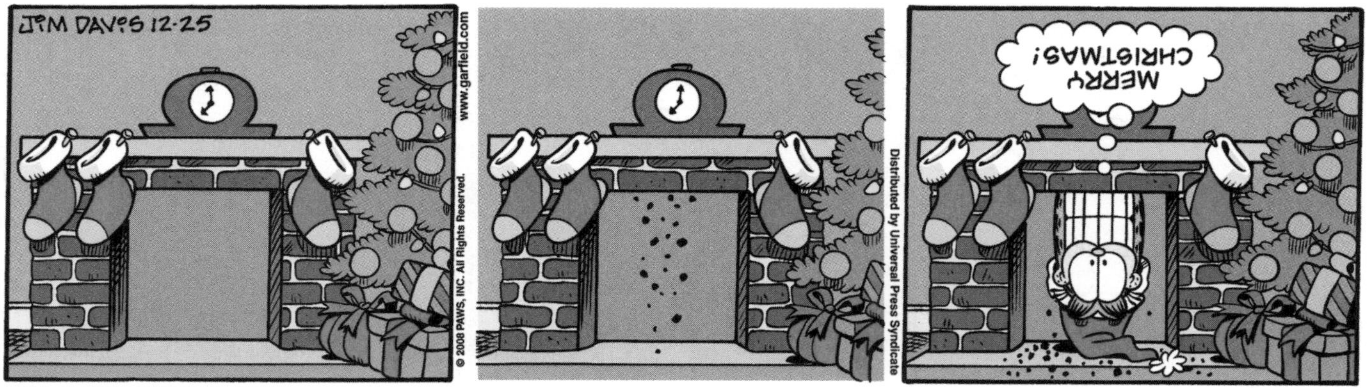
JIM DAVIS 12-25
MERRY CHRISTMAS!
© 2008 PAWS, INC. All Rights Reserved.
www.garfield.com
Distributed by Universal Press Syndicate

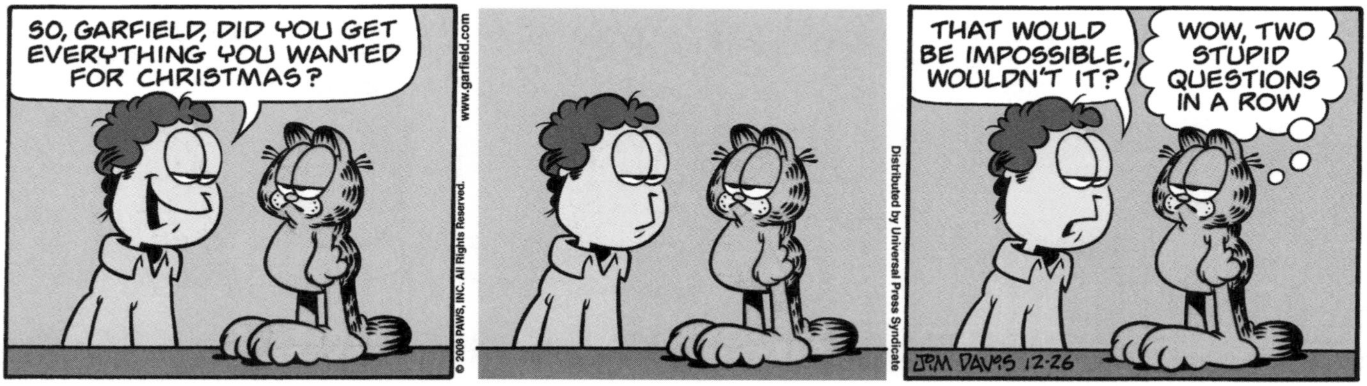
SO, GARFIELD, DID YOU GET EVERYTHING YOU WANTED FOR CHRISTMAS?
THAT WOULD BE IMPOSSIBLE, WOULDN'T IT?
WOW, TWO STUPID QUESTIONS IN A ROW
JIM DAVIS 12-26
© 2008 PAWS, INC. All Rights Reserved.
www.garfield.com
Distributed by Universal Press Syndicate

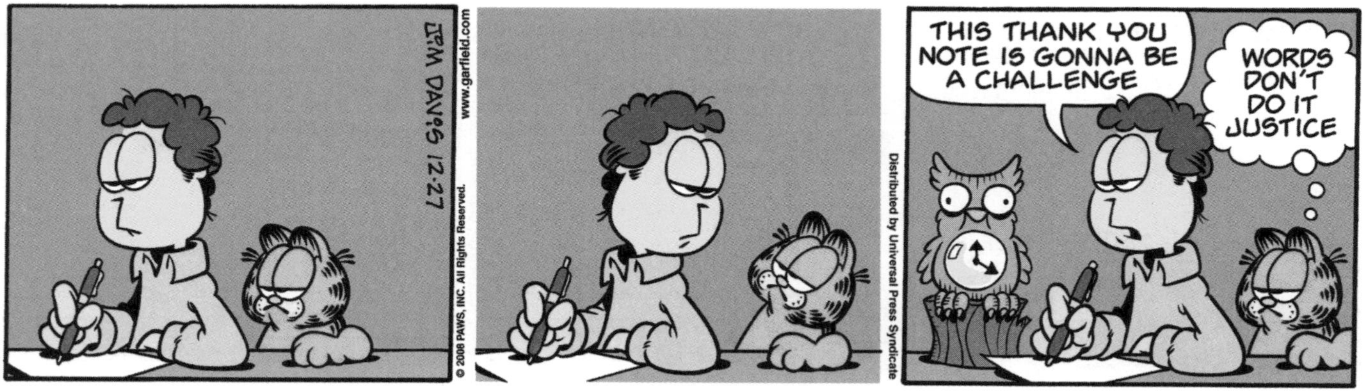
JIM DAVIS 12-27
THIS THANK YOU NOTE IS GONNA BE A CHALLENGE
WORDS DON'T DO IT JUSTICE
© 2008 PAWS, INC. All Rights Reserved.
www.garfield.com
Distributed by Universal Press Syndicate

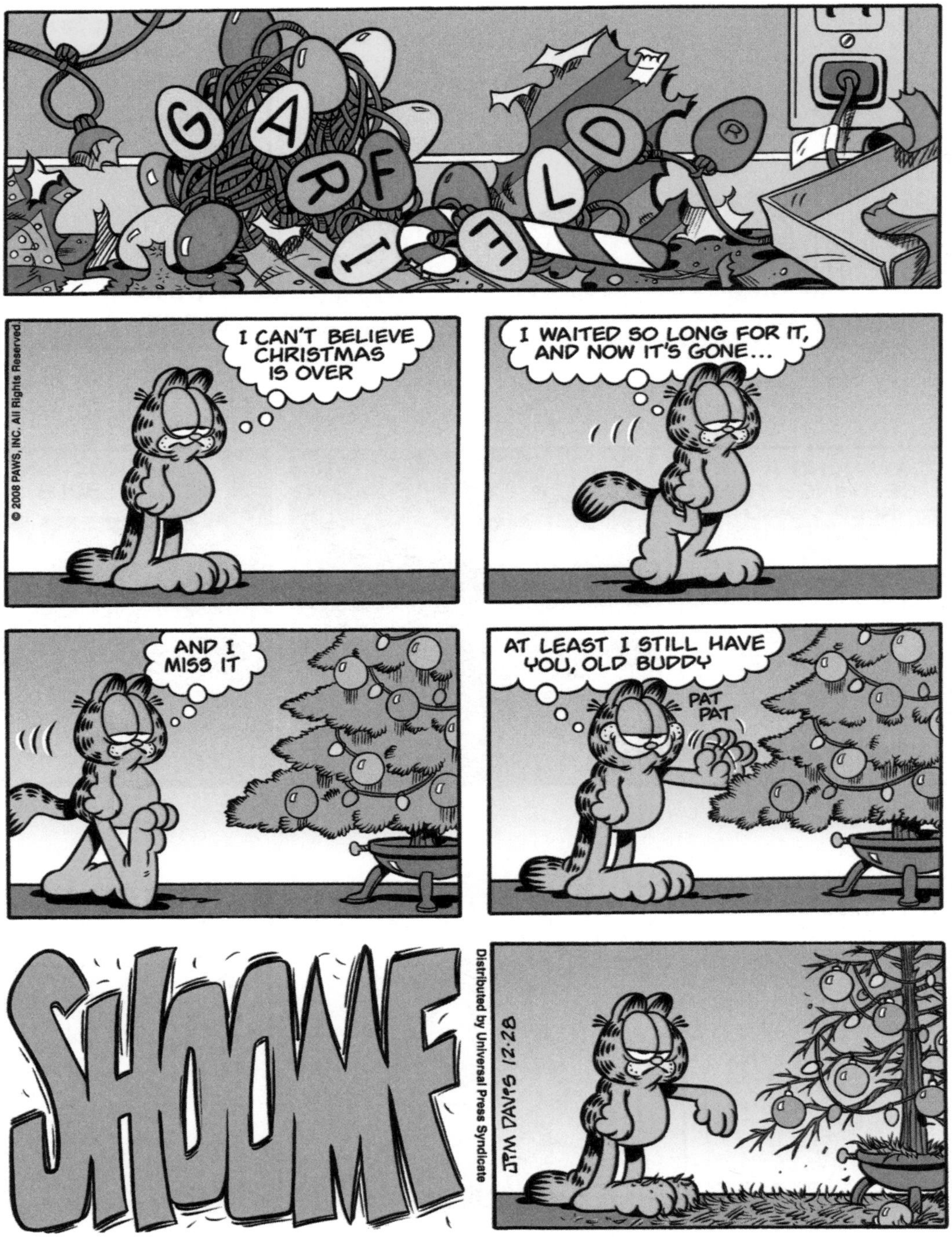
GARFIELD®
© 2008 PAWS, INC. All Rights Reserved.
I CAN'T BELIEVE CHRISTMAS IS OVER
I WAITED SO LONG FOR IT, AND NOW IT'S GONE...
AND I MISS IT
AT LEAST I STILL HAVE YOU, OLD BUDDY
PAT PAT
SHOOMF
Distributed by Universal Press Syndicate
JPM DAVIS 12-28

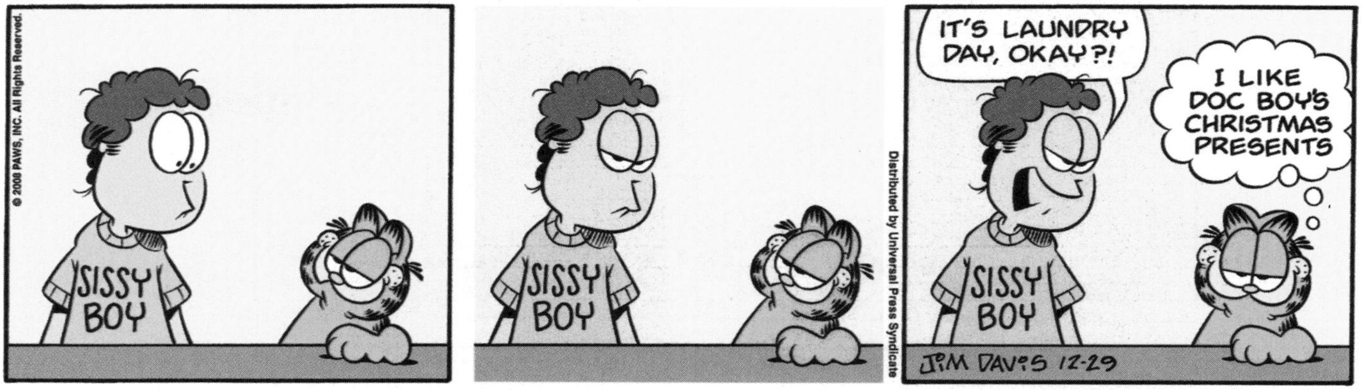
© 2008 PAWS, INC. All Rights Reserved.
SISSY BOY
SISSY BOY
IT'S LAUNDRY DAY, OKAY?!
I LIKE DOC BOY'S CHRISTMAS PRESENTS
SISSY BOY
JIM DAVIS 12-29
Distributed by Universal Press Syndicate

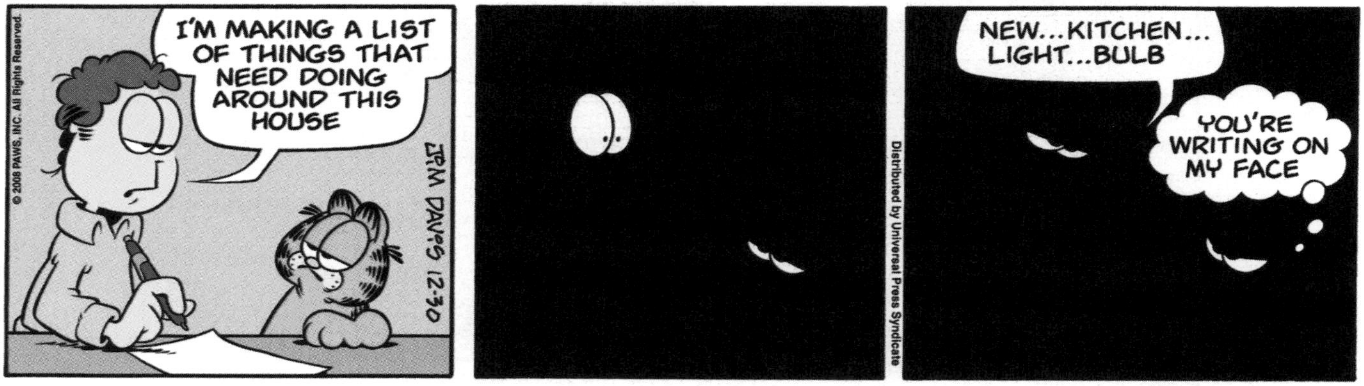
© 2008 PAWS, INC. All Rights Reserved.
I'M MAKING A LIST OF THINGS THAT NEED DOING AROUND THIS HOUSE
JIM DAVIS 12-30
NEW... KITCHEN... LIGHT... BULB
YOU'RE WRITING ON MY FACE
Distributed by Universal Press Syndicate

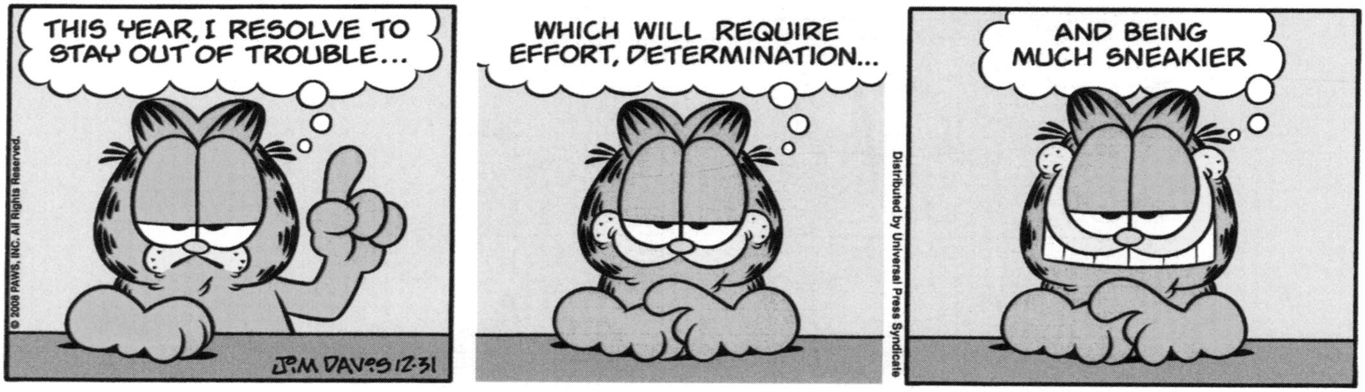
© 2008 PAWS, INC. All Rights Reserved.
THIS YEAR, I RESOLVE TO STAY OUT OF TROUBLE...
JIM DAVIS 12-31
WHICH WILL REQUIRE EFFORT, DETERMINATION...
AND BEING MUCH SNEAKIER
Distributed by Universal Press Syndicate

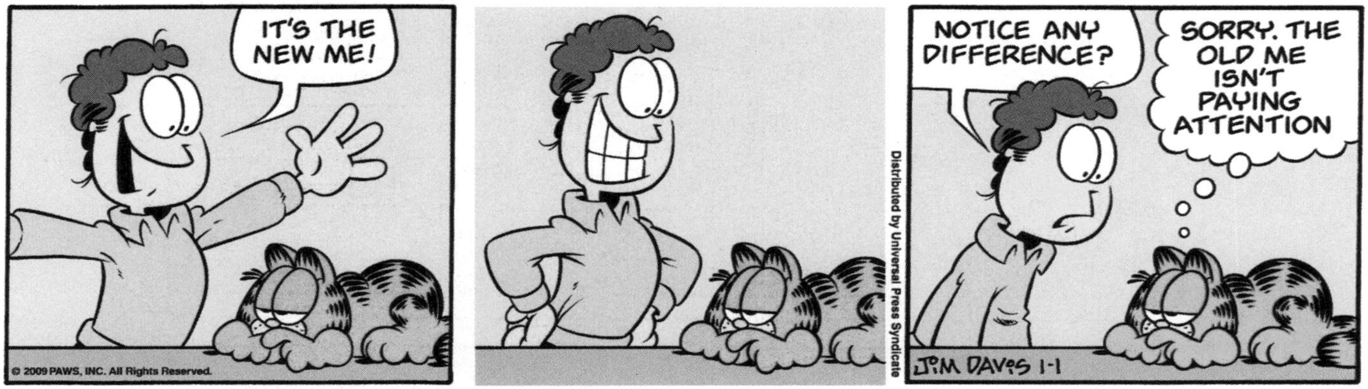
IT'S THE NEW ME!
NOTICE ANY DIFFERENCE?
SORRY. THE OLD ME ISN'T PAYING ATTENTION
© 2009 PAWS, INC. All Rights Reserved.
Distributed by Universal Press Syndicate
JIM DAVIS 1-1

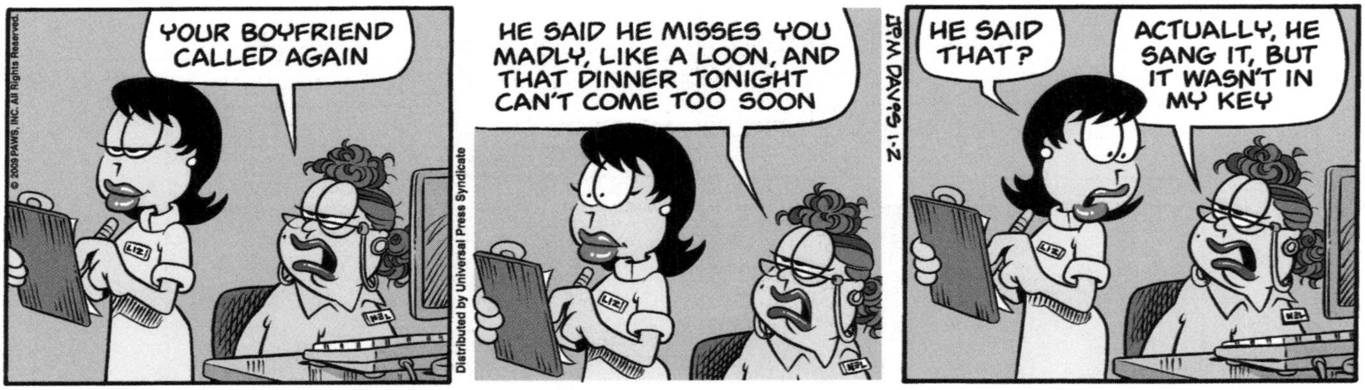
YOUR BOYFRIEND CALLED AGAIN
HE SAID HE MISSES YOU MADLY, LIKE A LOON, AND THAT DINNER TONIGHT CAN'T COME TOO SOON
HE SAID THAT?
ACTUALLY, HE SANG IT, BUT IT WASN'T IN MY KEY
© 2009 PAWS, INC. All Rights Reserved.
Distributed by Universal Press Syndicate
JIM DAVIS 1-2

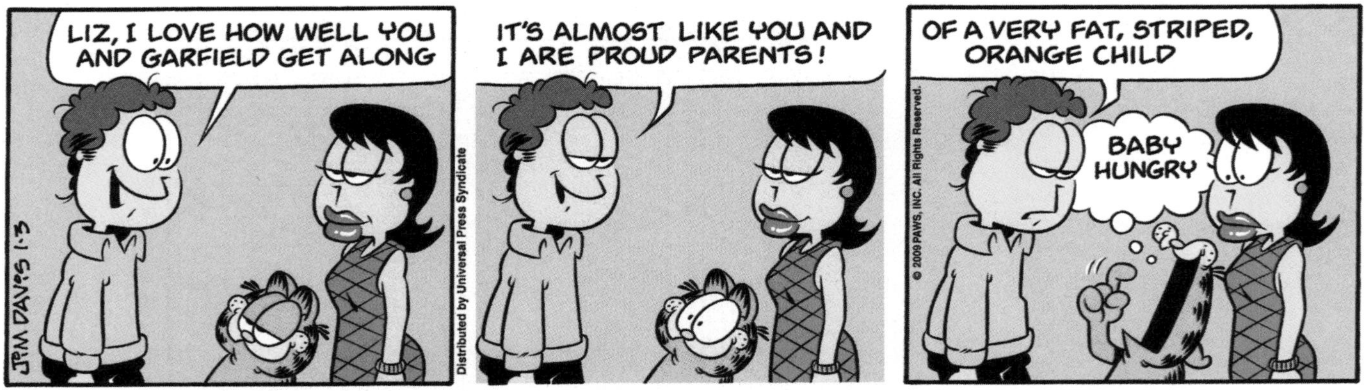
LIZ, I LOVE HOW WELL YOU AND GARFIELD GET ALONG
IT'S ALMOST LIKE YOU AND I ARE PROUD PARENTS!
OF A VERY FAT, STRIPED, ORANGE CHILD
BABY HUNGRY
JIM DAVIS 1-3
Distributed by Universal Press Syndicate
© 2009 PAWS, INC. All Rights Reserved.

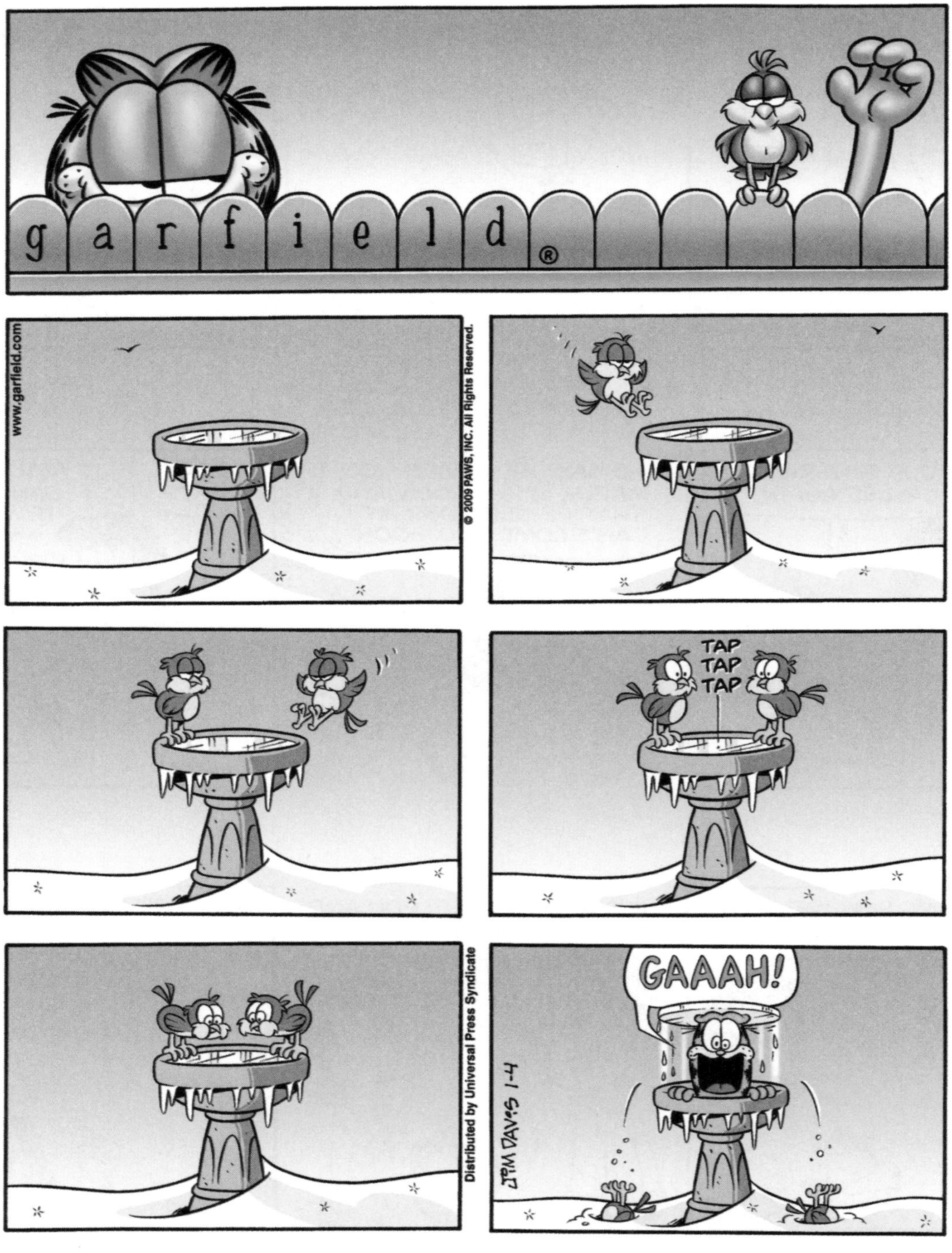
garfield®
www.garfield.com
© 2009 PAWS, INC. All Rights Reserved.
TAP
TAP
TAP
Distributed by Universal Press Syndicate
JIM DAVIS 1-4
GAAAH!

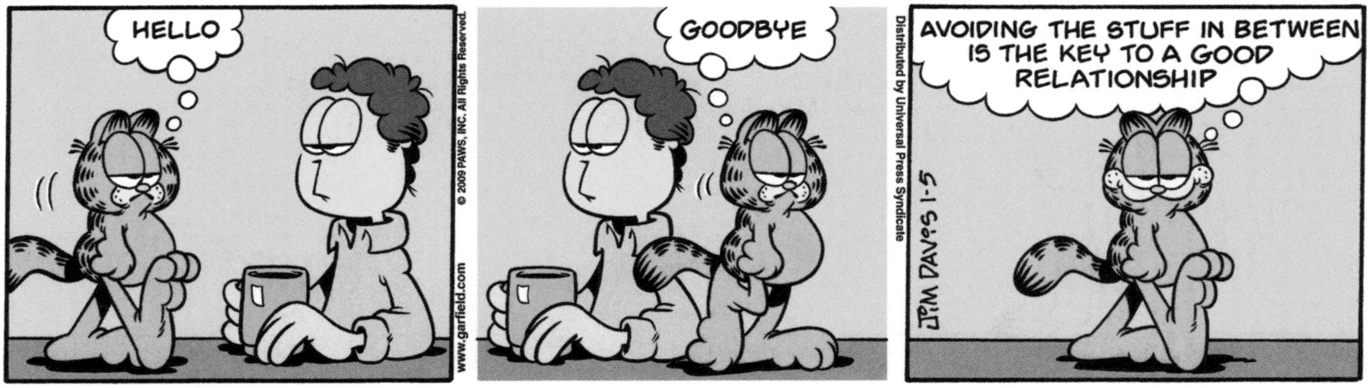
HELLO
© 2009 PAWS, INC. All Rights Reserved.
www.garfield.com
GOODBYE
Distributed by Universal Press Syndicate
AVOIDING THE STUFF IN BETWEEN IS THE KEY TO A GOOD RELATIONSHIP
JPM DAVPS 1-5

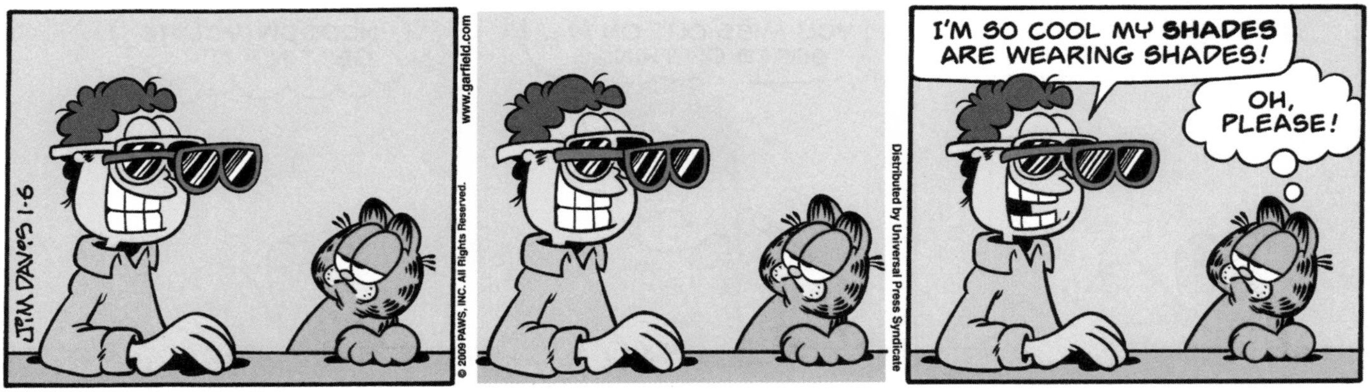
JPM DAVPS 1-6
www.garfield.com
© 2009 PAWS, INC. All Rights Reserved.
Distributed by Universal Press Syndicate
I'M SO COOL MY **SHADES** ARE WEARING SHADES!
OH, PLEASE!

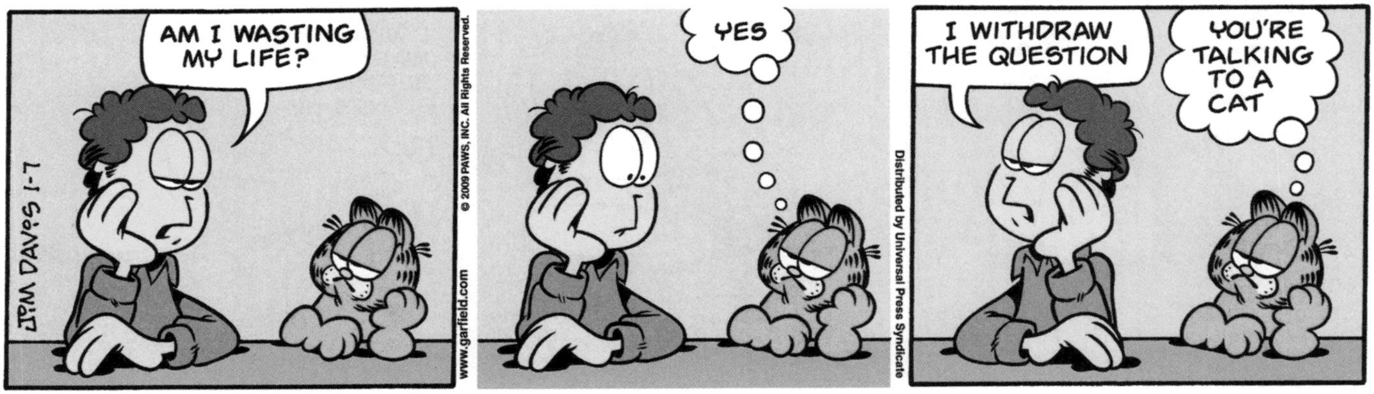
AM I WASTING MY LIFE?
JPM DAVPS 1-7
© 2009 PAWS, INC. All Rights Reserved.
www.garfield.com
YES
Distributed by Universal Press Syndicate
I WITHDRAW THE QUESTION
YOU'RE TALKING TO A CAT

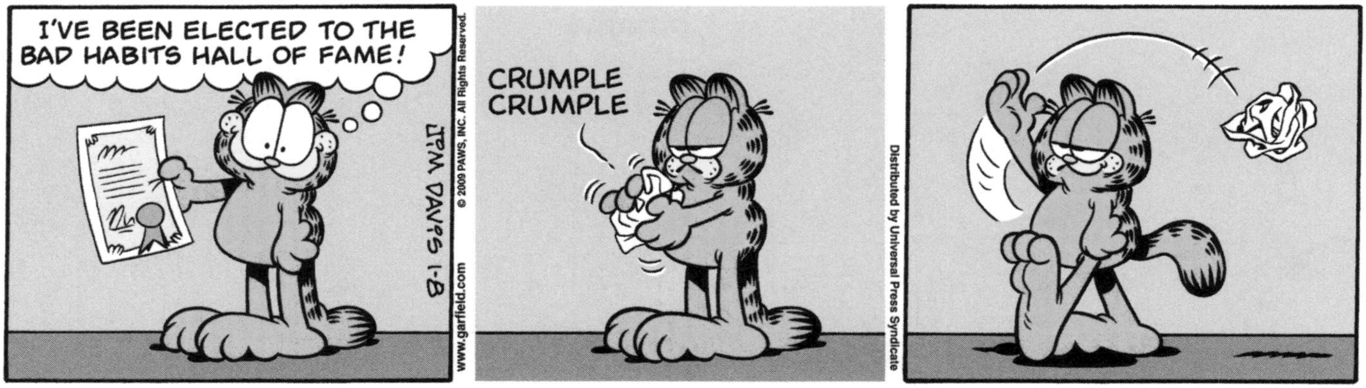
I'VE BEEN ELECTED TO THE BAD HABITS HALL OF FAME!
CRUMPLE CRUMPLE

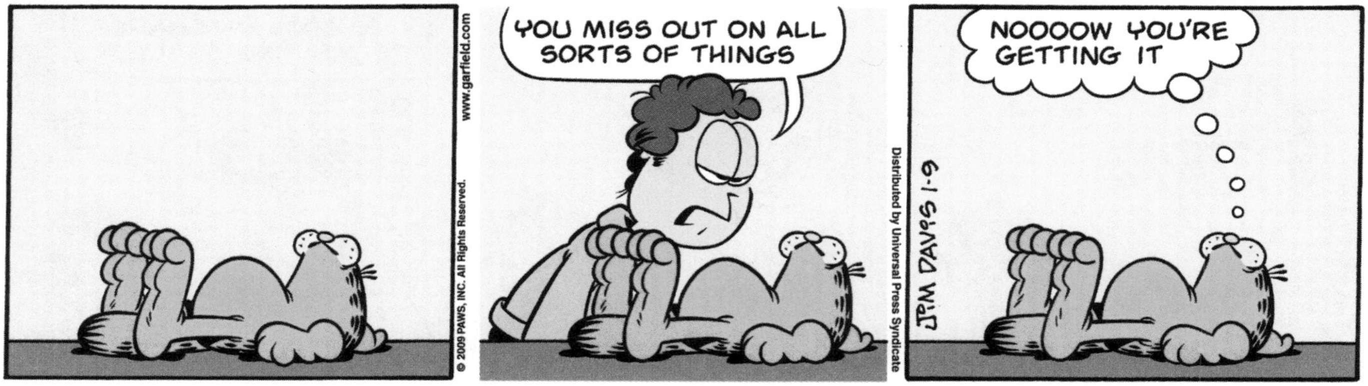
YOU MISS OUT ON ALL SORTS OF THINGS
NOOOOW YOU'RE GETTING IT

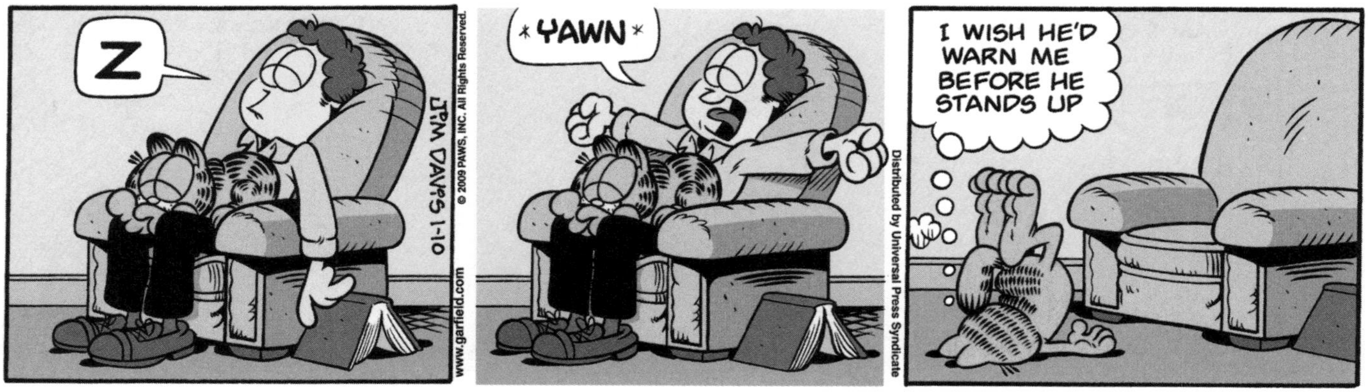
Z
YAWN
I WISH HE'D WARN ME BEFORE HE STANDS UP

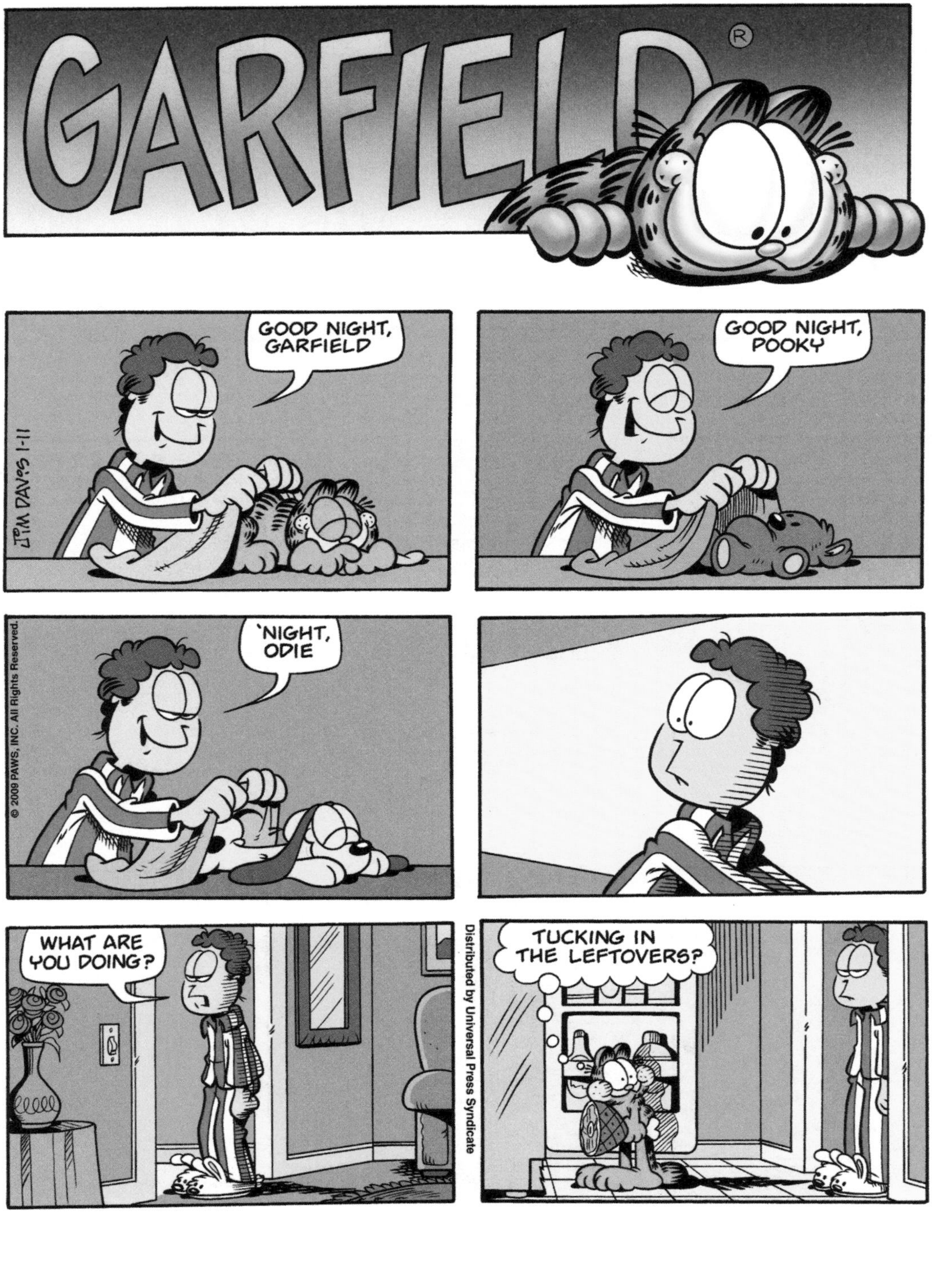
GARFIELD®
GOOD NIGHT, GARFIELD
JIM DAVIS 1-11
GOOD NIGHT, POOKY
'NIGHT, ODIE
WHAT ARE YOU DOING?
TUCKING IN THE LEFTOVERS?

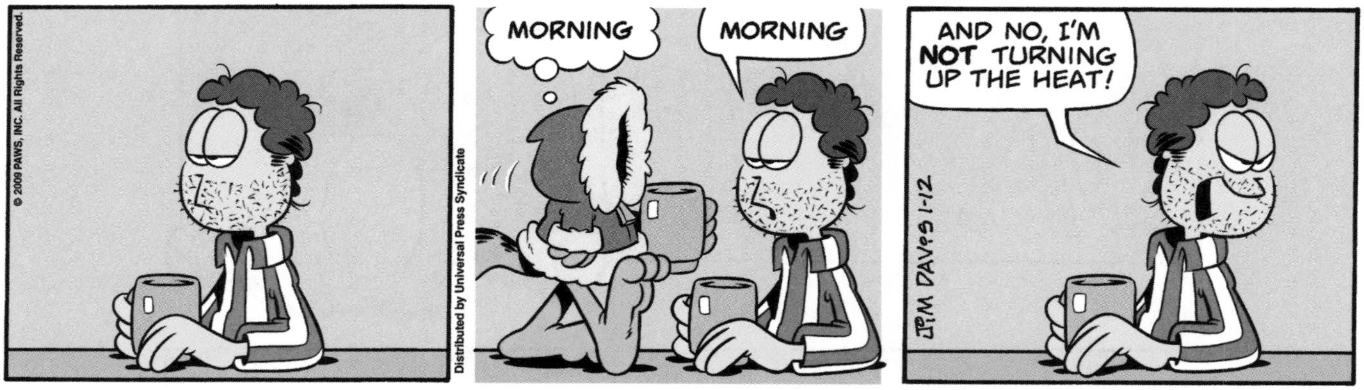
MORNING
MORNING
AND NO, I'M **NOT** TURNING UP THE HEAT!
JIM DAVIS 1-12

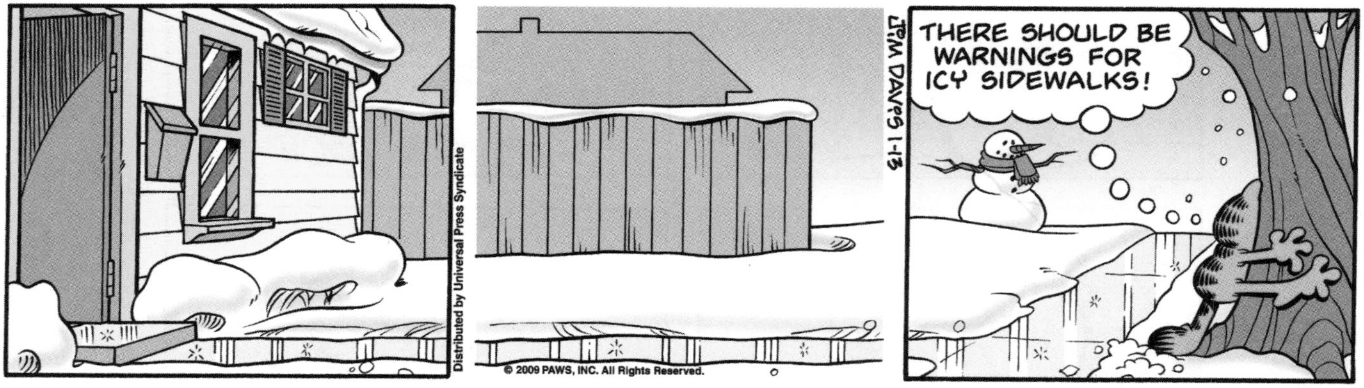
JIM DAVIS 1-13
THERE SHOULD BE WARNINGS FOR ICY SIDEWALKS!

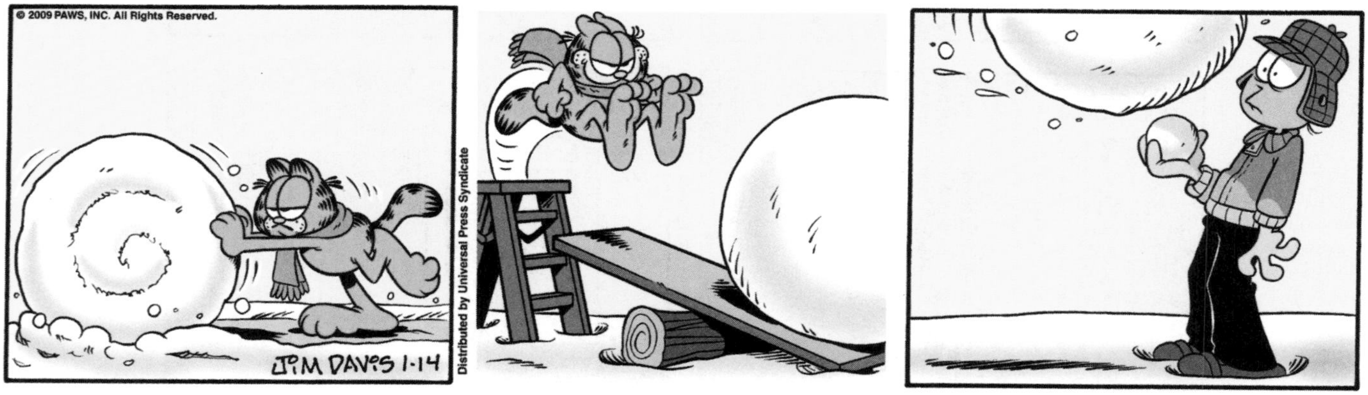
JIM DAVIS 1-14

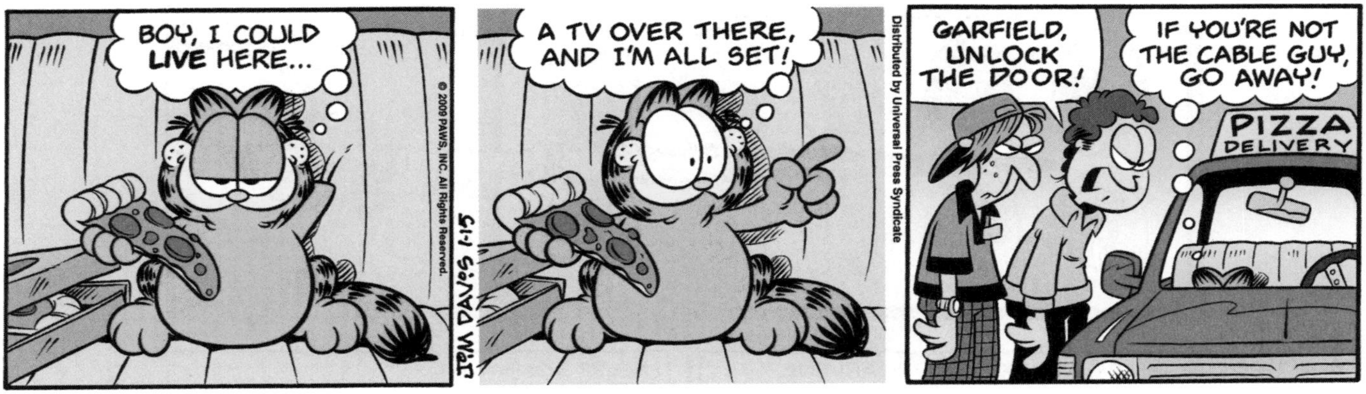
BOY, I COULD LIVE HERE...
© 2009 PAWS, INC. All Rights Reserved.
JPM DAVIS 1-15
A TV OVER THERE, AND I'M ALL SET!
Distributed by Universal Press Syndicate
GARFIELD, UNLOCK THE DOOR!
IF YOU'RE NOT THE CABLE GUY, GO AWAY!
PIZZA DELIVERY

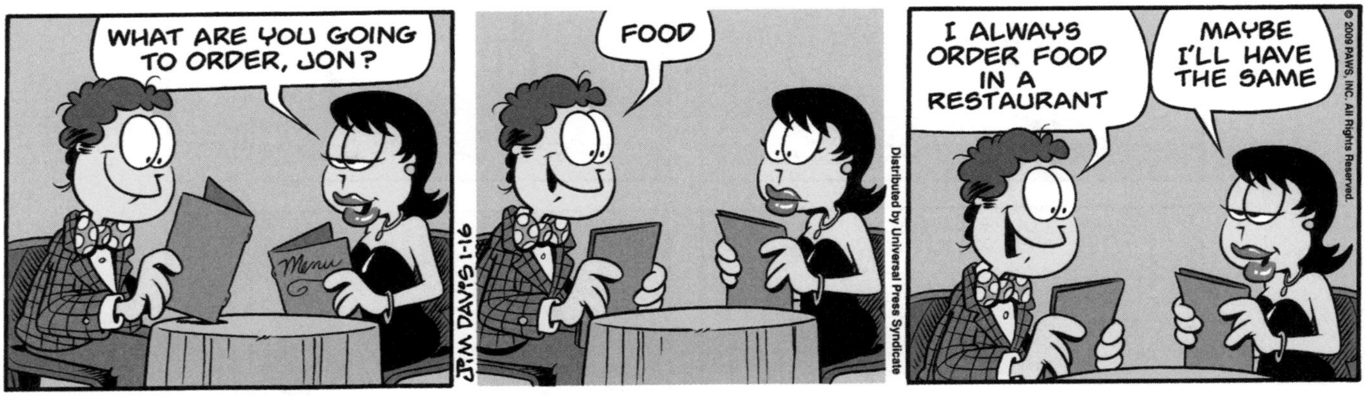
WHAT ARE YOU GOING TO ORDER, JON?
Menu
JPM DAVIS 1-16
FOOD
Distributed by Universal Press Syndicate
I ALWAYS ORDER FOOD IN A RESTAURANT
MAYBE I'LL HAVE THE SAME
© 2009 PAWS, INC. All Rights Reserved.

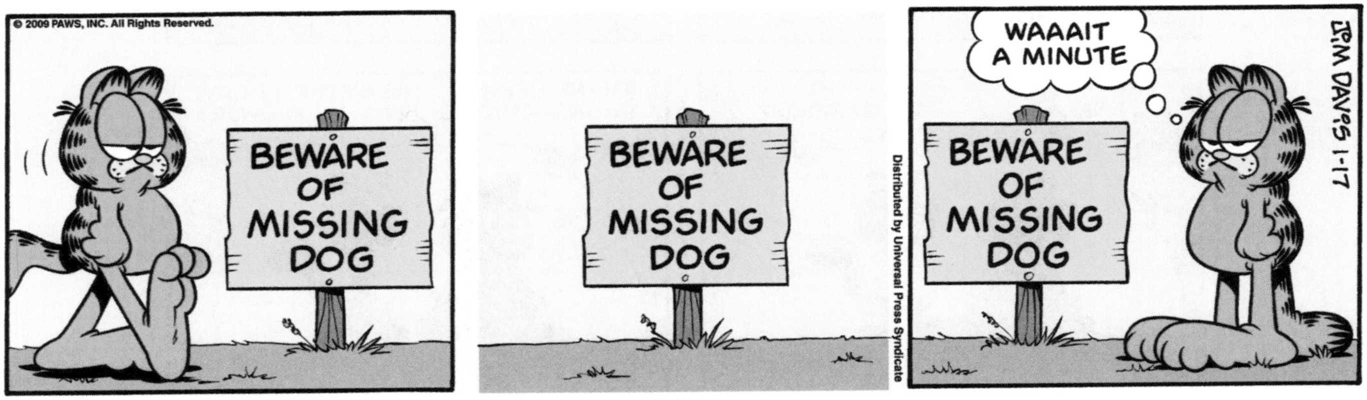
© 2009 PAWS, INC. All Rights Reserved.
BEWARE OF MISSING DOG
BEWARE OF MISSING DOG
Distributed by Universal Press Syndicate
WAAAIT A MINUTE
BEWARE OF MISSING DOG
JPM DAVIS 1-17

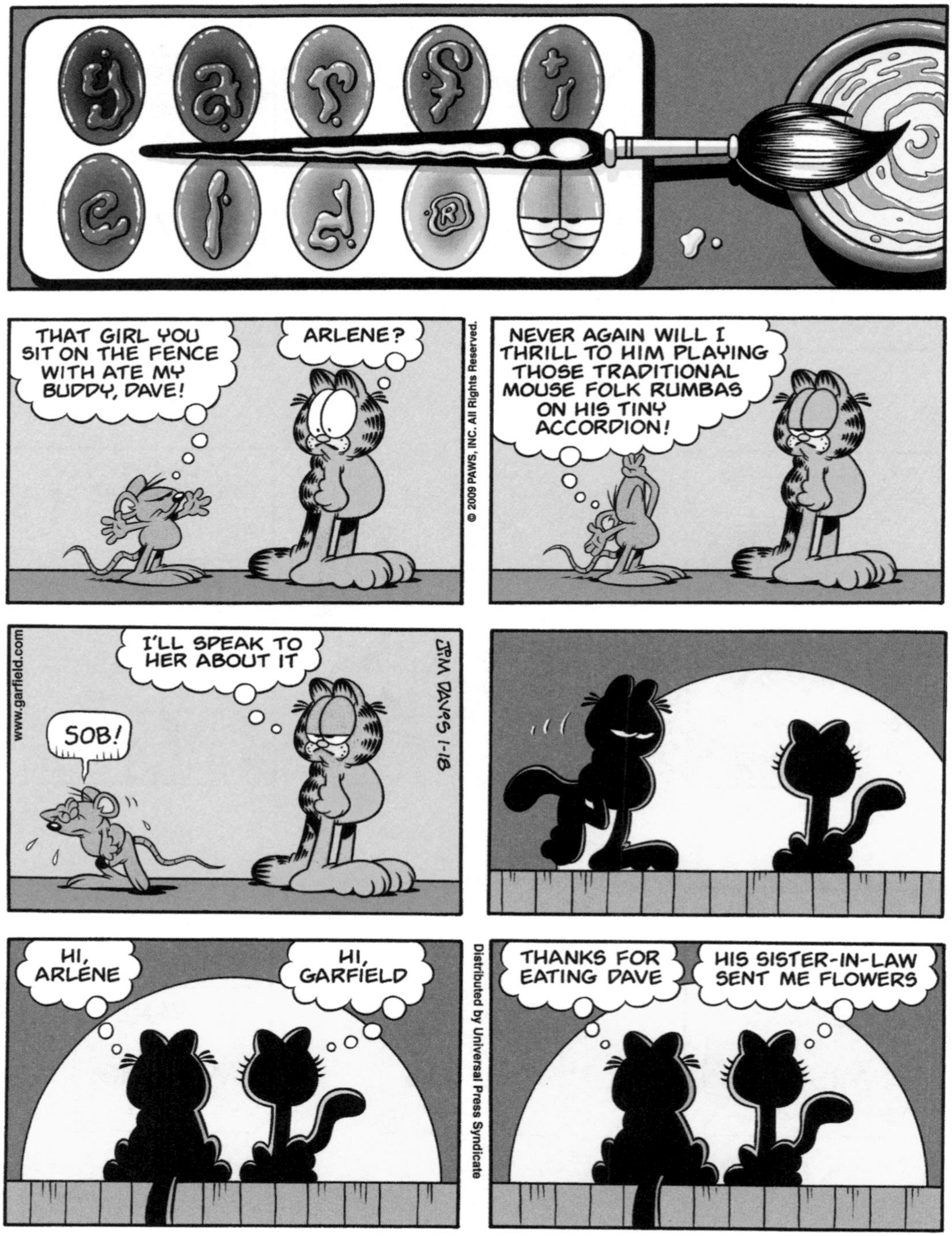
garfield ®
THAT GIRL YOU SIT ON THE FENCE WITH ATE MY BUDDY, DAVE!
ARLENE?
© 2009 PAWS, INC. All Rights Reserved.
NEVER AGAIN WILL I THRILL TO HIM PLAYING THOSE TRADITIONAL MOUSE FOLK RUMBAS ON HIS TINY ACCORDION!
www.garfield.com
I'LL SPEAK TO HER ABOUT IT
SOB!
JIM DAVIS 1-18
HI, ARLENE
HI, GARFIELD
Distributed by Universal Press Syndicate
THANKS FOR EATING DAVE
HIS SISTER-IN-LAW SENT ME FLOWERS

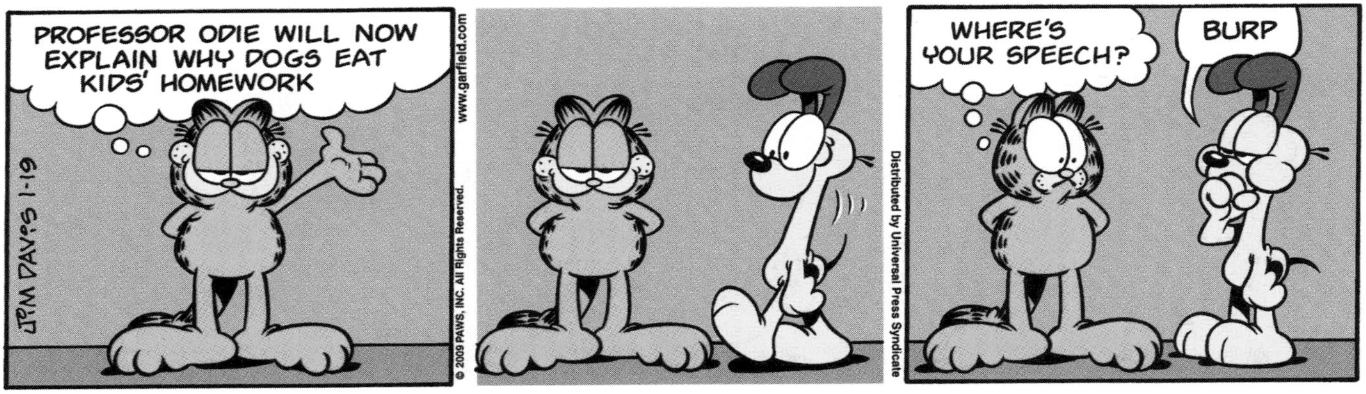
PROFESSOR ODIE WILL NOW EXPLAIN WHY DOGS EAT KIDS' HOMEWORK
JIM DAVIS 1-19
© 2009 PAWS, INC. All Rights Reserved.
www.garfield.com
WHERE'S YOUR SPEECH?
BURP
Distributed by Universal Press Syndicate

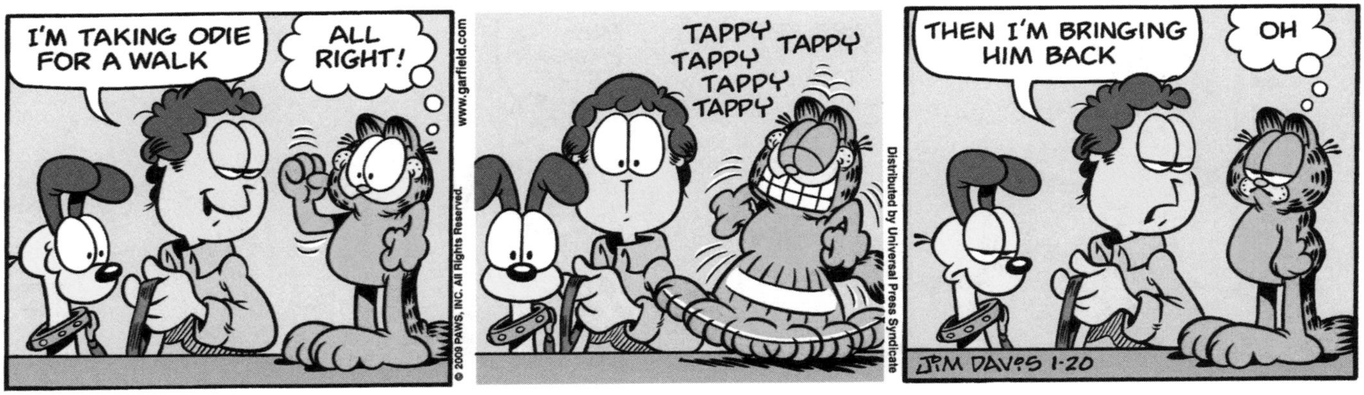
I'M TAKING ODIE FOR A WALK
ALL RIGHT!
© 2009 PAWS, INC. All Rights Reserved.
www.garfield.com
TAPPY TAPPY TAPPY TAPPY TAPPY
THEN I'M BRINGING HIM BACK
OH
JIM DAVIS 1-20
Distributed by Universal Press Syndicate

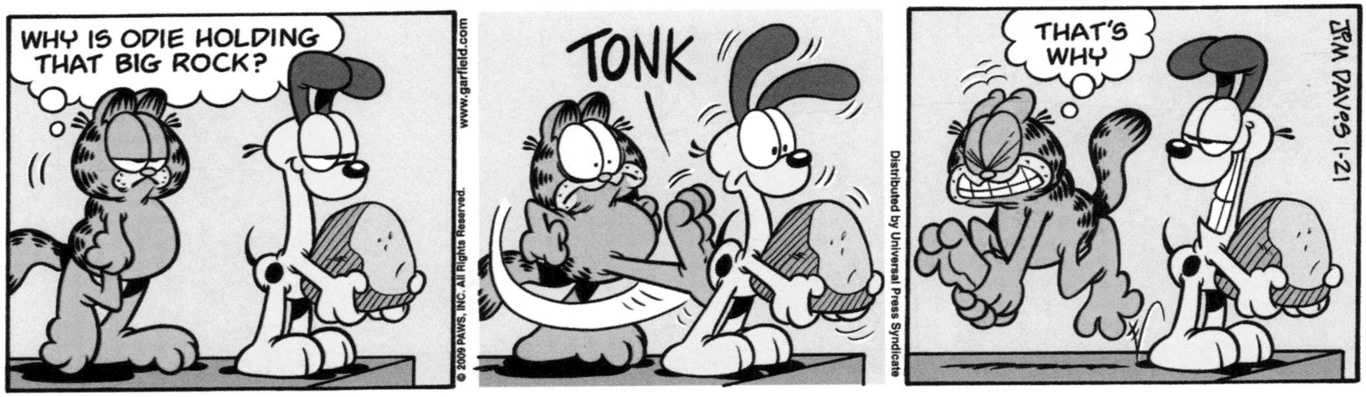
WHY IS ODIE HOLDING THAT BIG ROCK?
© 2009 PAWS, INC. All Rights Reserved.
www.garfield.com
TONK
THAT'S WHY
JIM DAVIS 1-21
Distributed by Universal Press Syndicate

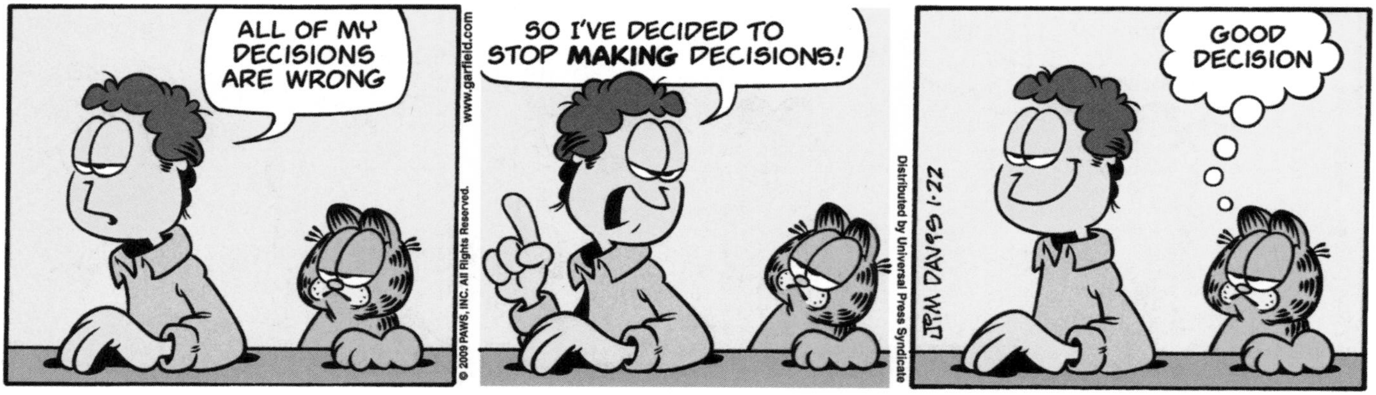
ALL OF MY DECISIONS ARE WRONG
© 2009 PAWS, INC. All Rights Reserved. www.garfield.com
SO I'VE DECIDED TO STOP **MAKING** DECISIONS!
Distributed by Universal Press Syndicate
JIM DAVIS 1·22
GOOD DECISION

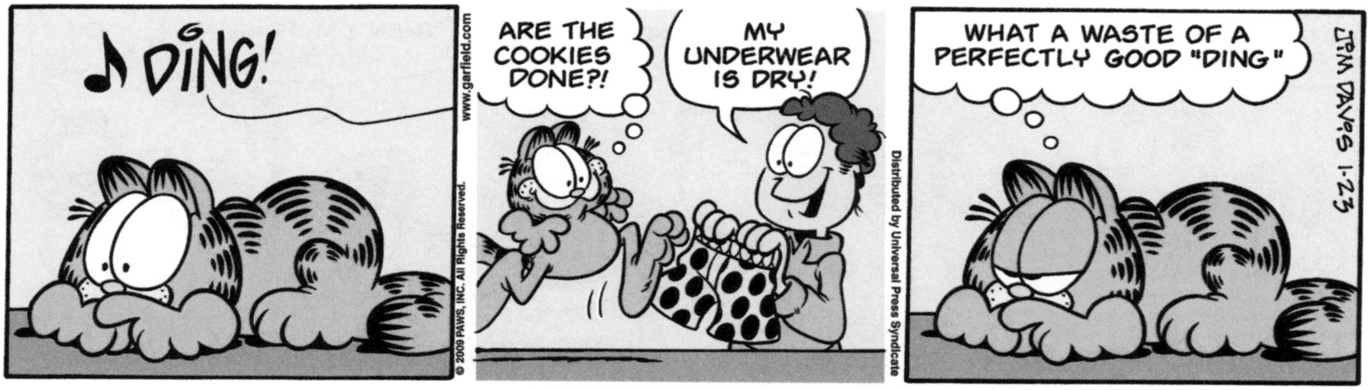
♪ DING!
© 2009 PAWS, INC. All Rights Reserved. www.garfield.com
ARE THE COOKIES DONE?!
MY UNDERWEAR IS DRY!
Distributed by Universal Press Syndicate
WHAT A WASTE OF A PERFECTLY GOOD "DING"
JIM DAVIS 1·23

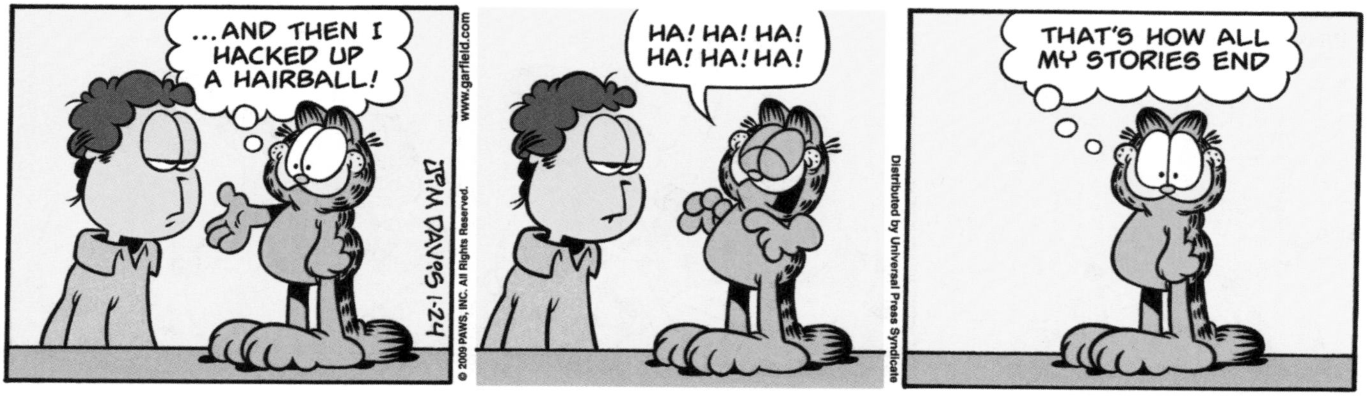
...AND THEN I HACKED UP A HAIRBALL!
JIM DAVIS 1·24
© 2009 PAWS, INC. All Rights Reserved. www.garfield.com
HA! HA! HA! HA! HA! HA!
Distributed by Universal Press Syndicate
THAT'S HOW ALL MY STORIES END

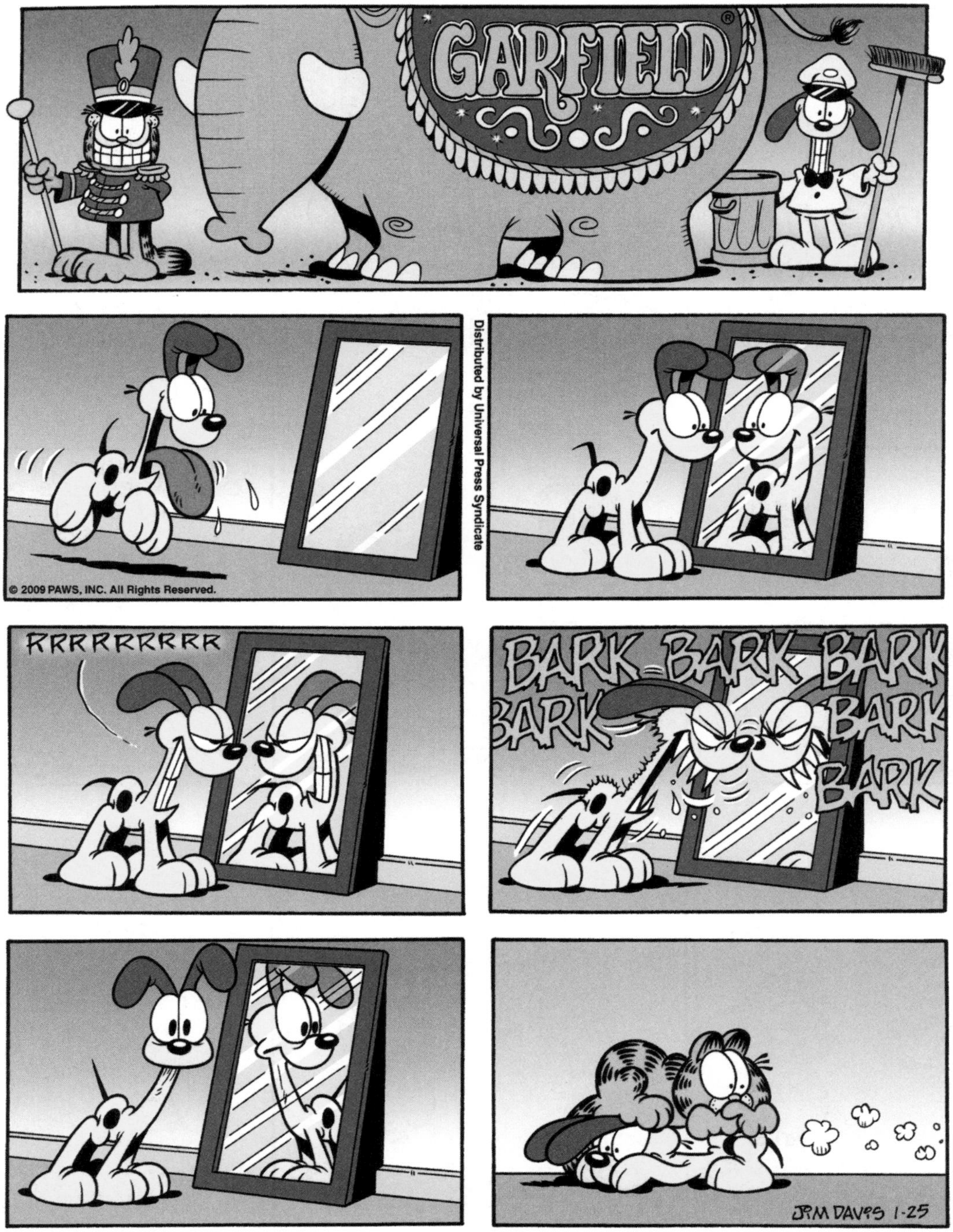
GARFIELD®
Distributed by Universal Press Syndicate
© 2009 PAWS, INC. All Rights Reserved.
RRRRRRRRR
BARK BARK BARK
BARK BARK
BARK
JIM DAVIS 1-25

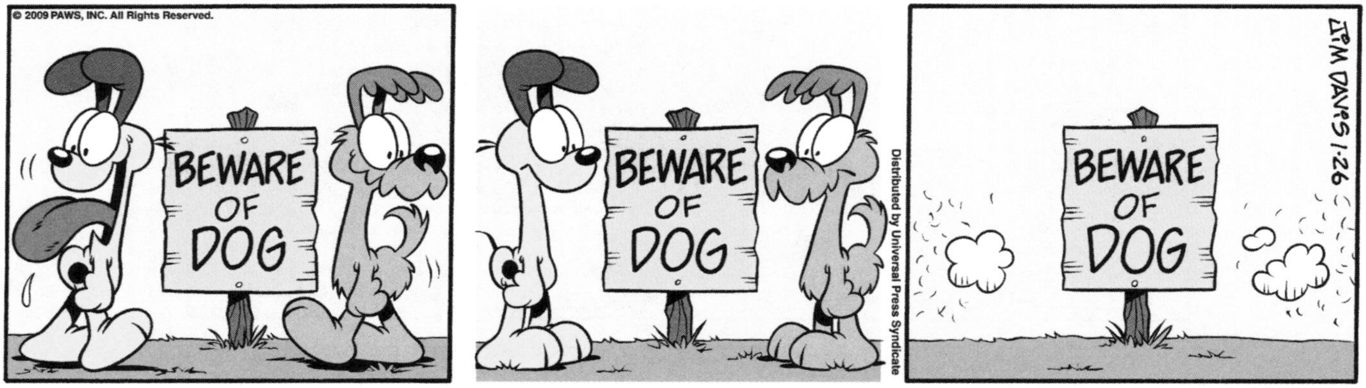
© 2009 PAWS, INC. All Rights Reserved.
BEWARE OF DOG
BEWARE OF DOG
Distributed by Universal Press Syndicate
BEWARE OF DOG
JIM DAVIS 1-26

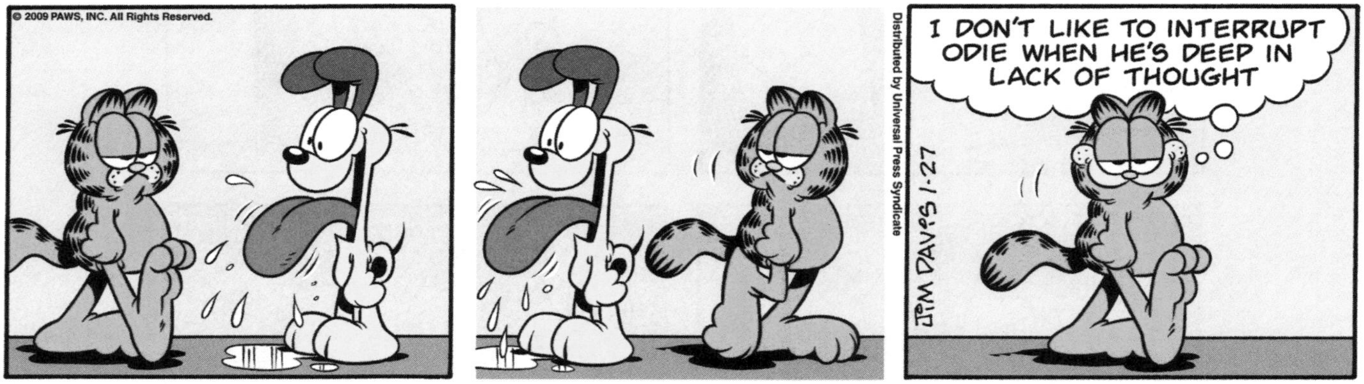
© 2009 PAWS, INC. All Rights Reserved.
Distributed by Universal Press Syndicate
JIM DAVIS 1-27
I DON'T LIKE TO INTERRUPT ODIE WHEN HE'S DEEP IN LACK OF THOUGHT

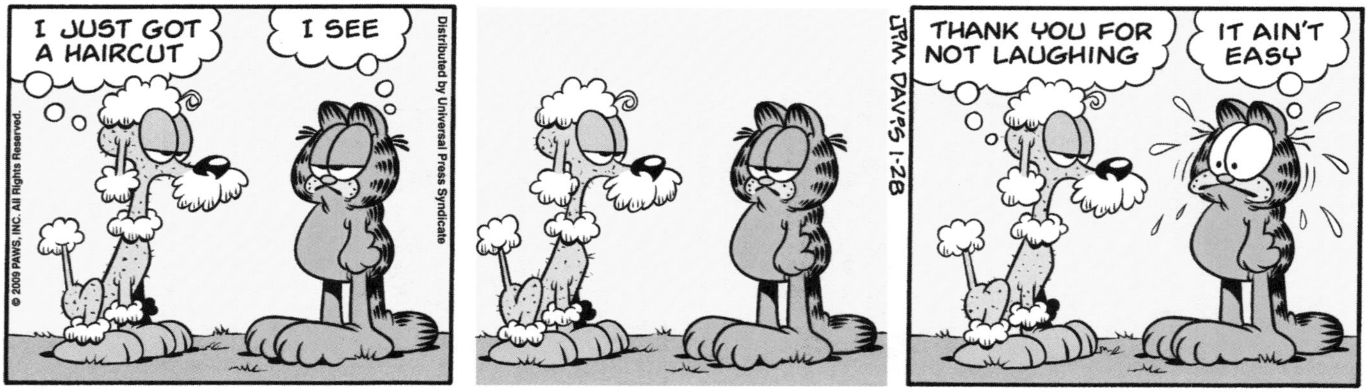
I JUST GOT A HAIRCUT
I SEE
© 2009 PAWS, INC. All Rights Reserved.
Distributed by Universal Press Syndicate
JIM DAVIS 1-28
THANK YOU FOR NOT LAUGHING
IT AIN'T EASY

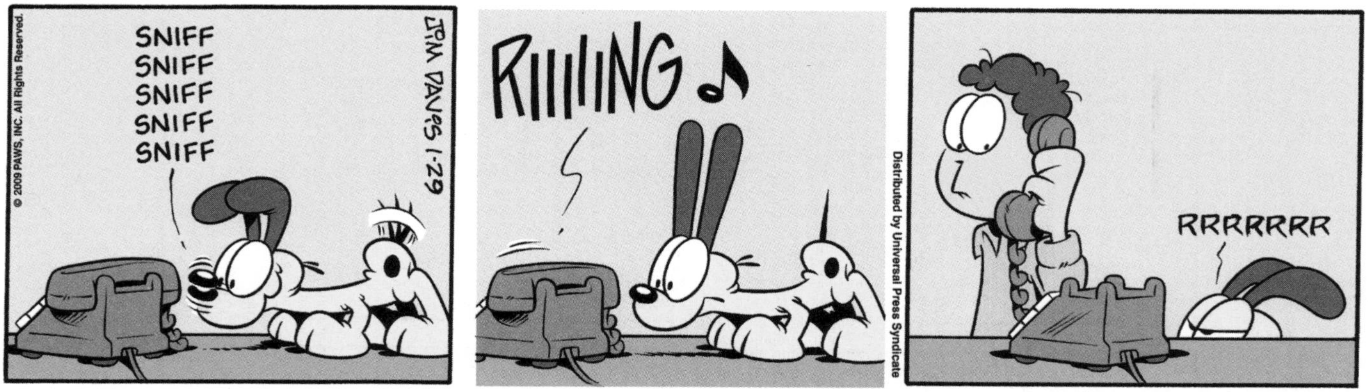
© 2009 PAWS, INC. All Rights Reserved.
SNIFF SNIFF SNIFF SNIFF SNIFF
JIM DAVIS 1-29
RIIIIING ♪
Distributed by Universal Press Syndicate
RRRRRRR

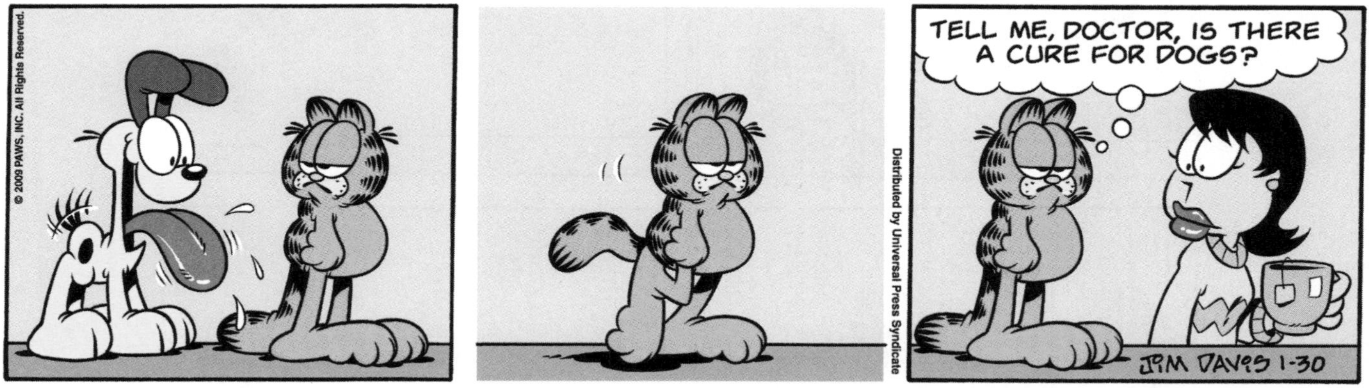
© 2009 PAWS, INC. All Rights Reserved.
Distributed by Universal Press Syndicate
TELL ME, DOCTOR, IS THERE A CURE FOR DOGS?
JIM DAVIS 1-30

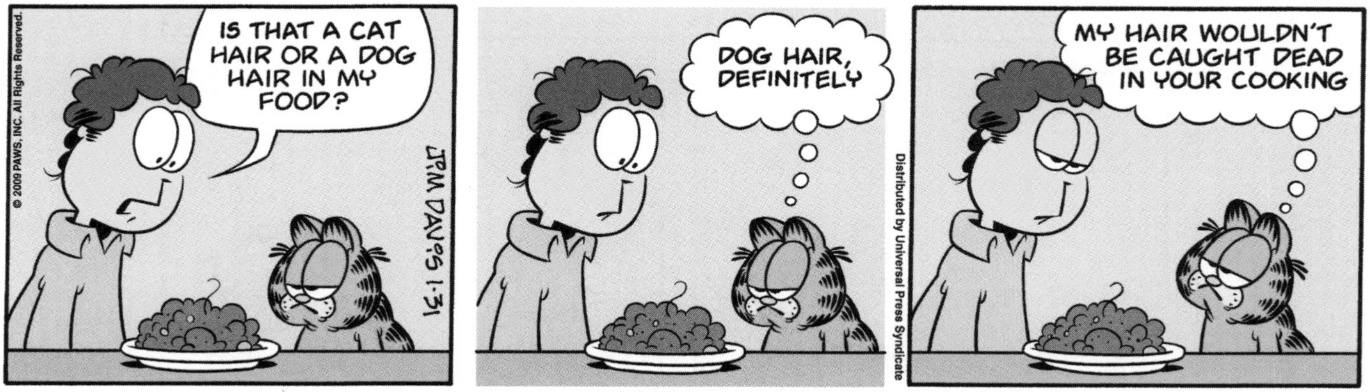
© 2009 PAWS, INC. All Rights Reserved.
IS THAT A CAT HAIR OR A DOG HAIR IN MY FOOD?
JIM DAVIS 1-31
DOG HAIR, DEFINITELY
Distributed by Universal Press Syndicate
MY HAIR WOULDN'T BE CAUGHT DEAD IN YOUR COOKING

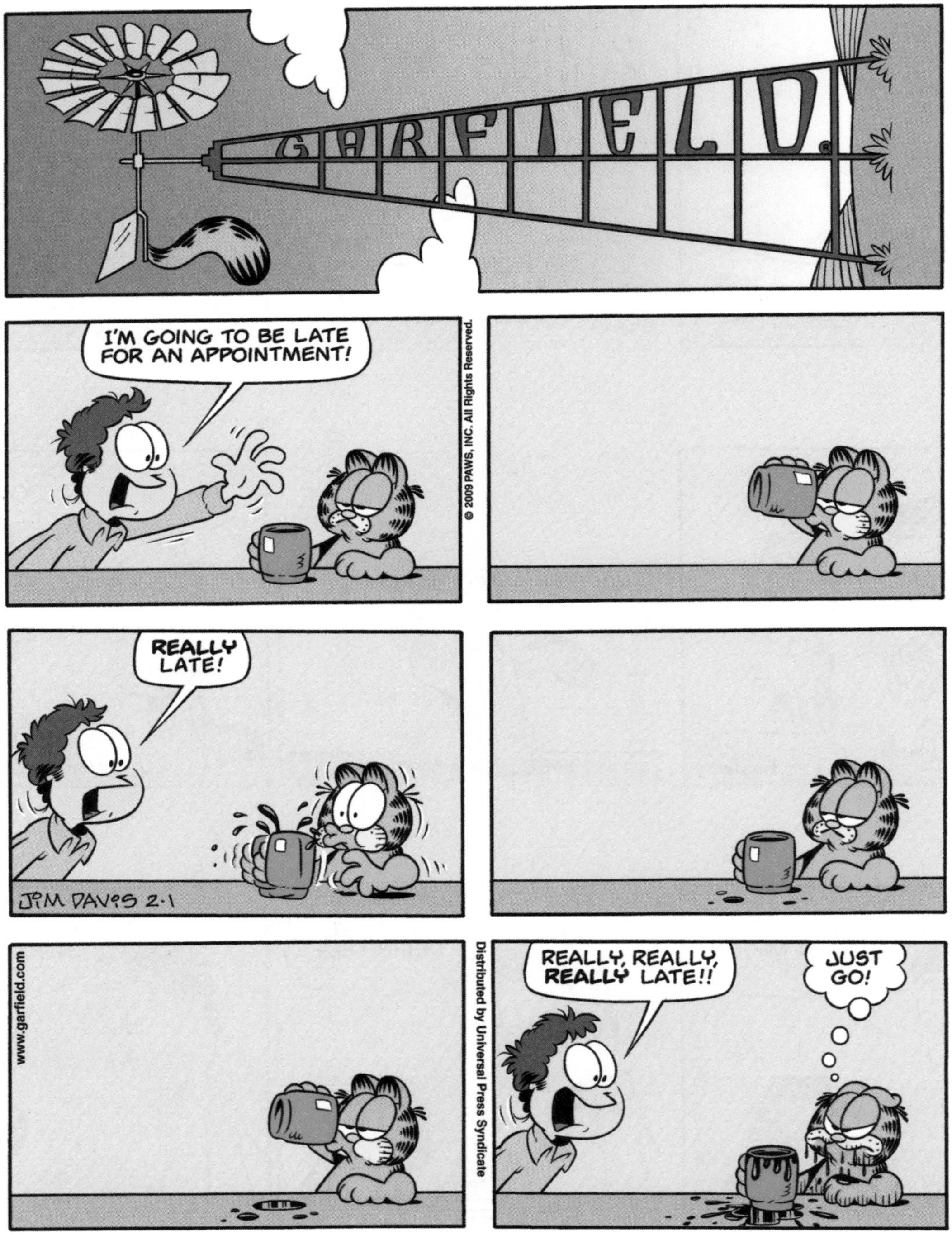
GARFIELD®
I'M GOING TO BE LATE FOR AN APPOINTMENT!
© 2009 PAWS, INC. All Rights Reserved.
REALLY LATE!
JIM DAVIS 2-1
www.garfield.com
Distributed by Universal Press Syndicate
REALLY, REALLY, REALLY LATE!!
JUST GO!

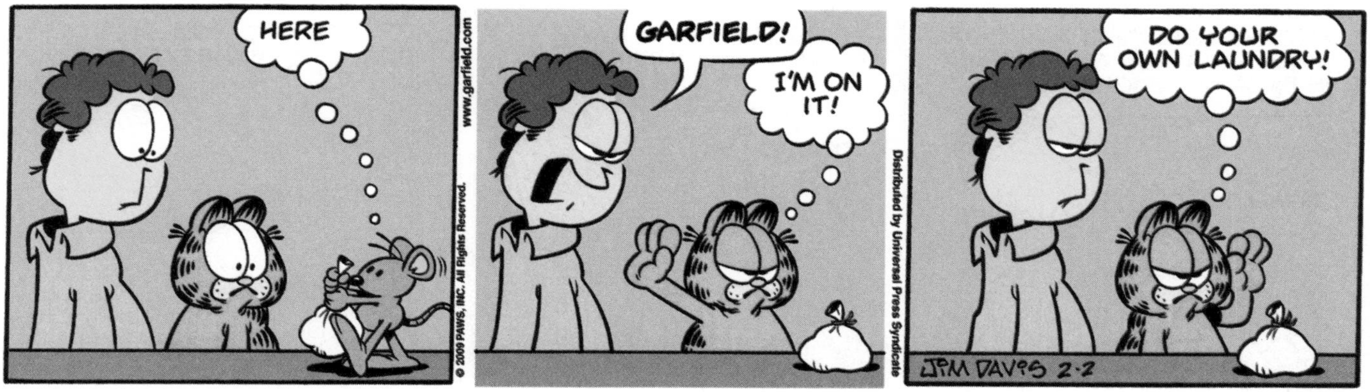
HERE
© 2009 PAWS, INC. All Rights Reserved.
www.garfield.com
GARFIELD!
I'M ON IT!
Distributed by Universal Press Syndicate
DO YOUR OWN LAUNDRY!
JIM DAVIS 2-2

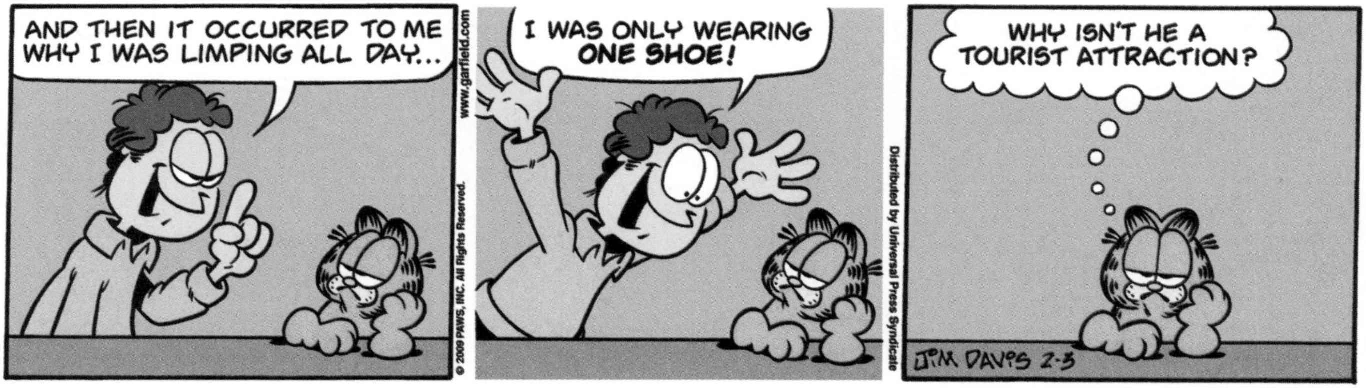
AND THEN IT OCCURRED TO ME WHY I WAS LIMPING ALL DAY...
© 2009 PAWS, INC. All Rights Reserved.
www.garfield.com
I WAS ONLY WEARING ONE SHOE!
Distributed by Universal Press Syndicate
WHY ISN'T HE A TOURIST ATTRACTION?
JIM DAVIS 2-3

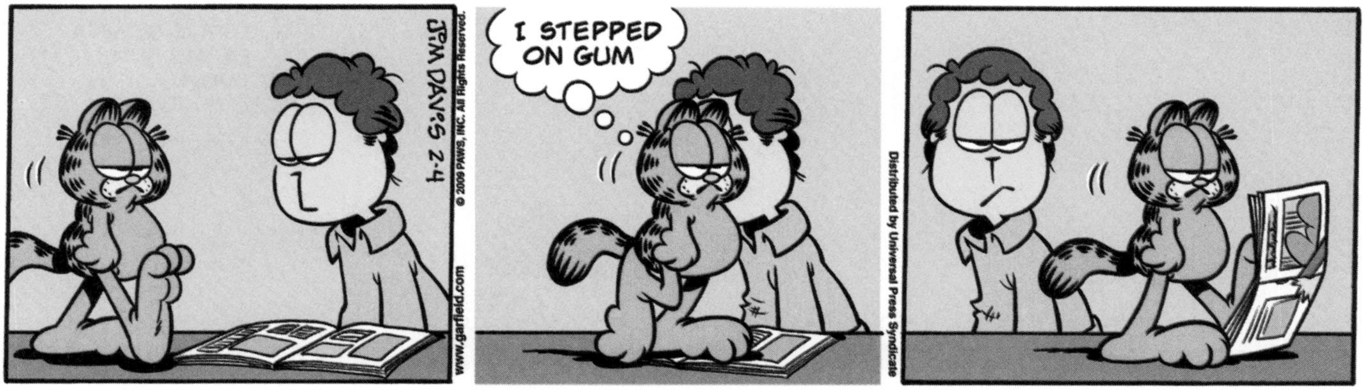
JIM DAVIS 2-4
© 2009 PAWS, INC. All Rights Reserved.
www.garfield.com
I STEPPED ON GUM
Distributed by Universal Press Syndicate

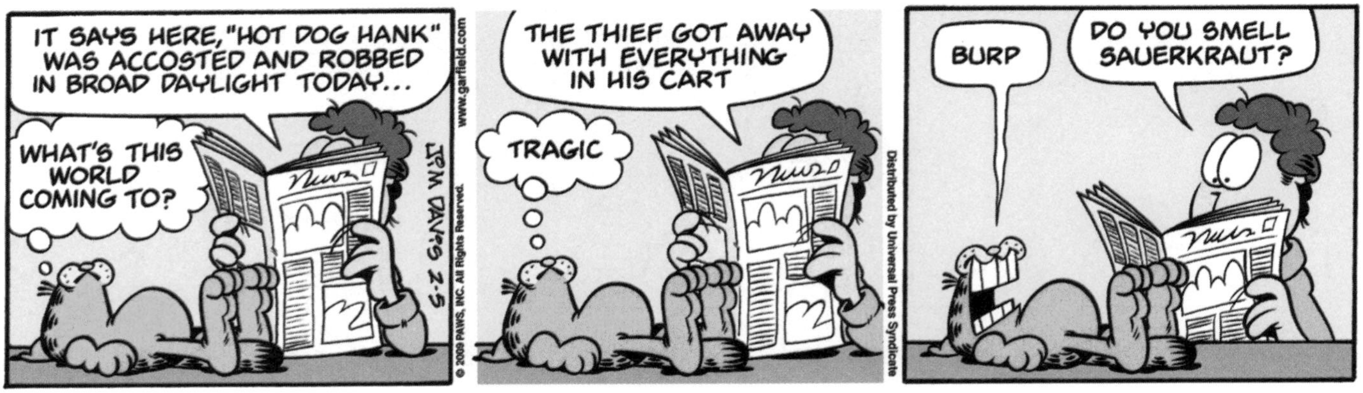
IT SAYS HERE, "HOT DOG HANK" WAS ACCOSTED AND ROBBED IN BROAD DAYLIGHT TODAY...
WHAT'S THIS WORLD COMING TO?
News
JIM DAVIS 2-5
www.garfield.com
© 2009 PAWS, INC. All Rights Reserved.
THE THIEF GOT AWAY WITH EVERYTHING IN HIS CART
TRAGIC
Distributed by Universal Press Syndicate
BURP
DO YOU SMELL SAUERKRAUT?

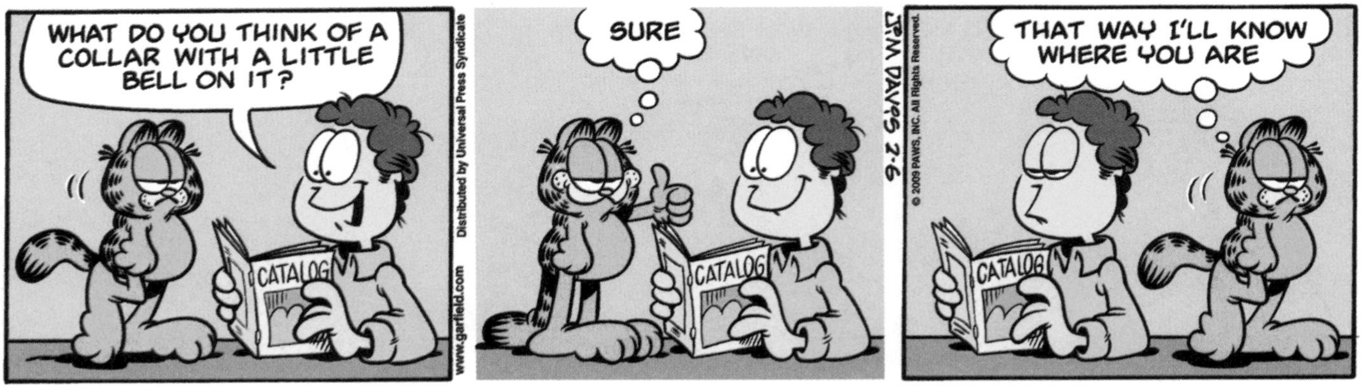
WHAT DO YOU THINK OF A COLLAR WITH A LITTLE BELL ON IT?
CATALOG
www.garfield.com
Distributed by Universal Press Syndicate
SURE
JIM DAVIS 2-6
© 2009 PAWS, INC. All Rights Reserved.
THAT WAY I'LL KNOW WHERE YOU ARE

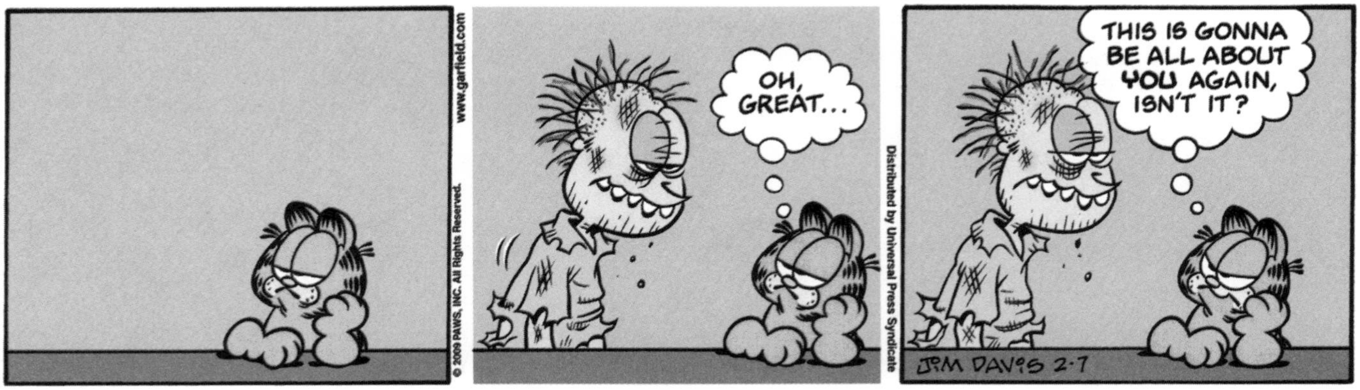
www.garfield.com
© 2009 PAWS, INC. All Rights Reserved.
OH, GREAT...
Distributed by Universal Press Syndicate
THIS IS GONNA BE ALL ABOUT YOU AGAIN, ISN'T IT?
JIM DAVIS 2-7

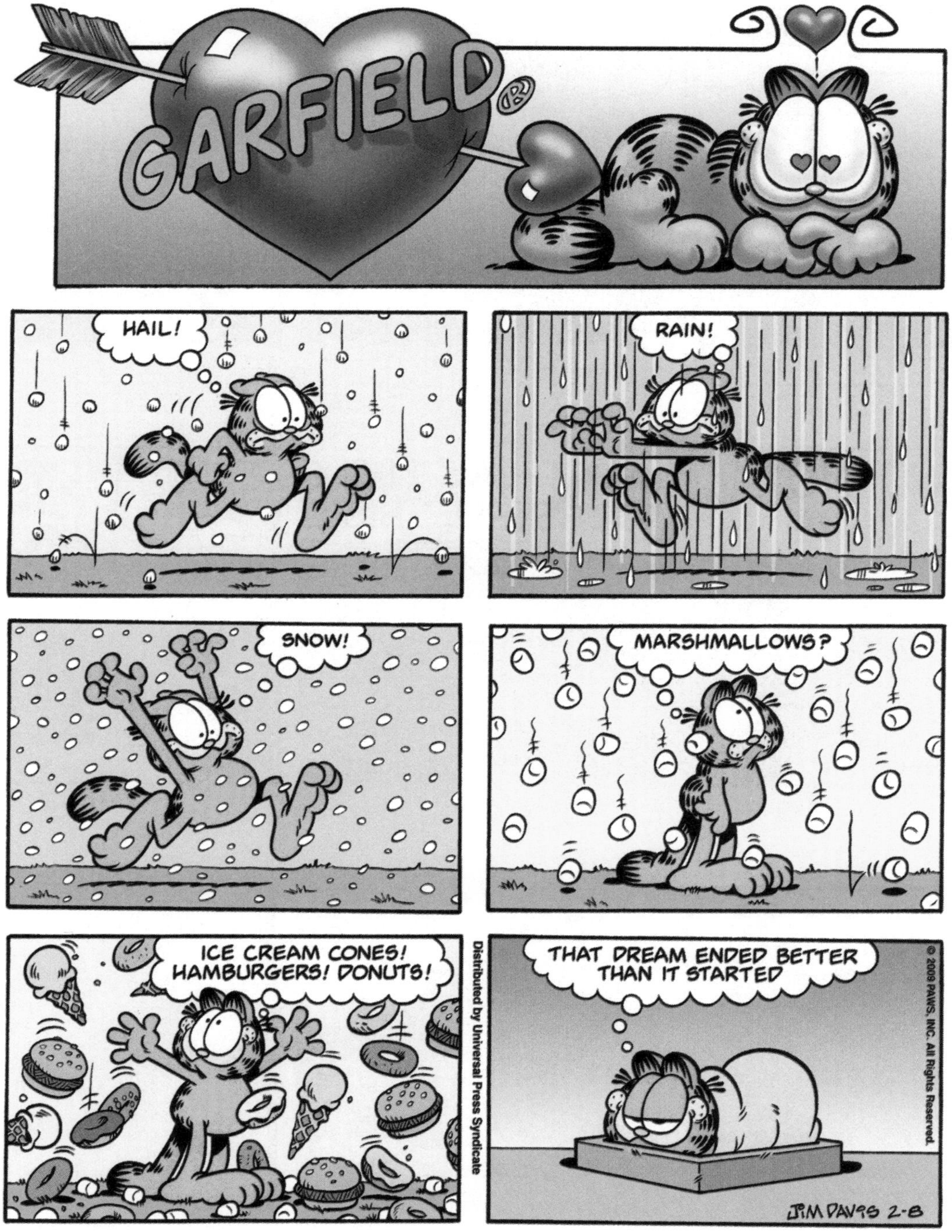
GARFIELD®
HAIL!
RAIN!
SNOW!
MARSHMALLOWS?
ICE CREAM CONES! HAMBURGERS! DONUTS!
Distributed by Universal Press Syndicate
THAT DREAM ENDED BETTER THAN IT STARTED
© 2009 PAWS, INC. All Rights Reserved.
JIM DAVIS 2-8

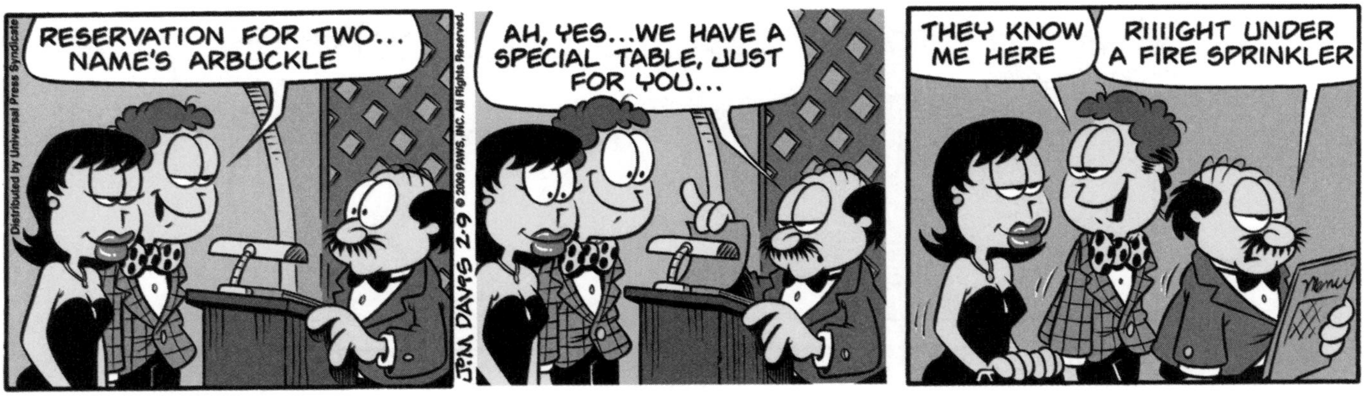
RESERVATION FOR TWO... NAME'S ARBUCKLE
Distributed by Universal Press Syndicate
AH, YES...WE HAVE A SPECIAL TABLE, JUST FOR YOU...
JIM DAVIS 2-9 © 2009 PAWS, INC. All Rights Reserved.
THEY KNOW ME HERE
RIIIIGHT UNDER A FIRE SPRINKLER
Menu

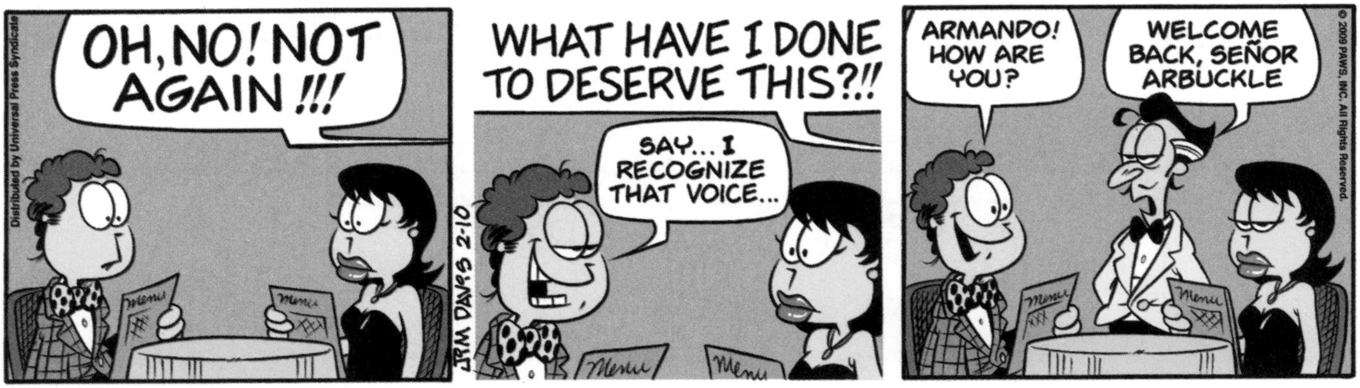
Distributed by Universal Press Syndicate
OH, NO! NOT AGAIN!!!
Menu
Menu
WHAT HAVE I DONE TO DESERVE THIS?!!
SAY... I RECOGNIZE THAT VOICE...
JIM DAVIS 2-10
ARMANDO! HOW ARE YOU?
WELCOME BACK, SEÑOR ARBUCKLE
© 2009 PAWS, INC. All Rights Reserved.

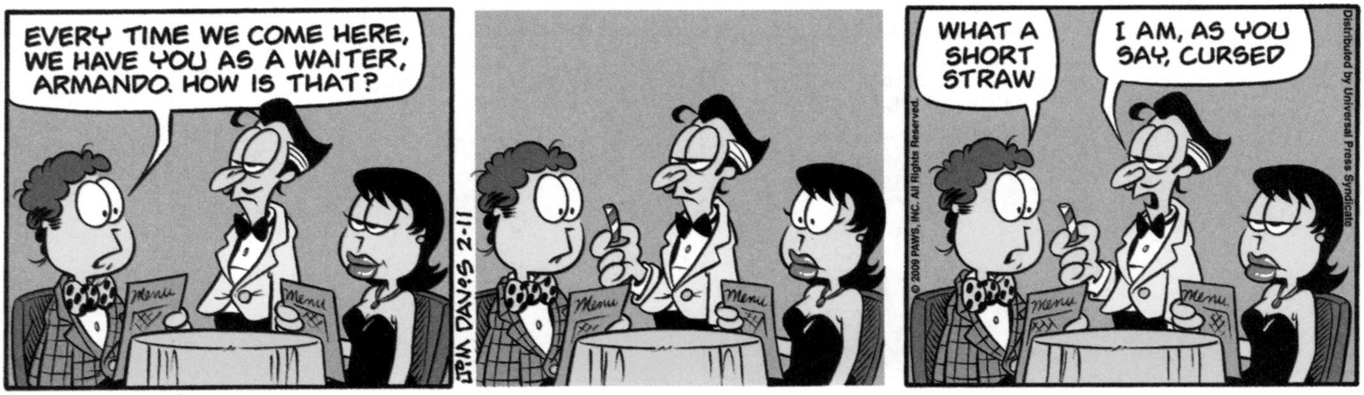
EVERY TIME WE COME HERE, WE HAVE YOU AS A WAITER, ARMANDO. HOW IS THAT?
Menu
JIM DAVIS 2-11
© 2009 PAWS, INC. All Rights Reserved.
WHAT A SHORT STRAW
I AM, AS YOU SAY, CURSED
Distributed by Universal Press Syndicate

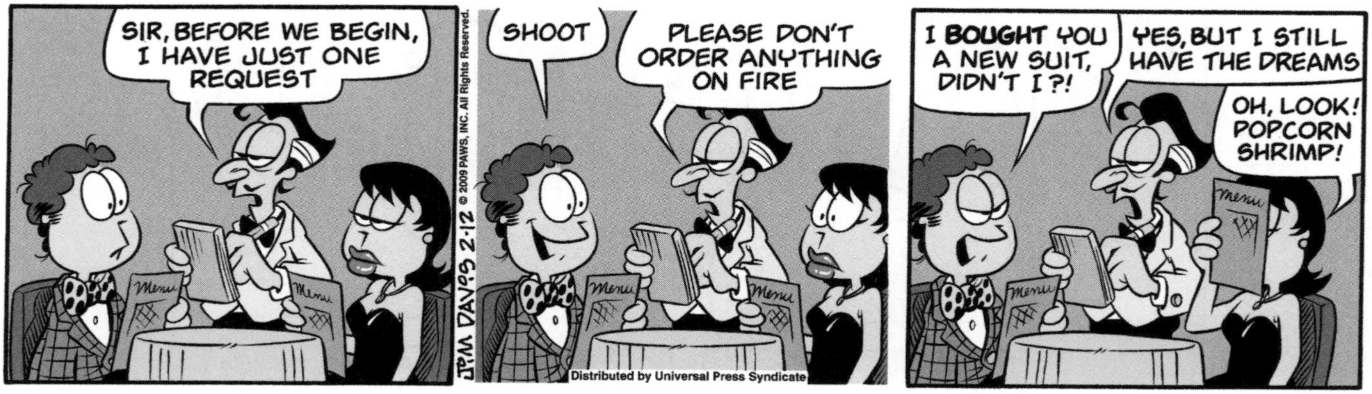
SIR, BEFORE WE BEGIN, I HAVE JUST ONE REQUEST
SHOOT
PLEASE DON'T ORDER ANYTHING ON FIRE
I **BOUGHT** YOU A NEW SUIT, DIDN'T I?!
YES, BUT I STILL HAVE THE DREAMS
OH, LOOK! POPCORN SHRIMP!
JIM DAVIS 2·12 © 2009 PAWS, INC. All Rights Reserved.
Distributed by Universal Press Syndicate

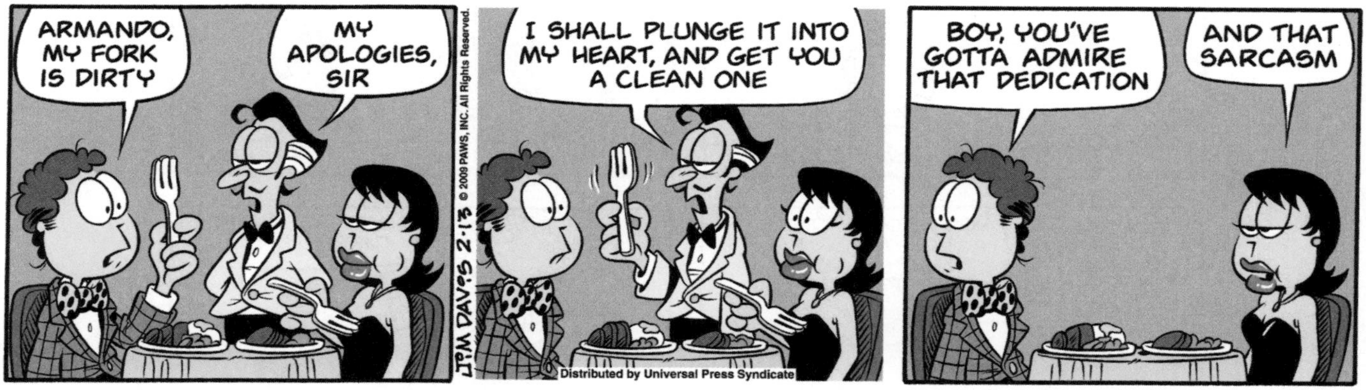
ARMANDO, MY FORK IS DIRTY
MY APOLOGIES, SIR
I SHALL PLUNGE IT INTO MY HEART, AND GET YOU A CLEAN ONE
BOY, YOU'VE GOTTA ADMIRE THAT DEDICATION
AND THAT SARCASM
JIM DAVIS 2·13 © 2009 PAWS, INC. All Rights Reserved.
Distributed by Universal Press Syndicate

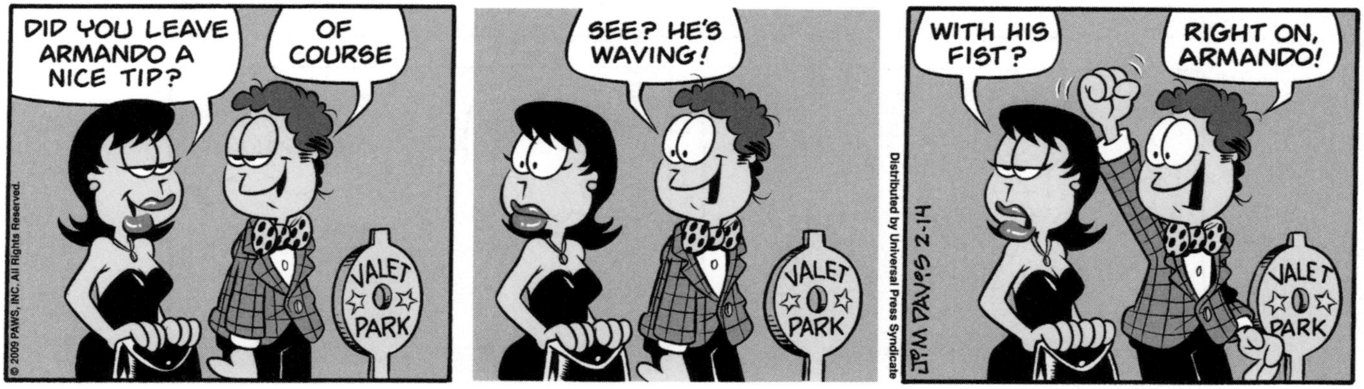
DID YOU LEAVE ARMANDO A NICE TIP?
OF COURSE
VALET PARK
SEE? HE'S WAVING!
WITH HIS FIST?
RIGHT ON, ARMANDO!
© 2009 PAWS, INC. All Rights Reserved.
JIM DAVIS 2-14
Distributed by Universal Press Syndicate

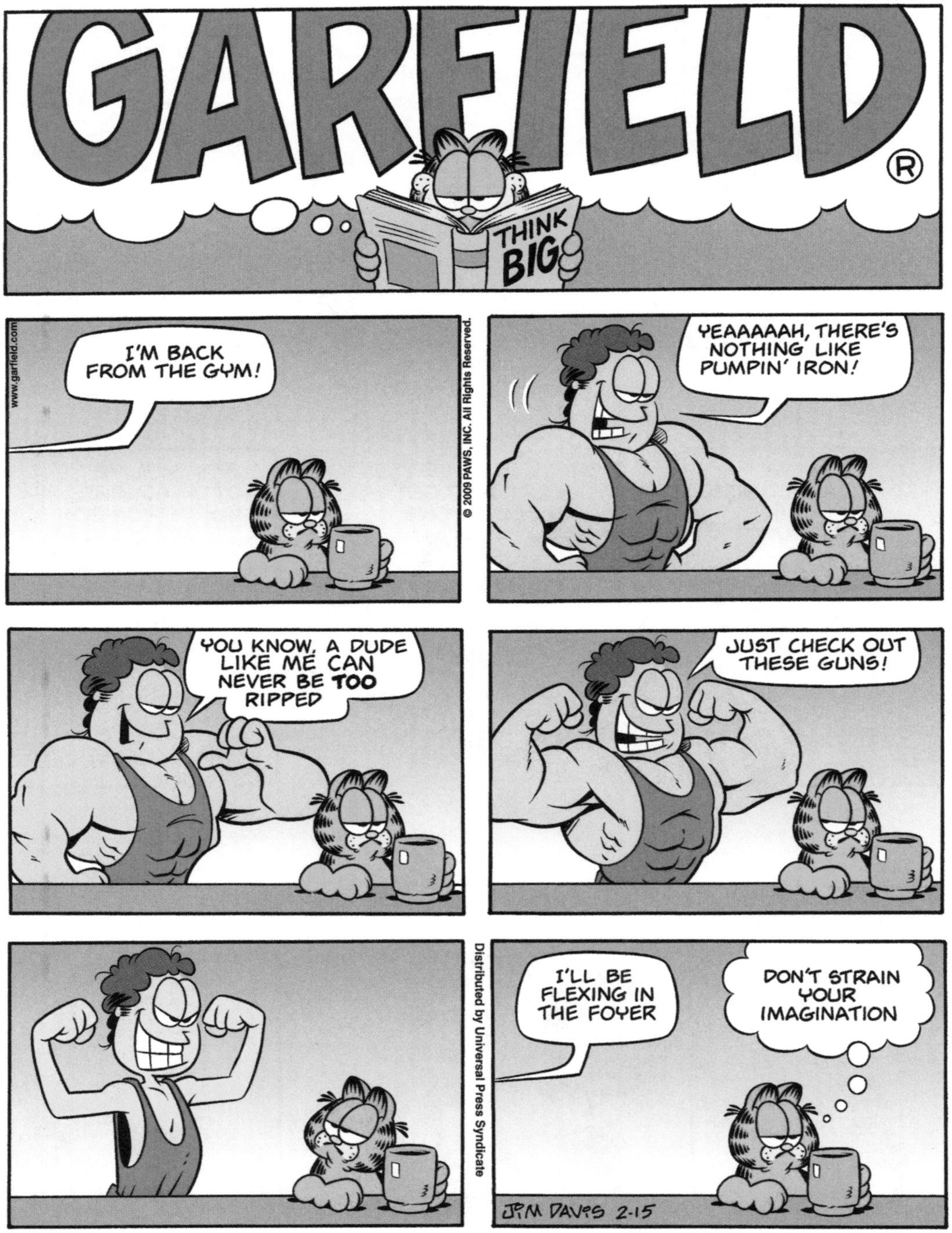
GARFIELD
THINK BIG
www.garfield.com
I'M BACK FROM THE GYM!
© 2009 PAWS, INC. All Rights Reserved.
YEAAAAAH, THERE'S NOTHING LIKE PUMPIN' IRON!
YOU KNOW, A DUDE LIKE ME CAN NEVER BE TOO RIPPED
JUST CHECK OUT THESE GUNS!
Distributed by Universal Press Syndicate
I'LL BE FLEXING IN THE FOYER
DON'T STRAIN YOUR IMAGINATION
JIM DAVIS 2-15

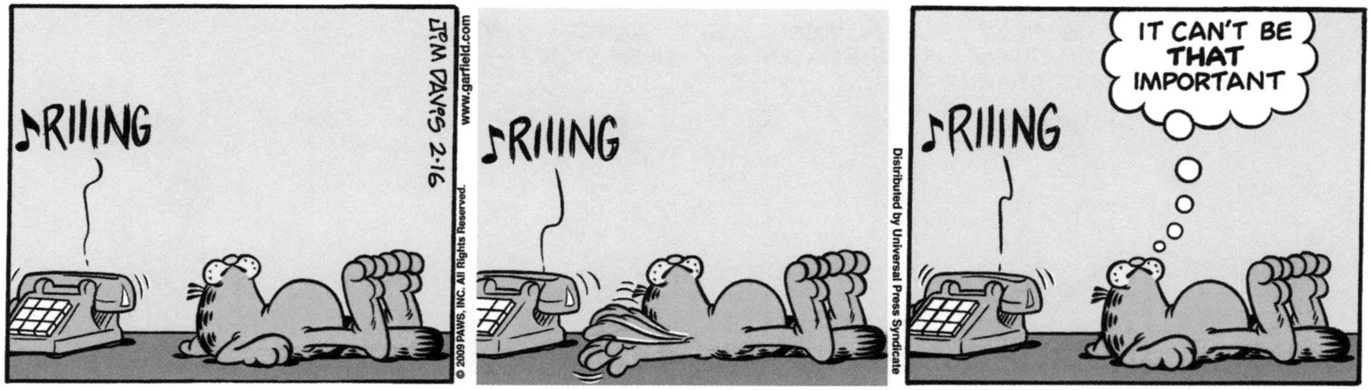
♪RIIING
JIM DAVIS 2·16
© 2009 PAWS, INC. All Rights Reserved. www.garfield.com
♪RIIING
Distributed by Universal Press Syndicate
♪RIIING
IT CAN'T BE **THAT** IMPORTANT

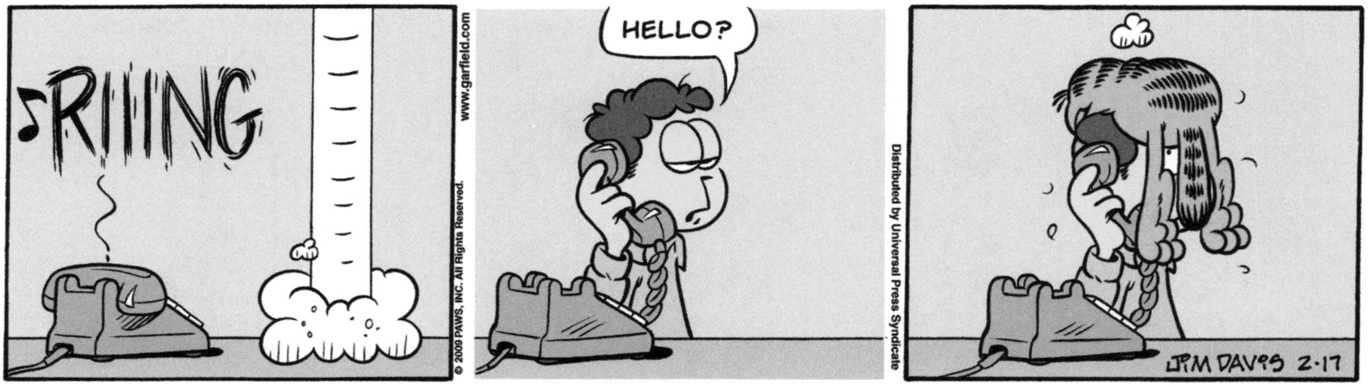
♪RIIING
© 2009 PAWS, INC. All Rights Reserved. www.garfield.com
HELLO?
Distributed by Universal Press Syndicate
JIM DAVIS 2·17

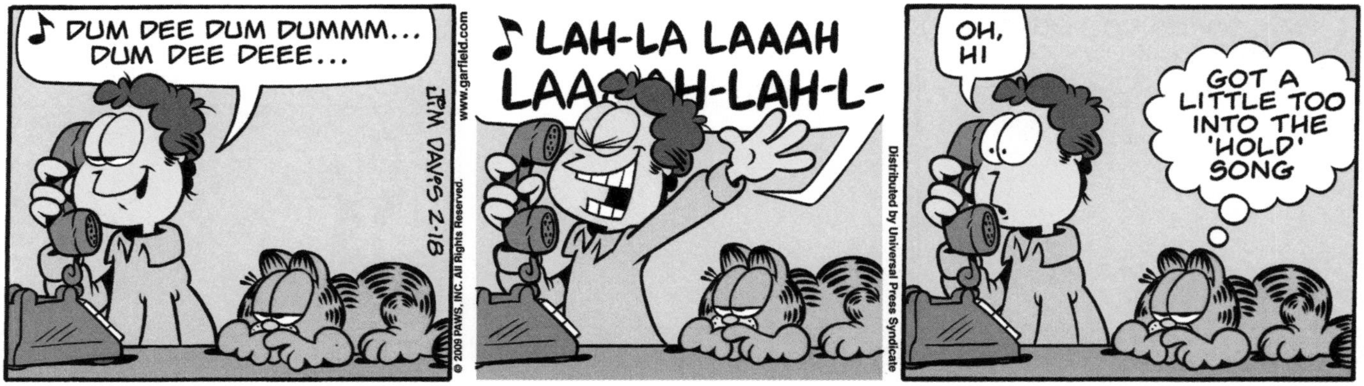
♪ DUM DEE DUM DUMMM... DUM DEE DEEE...
JIM DAVIS 2·18
© 2009 PAWS, INC. All Rights Reserved. www.garfield.com
♪ LAH-LA LAAAH
LAA H-LAH-L-
Distributed by Universal Press Syndicate
OH, HI
GOT A LITTLE TOO INTO THE 'HOLD' SONG

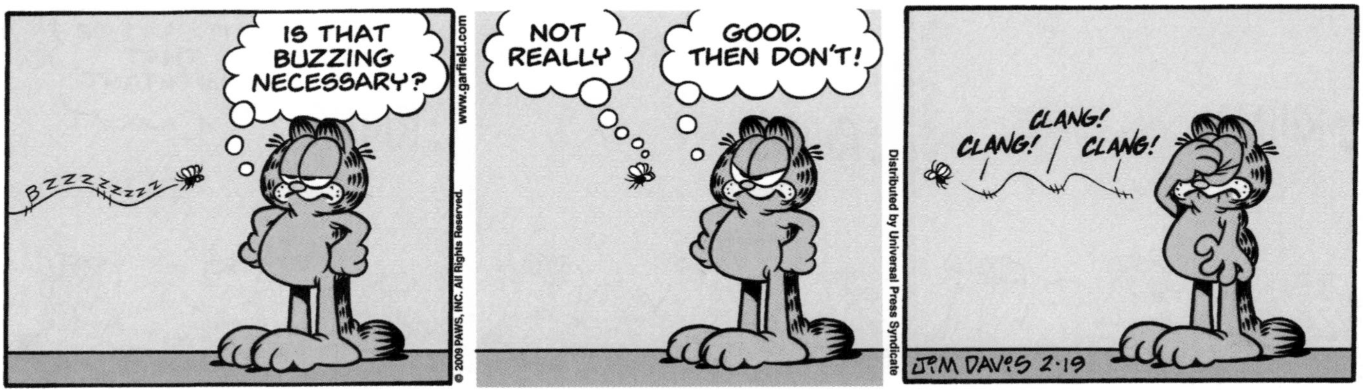
IS THAT BUZZING NECESSARY?
BZZZZZZZZZ
www.garfield.com
© 2009 PAWS, INC. All Rights Reserved.
NOT REALLY
GOOD. THEN DON'T!
Distributed by Universal Press Syndicate
CLANG!
CLANG!
CLANG!
JIM DAVIS 2-19

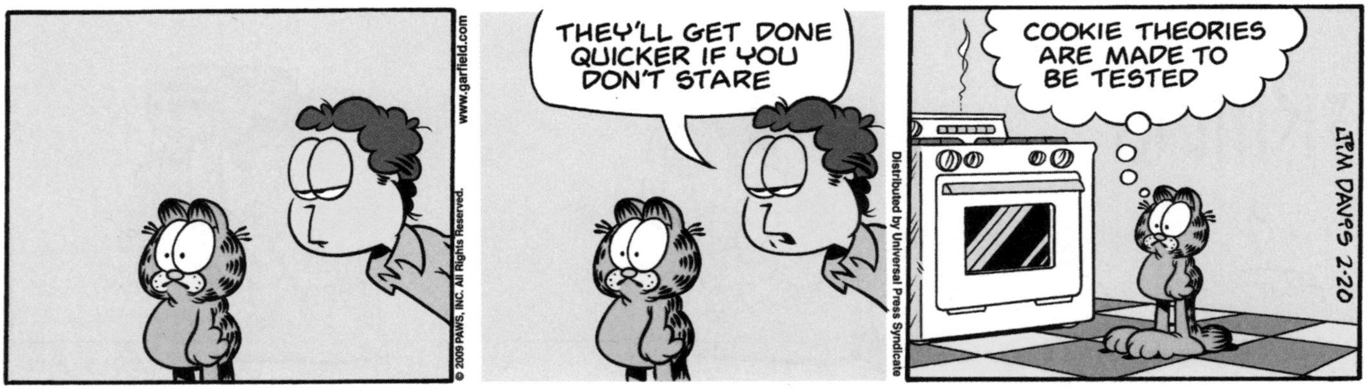
www.garfield.com
© 2009 PAWS, INC. All Rights Reserved.
THEY'LL GET DONE QUICKER IF YOU DON'T STARE
Distributed by Universal Press Syndicate
COOKIE THEORIES ARE MADE TO BE TESTED
JIM DAVIS 2-20

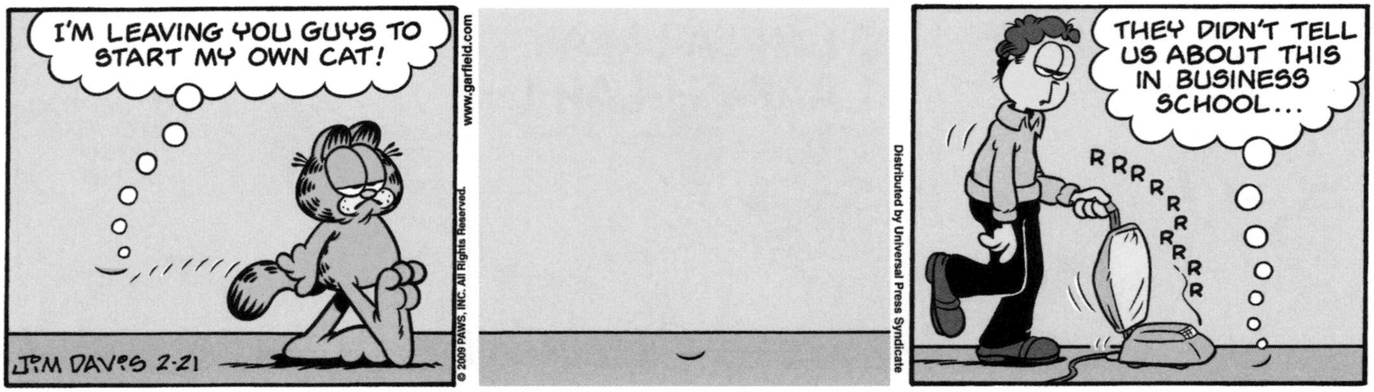
I'M LEAVING YOU GUYS TO START MY OWN CAT!
JIM DAVIS 2-21
www.garfield.com
© 2009 PAWS, INC. All Rights Reserved.
Distributed by Universal Press Syndicate
THEY DIDN'T TELL US ABOUT THIS IN BUSINESS SCHOOL...
RRRRRRRRRRR

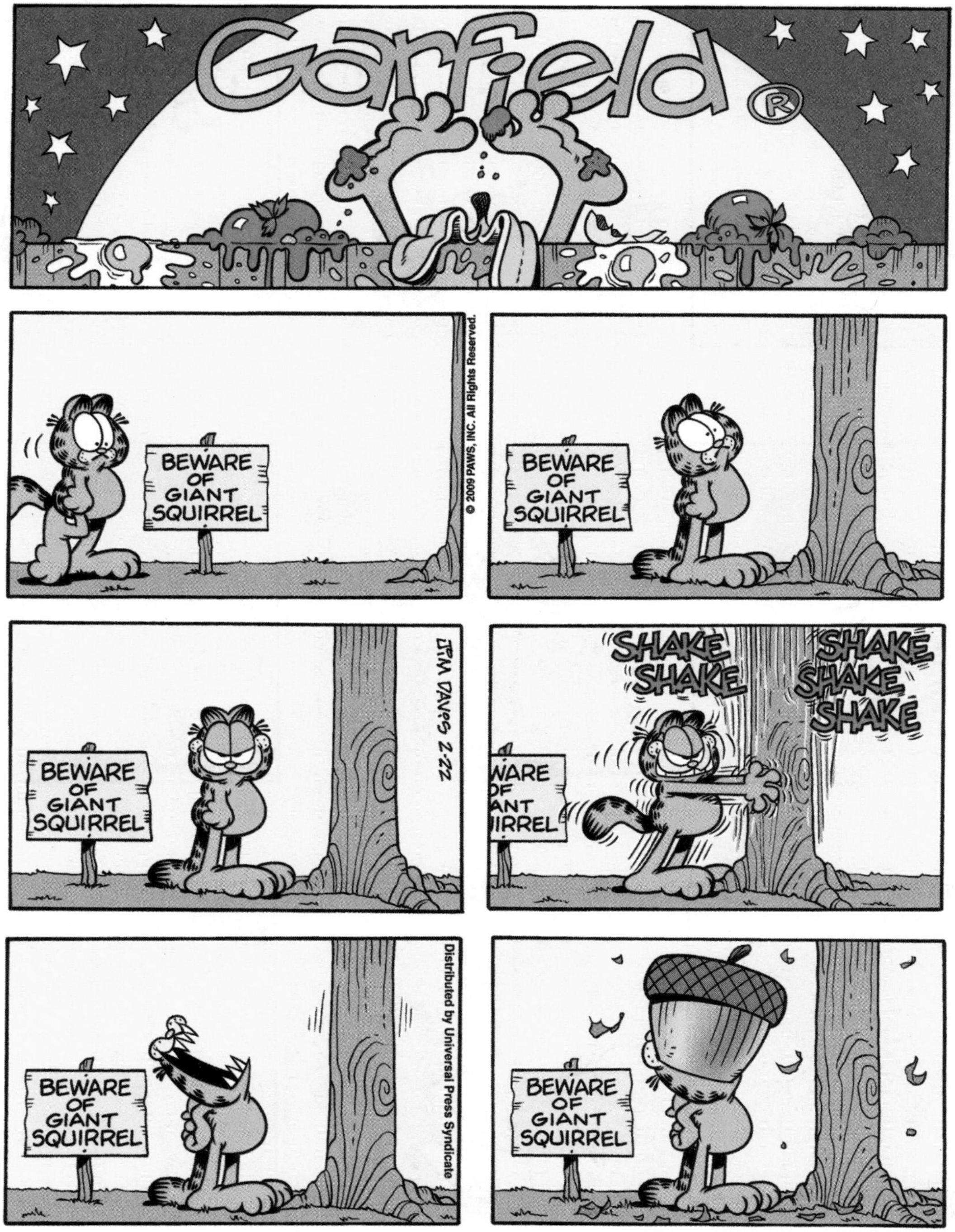
Garfield®
BEWARE OF GIANT SQUIRREL
© 2009 PAWS, INC. All Rights Reserved.
BEWARE OF GIANT SQUIRREL
BEWARE OF GIANT SQUIRREL
JPM DAVIS 2-22
SHAKE SHAKE
SHAKE SHAKE SHAKE
BEWARE OF GIANT SQUIRREL
Distributed by Universal Press Syndicate
BEWARE OF GIANT SQUIRREL

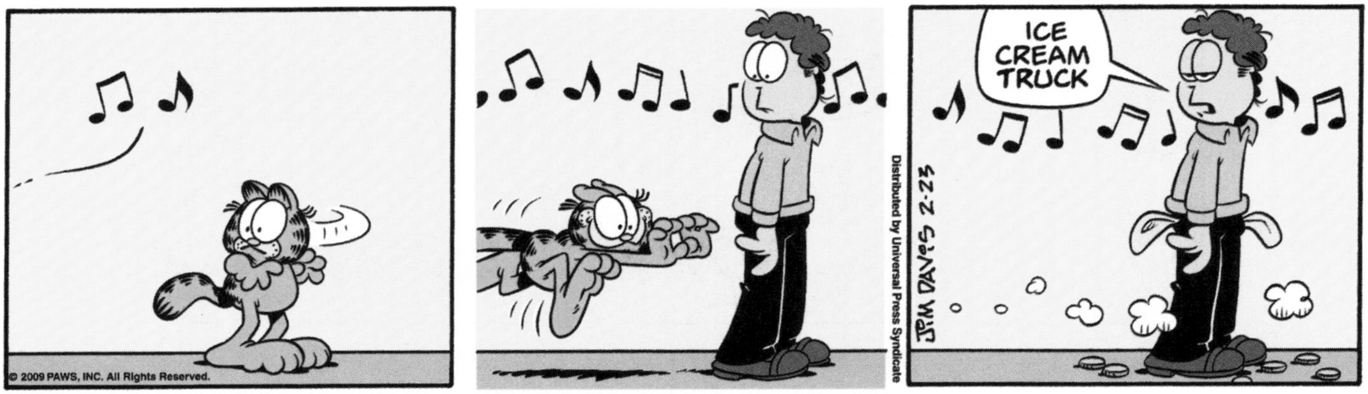
© 2009 PAWS, INC. All Rights Reserved.
Distributed by Universal Press Syndicate
JIM DAVIS 2-23
ICE CREAM TRUCK

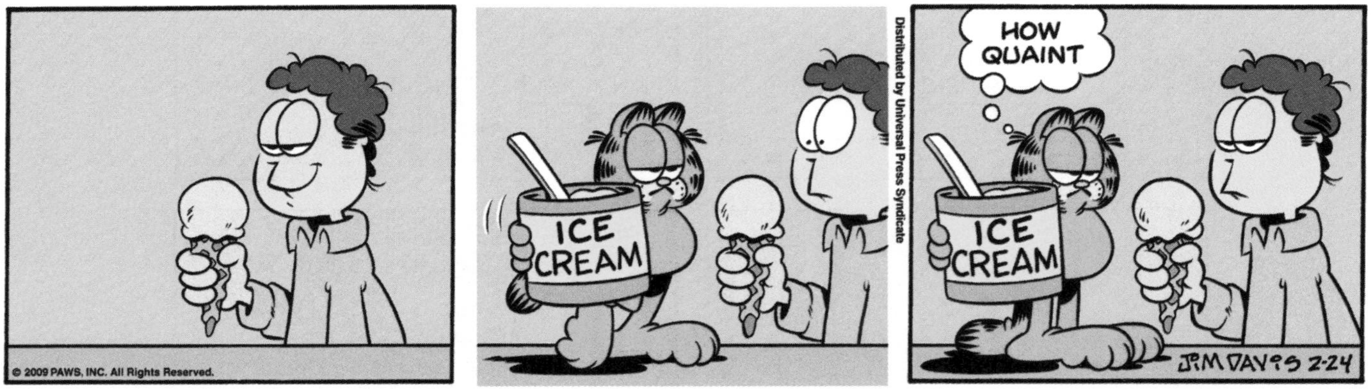
© 2009 PAWS, INC. All Rights Reserved.
Distributed by Universal Press Syndicate
ICE CREAM
ICE CREAM
HOW QUAINT
JIM DAVIS 2-24

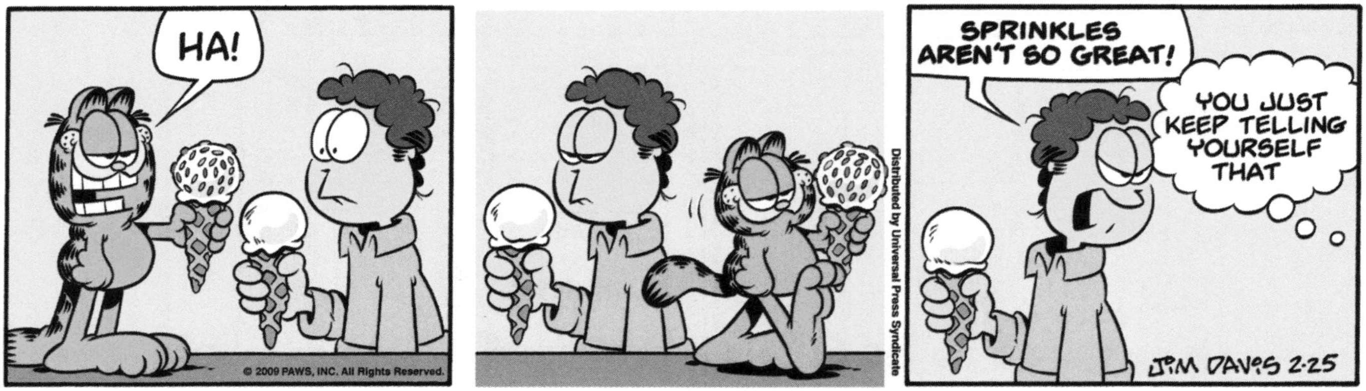
HA!
© 2009 PAWS, INC. All Rights Reserved.
Distributed by Universal Press Syndicate
SPRINKLES AREN'T SO GREAT!
YOU JUST KEEP TELLING YOURSELF THAT
JIM DAVIS 2-25

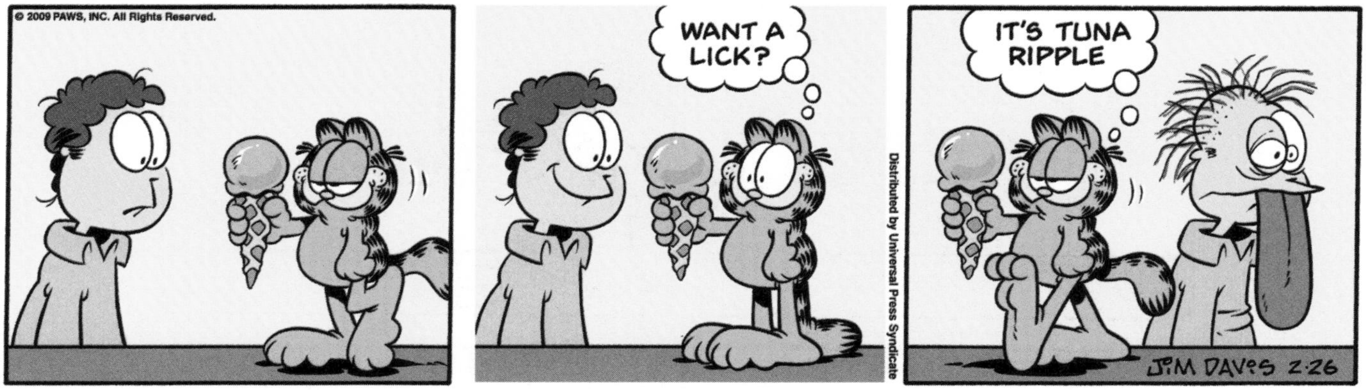
© 2009 PAWS, INC. All Rights Reserved.
WANT A LICK?
Distributed by Universal Press Syndicate
IT'S TUNA RIPPLE
JIM DAVIS 2-26

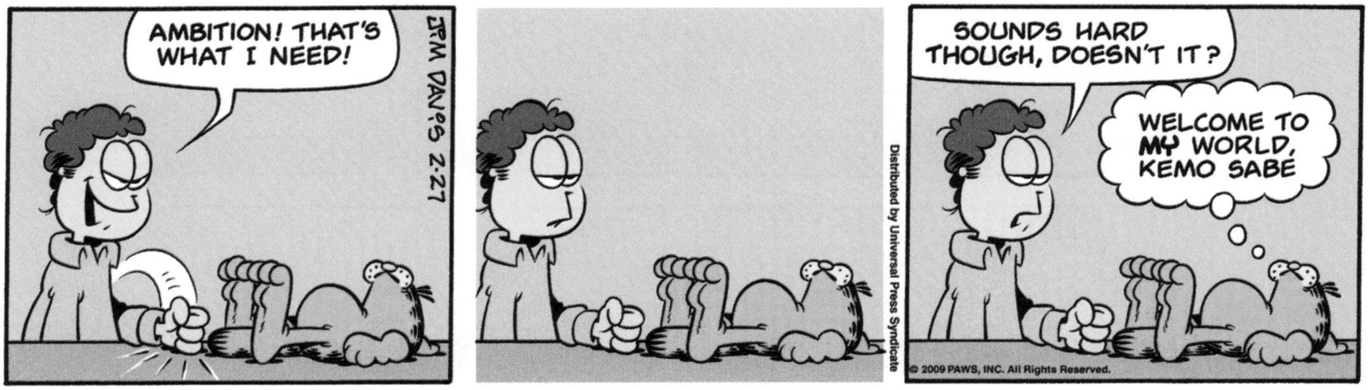
AMBITION! THAT'S WHAT I NEED!
JIM DAVIS 2-27
Distributed by Universal Press Syndicate
SOUNDS HARD THOUGH, DOESN'T IT?
WELCOME TO **MY** WORLD, KEMO SABE
© 2009 PAWS, INC. All Rights Reserved.

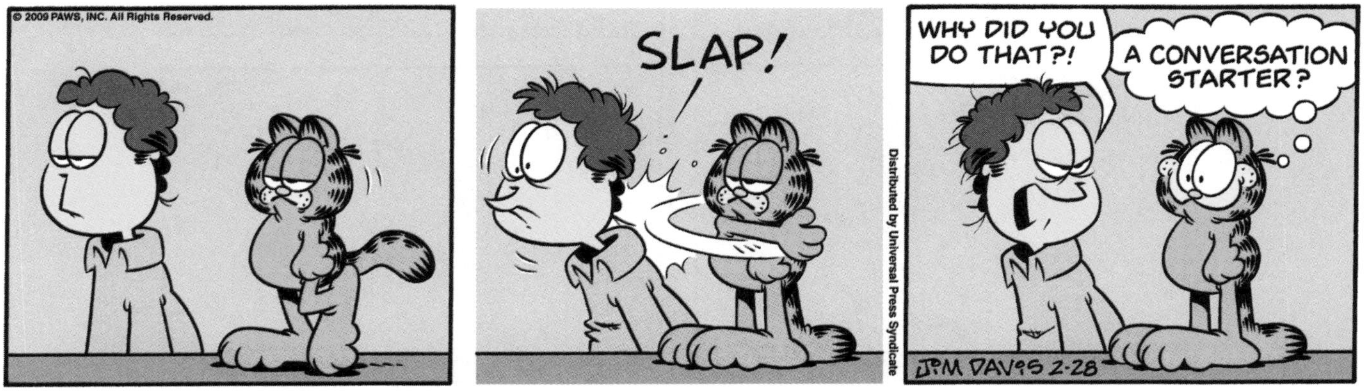
© 2009 PAWS, INC. All Rights Reserved.
SLAP!
Distributed by Universal Press Syndicate
WHY DID YOU DO THAT?!
A CONVERSATION STARTER?
JIM DAVIS 2-28

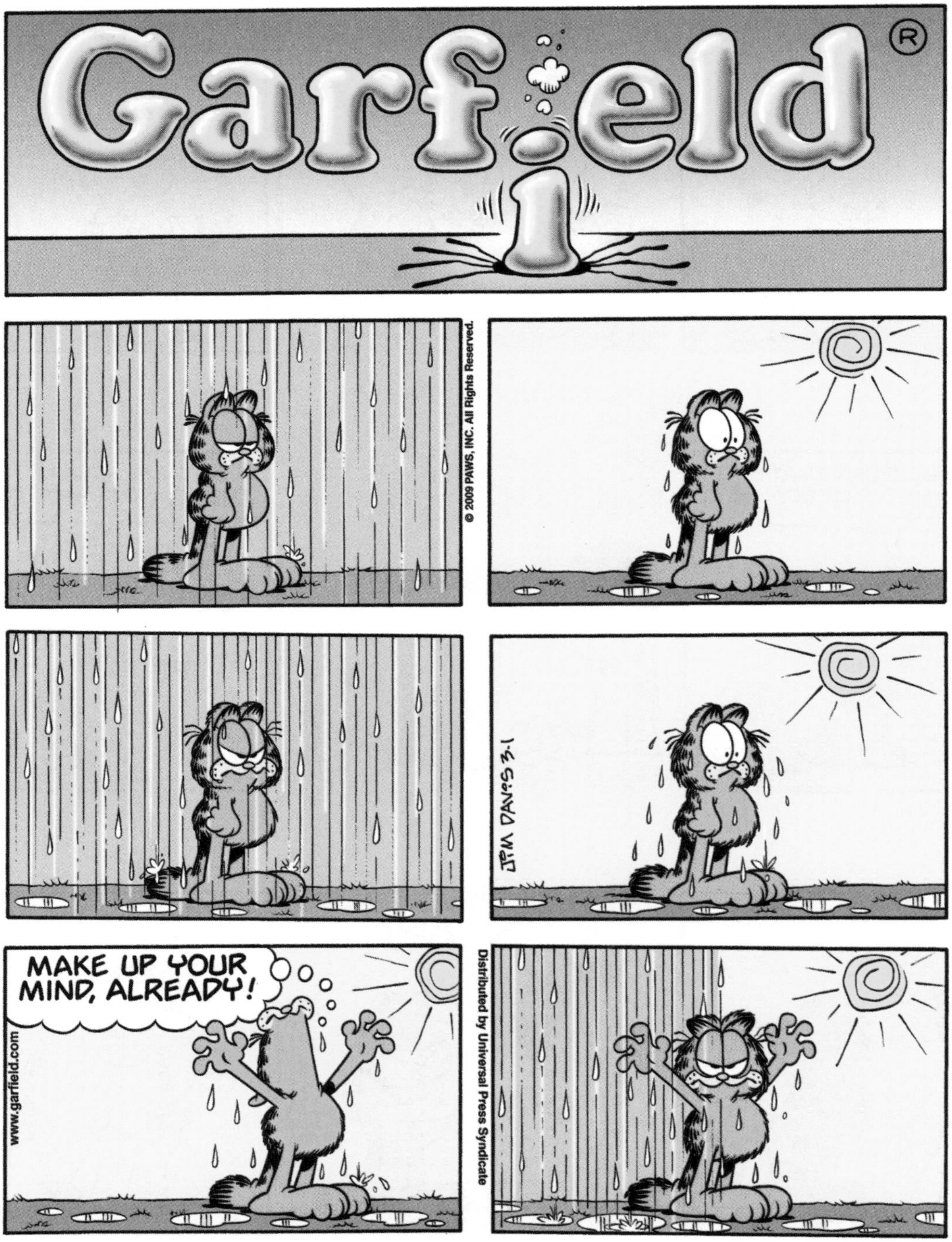
Garfield®
© 2009 PAWS, INC. All Rights Reserved.
JIM DAVIS 3-1
MAKE UP YOUR MIND, ALREADY!
www.garfield.com
Distributed by Universal Press Syndicate

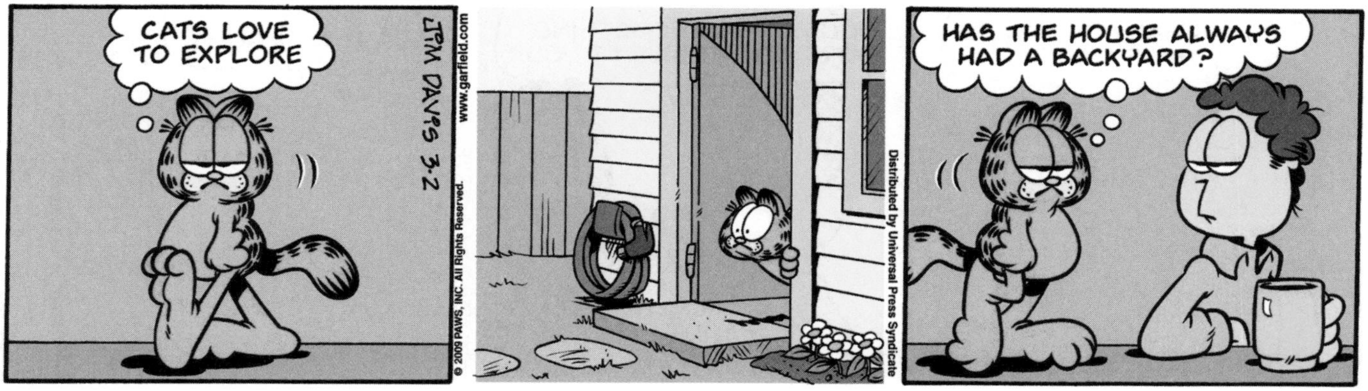
CATS LOVE TO EXPLORE
www.garfield.com
© 2009 PAWS, INC. All Rights Reserved.
Distributed by Universal Press Syndicate
HAS THE HOUSE ALWAYS HAD A BACKYARD?

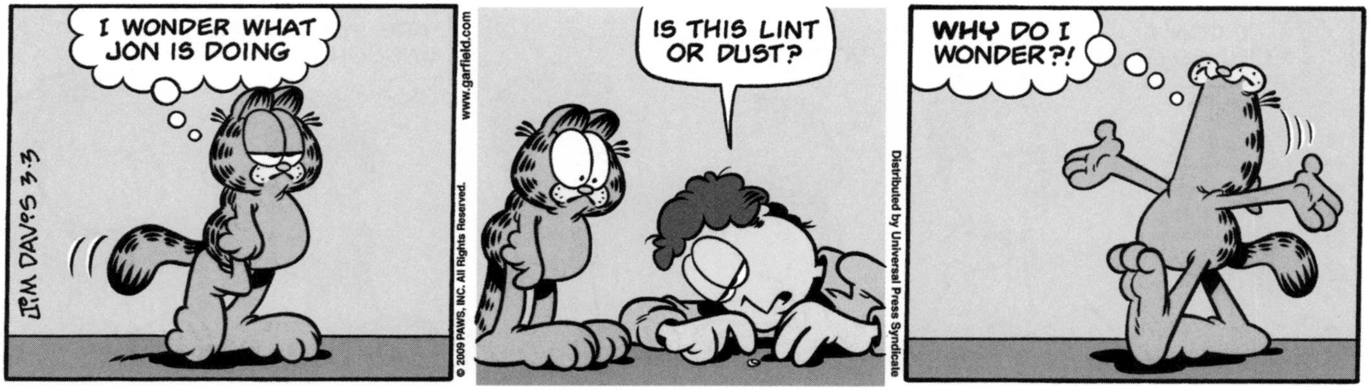
I WONDER WHAT JON IS DOING
www.garfield.com
© 2009 PAWS, INC. All Rights Reserved.
IS THIS LINT OR DUST?
Distributed by Universal Press Syndicate
WHY DO I WONDER?!

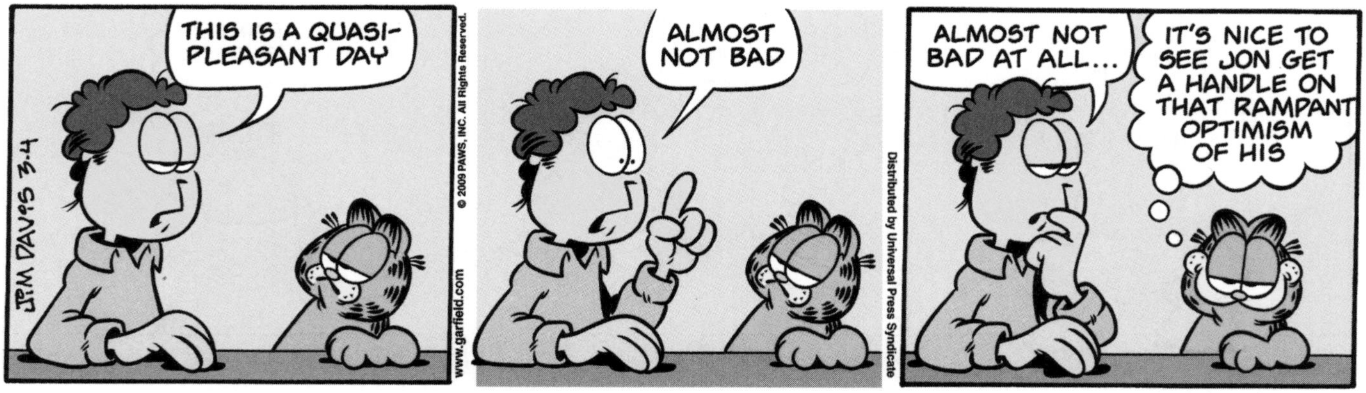
THIS IS A QUASI-PLEASANT DAY
www.garfield.com
© 2009 PAWS, INC. All Rights Reserved.
ALMOST NOT BAD
Distributed by Universal Press Syndicate
ALMOST NOT BAD AT ALL...
IT'S NICE TO SEE JON GET A HANDLE ON THAT RAMPANT OPTIMISM OF HIS

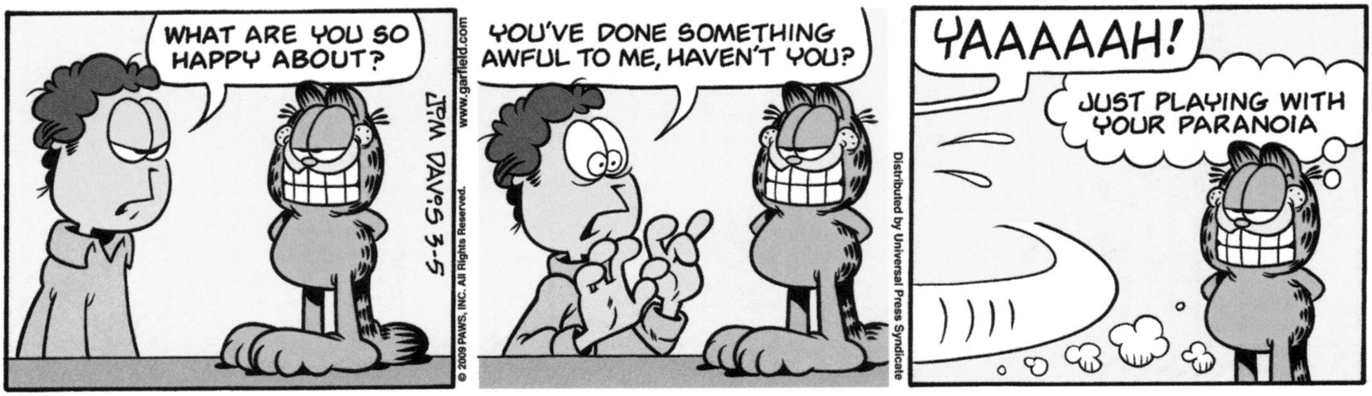
WHAT ARE YOU SO HAPPY ABOUT?
JIM DAVIS 3-5
www.garfield.com
© 2009 PAWS, INC. All Rights Reserved.
YOU'VE DONE SOMETHING AWFUL TO ME, HAVEN'T YOU?
Distributed by Universal Press Syndicate
YAAAAAH!
JUST PLAYING WITH YOUR PARANOIA

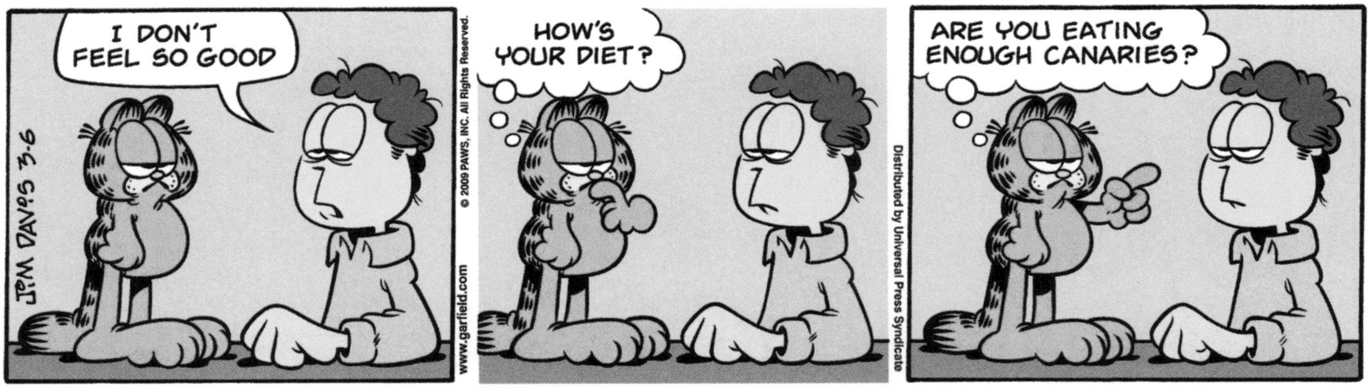
I DON'T FEEL SO GOOD
JIM DAVIS 3-6
www.garfield.com
© 2009 PAWS, INC. All Rights Reserved.
HOW'S YOUR DIET?
Distributed by Universal Press Syndicate
ARE YOU EATING ENOUGH CANARIES?

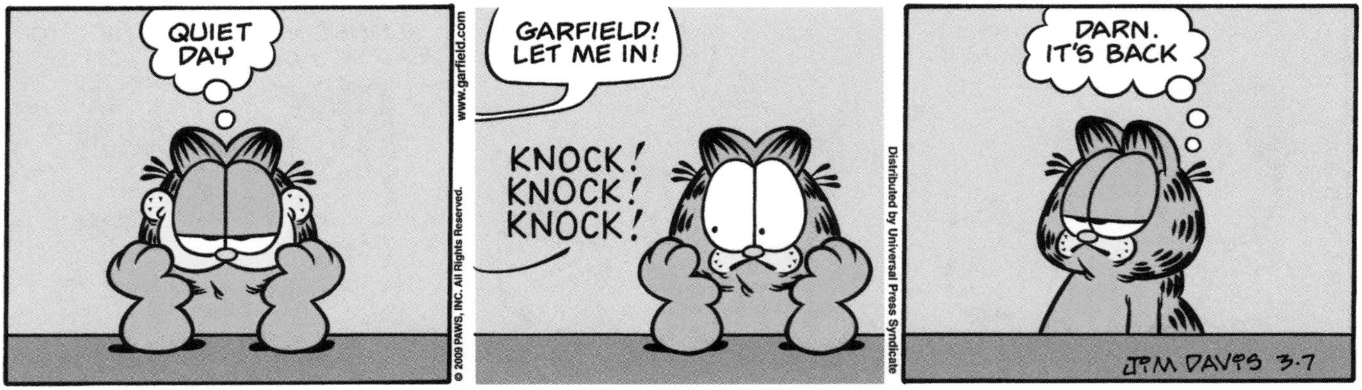
QUIET DAY
www.garfield.com
© 2009 PAWS, INC. All Rights Reserved.
GARFIELD! LET ME IN!
KNOCK! KNOCK! KNOCK!
Distributed by Universal Press Syndicate
DARN. IT'S BACK
JIM DAVIS 3-7

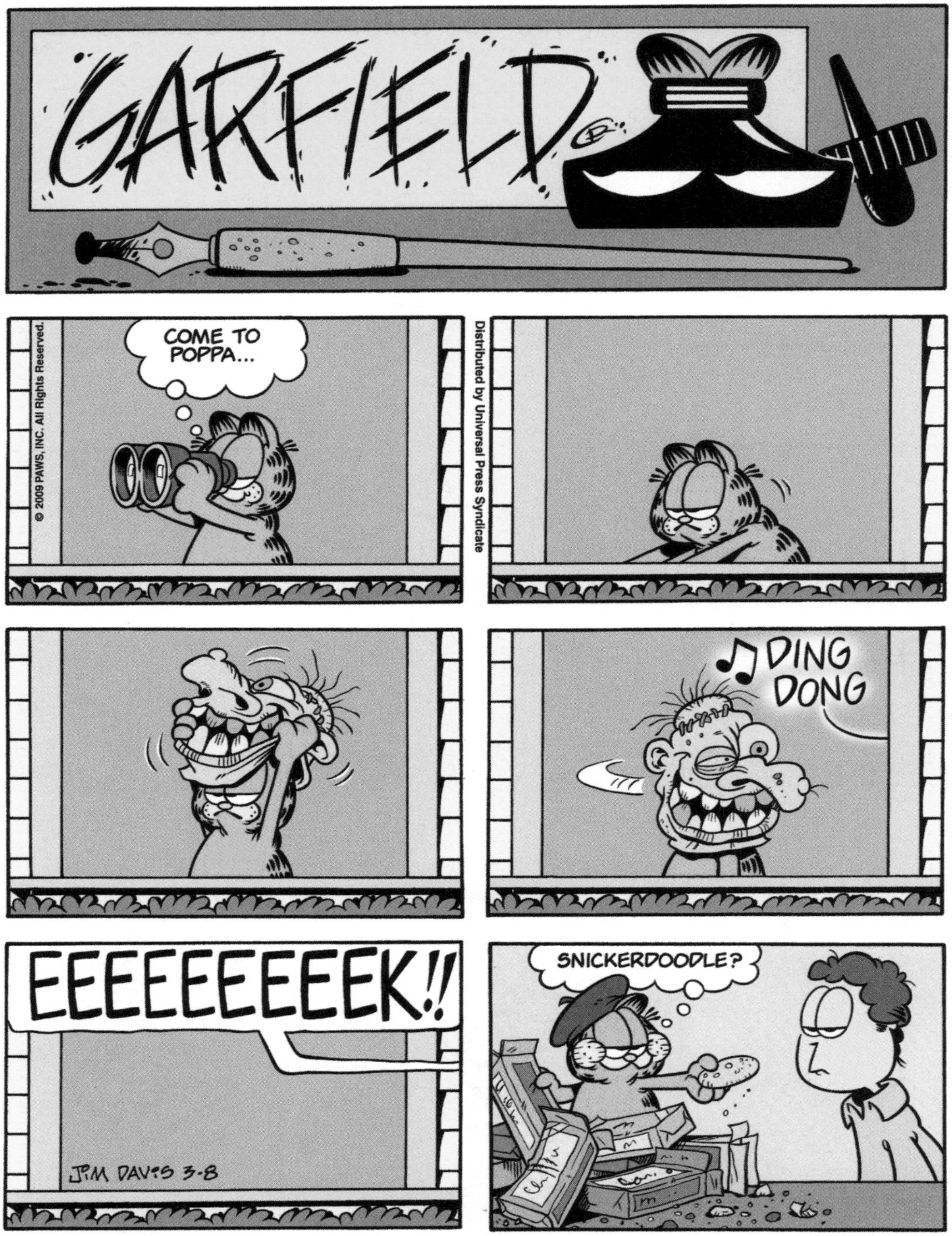
GARFIELD
© 2009 PAWS, INC. All Rights Reserved.
Distributed by Universal Press Syndicate
COME TO POPPA...
DING DONG
EEEEEEEEEK!!
JIM DAVIS 3-8
SNICKERDOODLE?

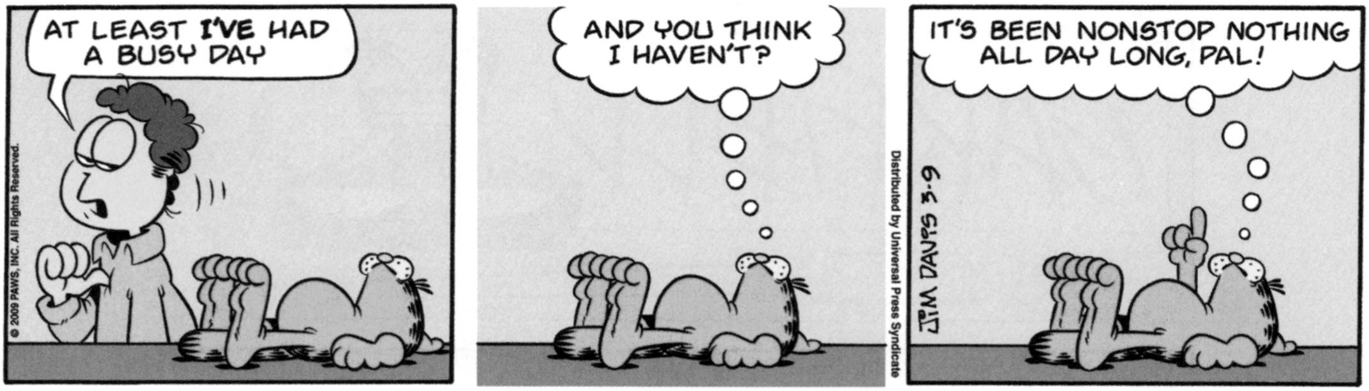
AT LEAST I'VE HAD A BUSY DAY
AND YOU THINK I HAVEN'T?
IT'S BEEN NONSTOP NOTHING ALL DAY LONG, PAL!

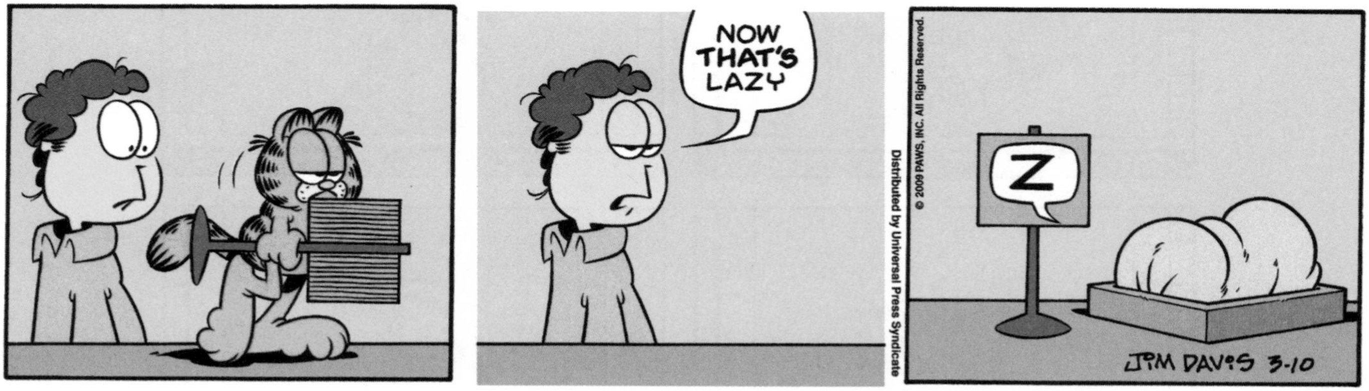
NOW THAT'S LAZY
Z

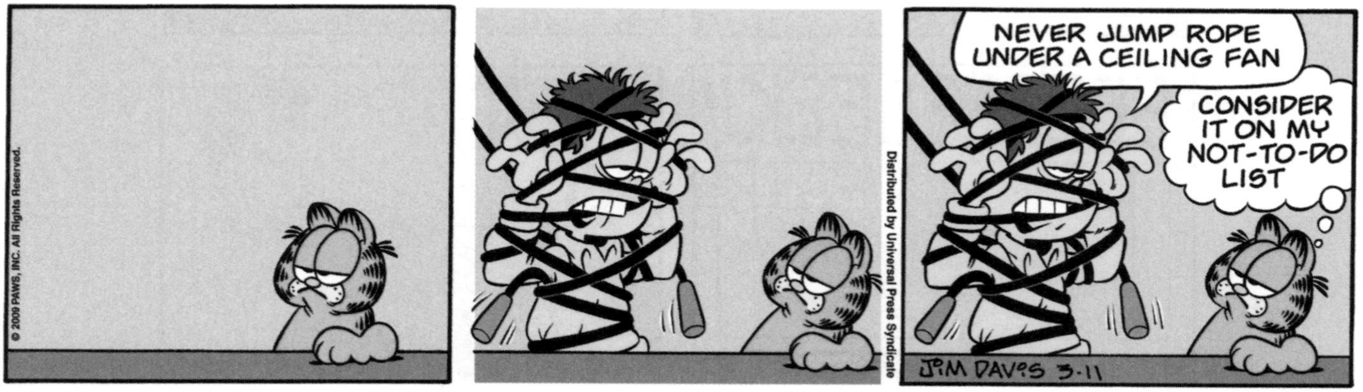
NEVER JUMP ROPE UNDER A CEILING FAN
CONSIDER IT ON MY NOT-TO-DO LIST

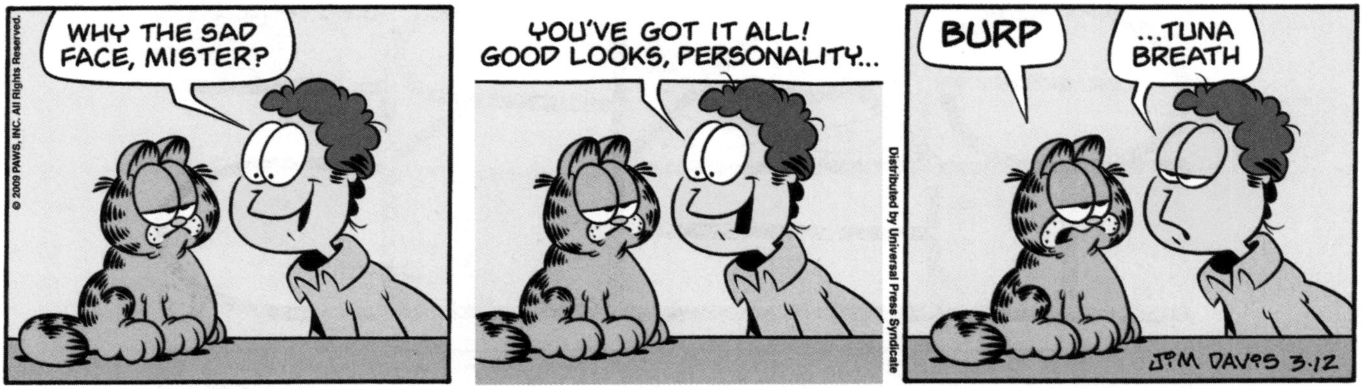
© 2009 PAWS, INC. All Rights Reserved.
WHY THE SAD FACE, MISTER?
YOU'VE GOT IT ALL! GOOD LOOKS, PERSONALITY...
Distributed by Universal Press Syndicate
BURP
...TUNA BREATH
JIM DAVIS 3-12

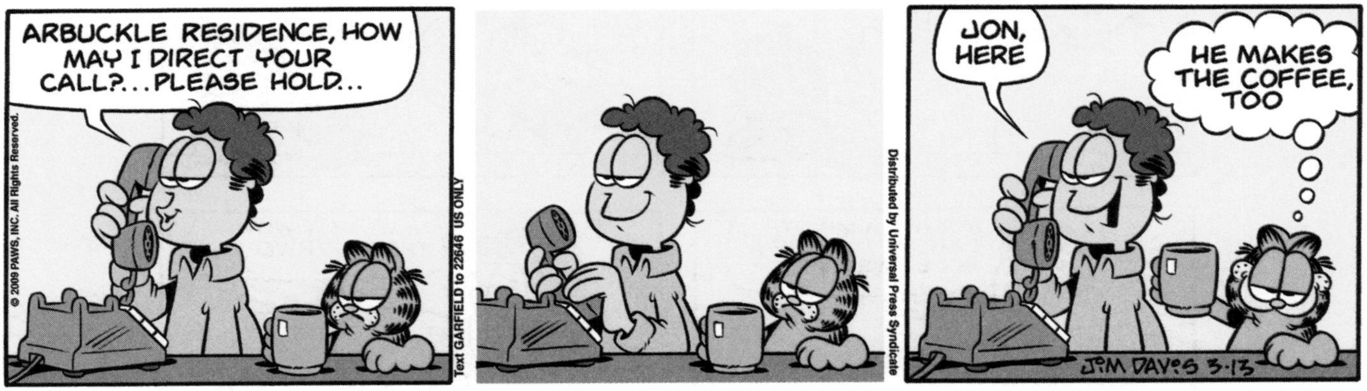
© 2009 PAWS, INC. All Rights Reserved.
ARBUCKLE RESIDENCE, HOW MAY I DIRECT YOUR CALL?...PLEASE HOLD...
Text GARFIELD to 22646 US ONLY
Distributed by Universal Press Syndicate
JON, HERE
HE MAKES THE COFFEE, TOO
JIM DAVIS 3-13

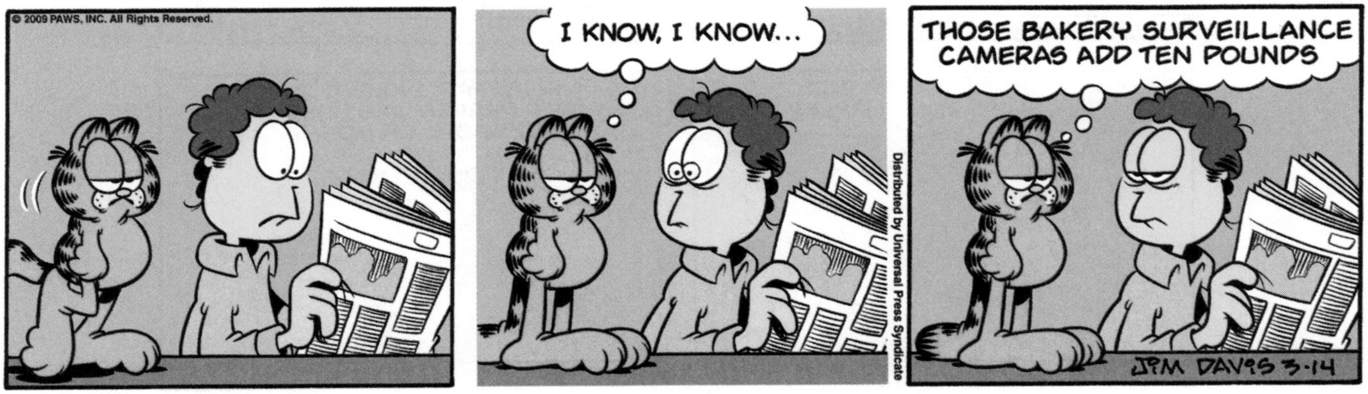
© 2009 PAWS, INC. All Rights Reserved.
I KNOW, I KNOW...
Distributed by Universal Press Syndicate
THOSE BAKERY SURVEILLANCE CAMERAS ADD TEN POUNDS
JIM DAVIS 3-14

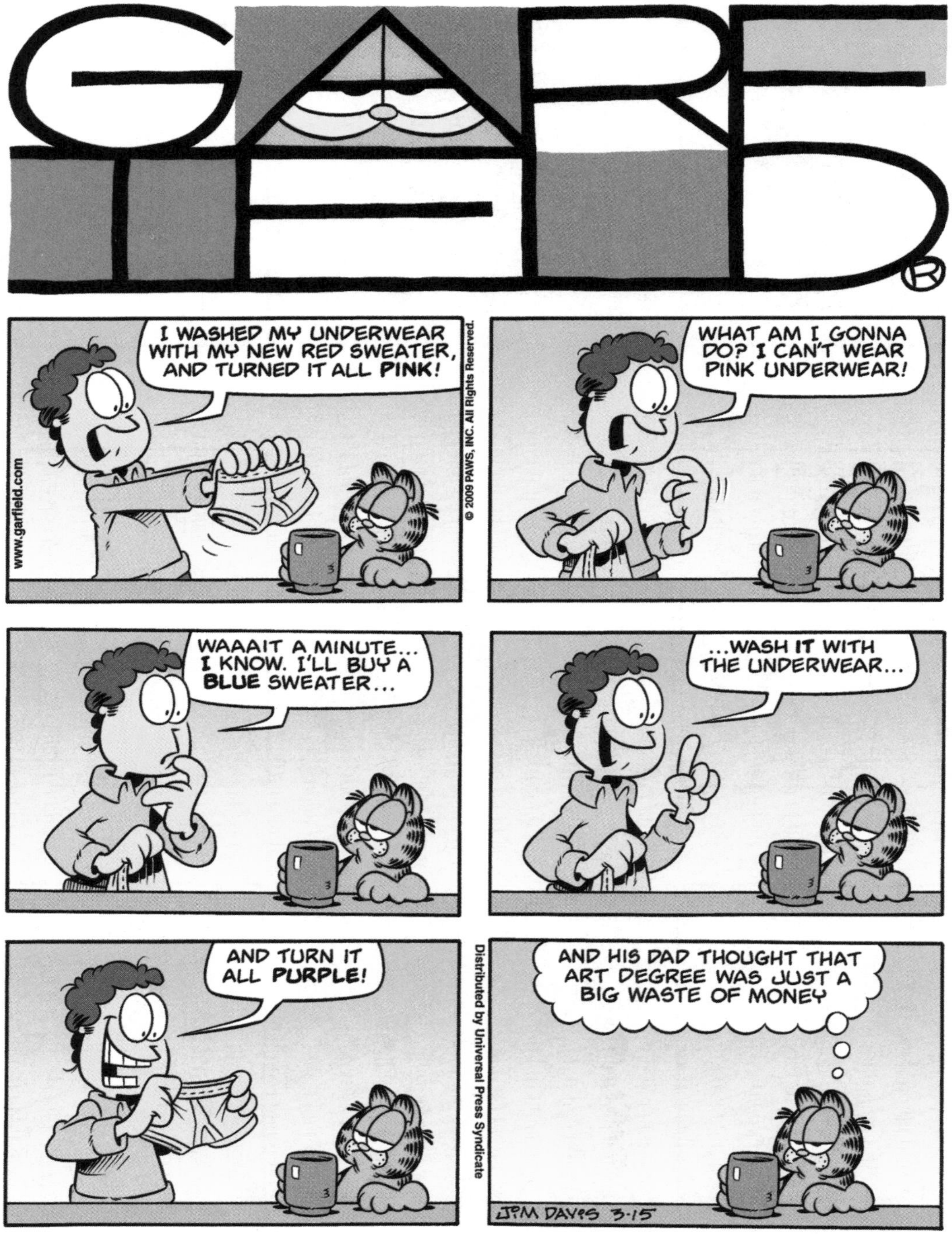
GARFIELD®
I WASHED MY UNDERWEAR WITH MY NEW RED SWEATER, AND TURNED IT ALL **PINK**!
www.garfield.com
© 2009 PAWS, INC. All Rights Reserved.
WHAT AM I GONNA DO? **I** CAN'T WEAR PINK UNDERWEAR!
WAAAIT A MINUTE... **I** KNOW. I'LL BUY A **BLUE** SWEATER...
...WASH **IT** WITH THE UNDERWEAR...
AND TURN IT ALL **PURPLE**!
Distributed by Universal Press Syndicate
AND HIS DAD THOUGHT THAT ART DEGREE WAS JUST A BIG WASTE OF MONEY
JIM DAVIS 3-15

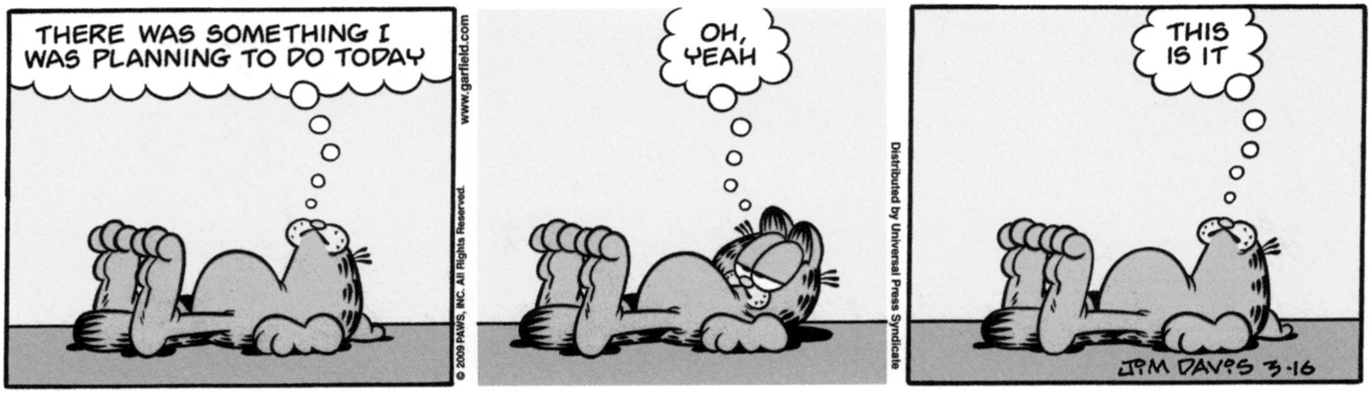
THERE WAS SOMETHING I WAS PLANNING TO DO TODAY
OH, YEAH
THIS IS IT
JIM DAVIS 3-16
© 2009 PAWS, INC. All Rights Reserved.
www.garfield.com
Distributed by Universal Press Syndicate

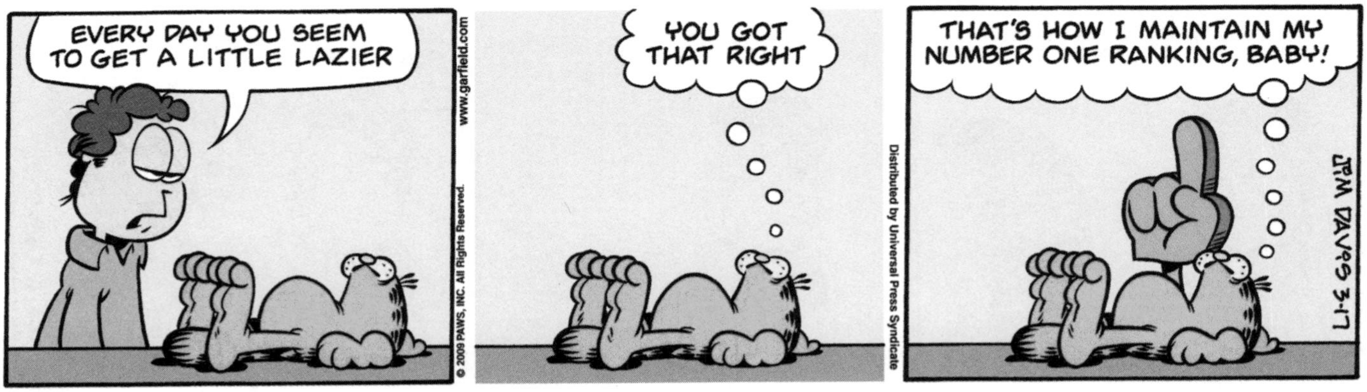
EVERY DAY YOU SEEM TO GET A LITTLE LAZIER
YOU GOT THAT RIGHT
THAT'S HOW I MAINTAIN MY NUMBER ONE RANKING, BABY!
JIM DAVIS 3-17
© 2009 PAWS, INC. All Rights Reserved.
www.garfield.com
Distributed by Universal Press Syndicate

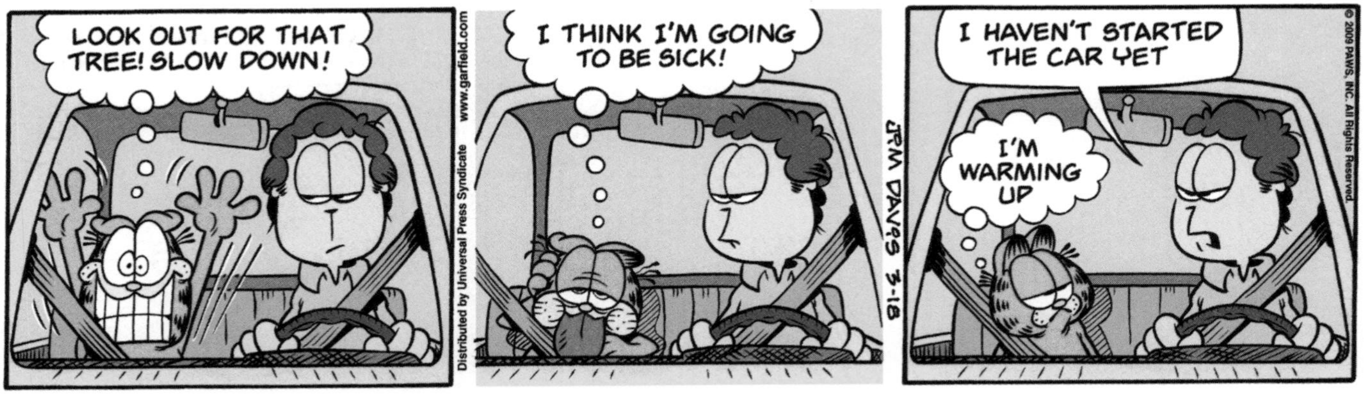
LOOK OUT FOR THAT TREE! SLOW DOWN!
I THINK I'M GOING TO BE SICK!
I HAVEN'T STARTED THE CAR YET
I'M WARMING UP
JIM DAVIS 3-18
© 2009 PAWS, INC. All Rights Reserved.
www.garfield.com
Distributed by Universal Press Syndicate

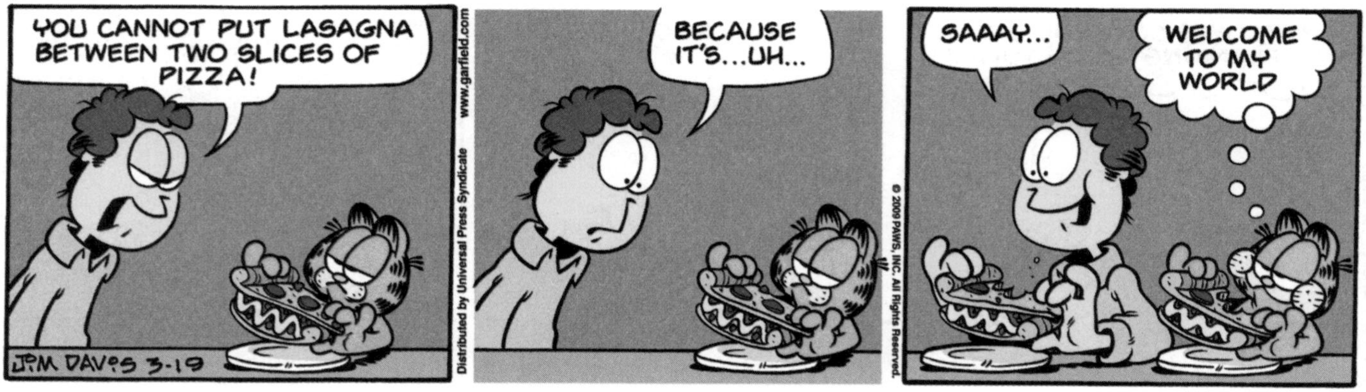
YOU CANNOT PUT LASAGNA BETWEEN TWO SLICES OF PIZZA!
JIM DAVIS 3-19
www.garfield.com
Distributed by Universal Press Syndicate
BECAUSE IT'S...UH...
© 2009 PAWS, INC. All Rights Reserved.
SAAAY...
WELCOME TO MY WORLD

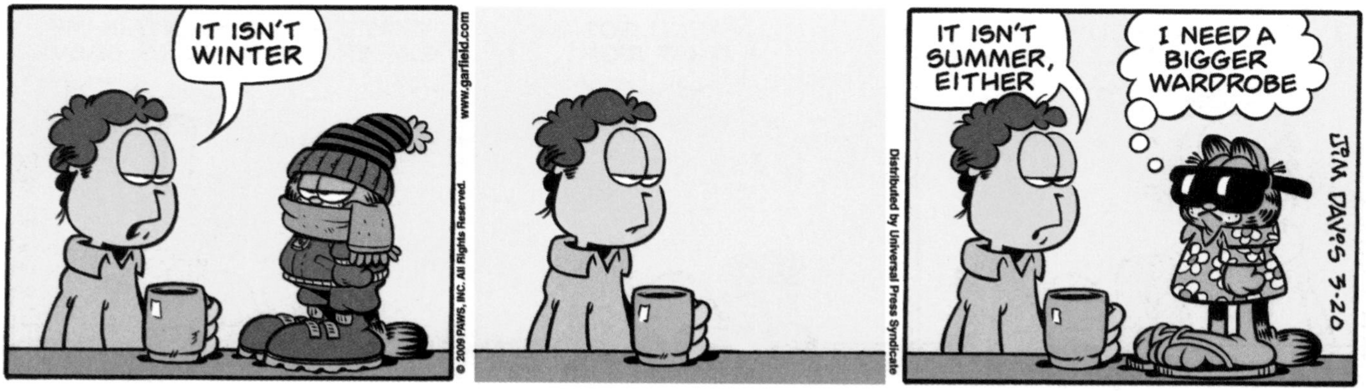
IT ISN'T WINTER
www.garfield.com
© 2009 PAWS, INC. All Rights Reserved.
Distributed by Universal Press Syndicate
IT ISN'T SUMMER, EITHER
I NEED A BIGGER WARDROBE
JIM DAVIS 3-20

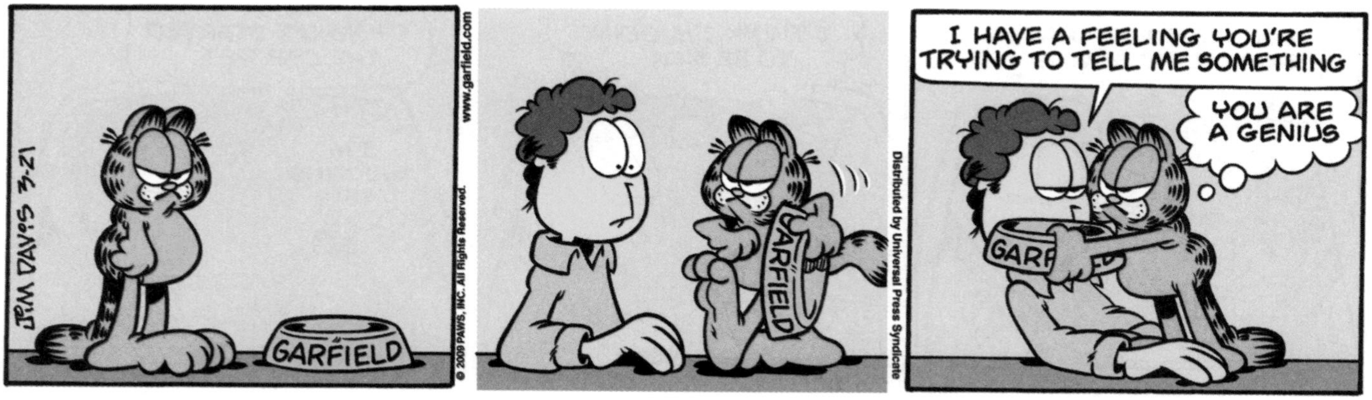
JIM DAVIS 3-21
GARFIELD
www.garfield.com
© 2009 PAWS, INC. All Rights Reserved.
GARFIELD
Distributed by Universal Press Syndicate
I HAVE A FEELING YOU'RE TRYING TO TELL ME SOMETHING
YOU ARE A GENIUS
GARF

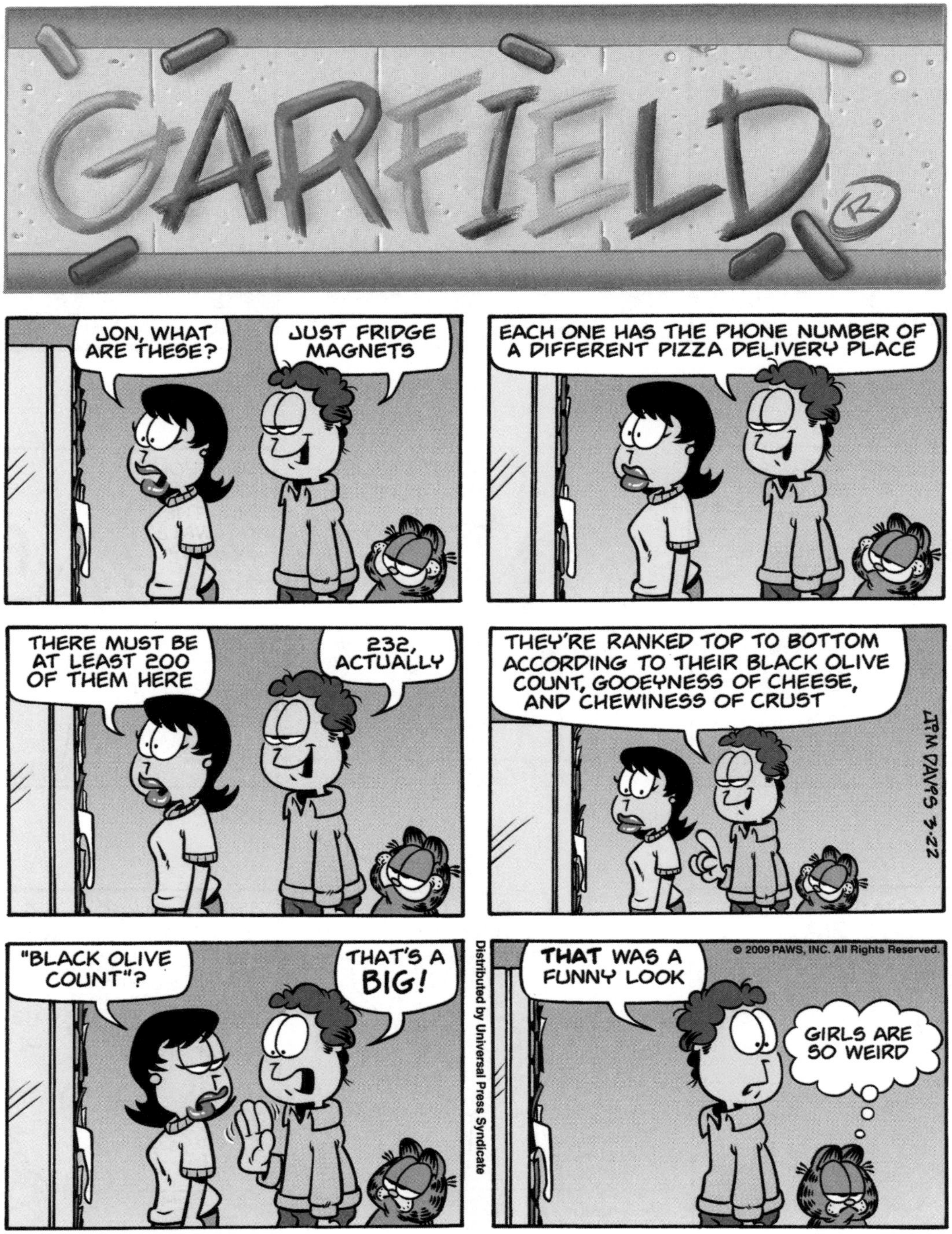
GARFIELD®
JON, WHAT ARE THESE?
JUST FRIDGE MAGNETS
EACH ONE HAS THE PHONE NUMBER OF A DIFFERENT PIZZA DELIVERY PLACE
THERE MUST BE AT LEAST 200 OF THEM HERE
232, ACTUALLY
THEY'RE RANKED TOP TO BOTTOM ACCORDING TO THEIR BLACK OLIVE COUNT, GOOEYNESS OF CHEESE, AND CHEWINESS OF CRUST
JIM DAVIS 3-22
"BLACK OLIVE COUNT"?
THAT'S A BIG!
Distributed by Universal Press Syndicate
© 2009 PAWS, INC. All Rights Reserved.
THAT WAS A FUNNY LOOK
GIRLS ARE SO WEIRD

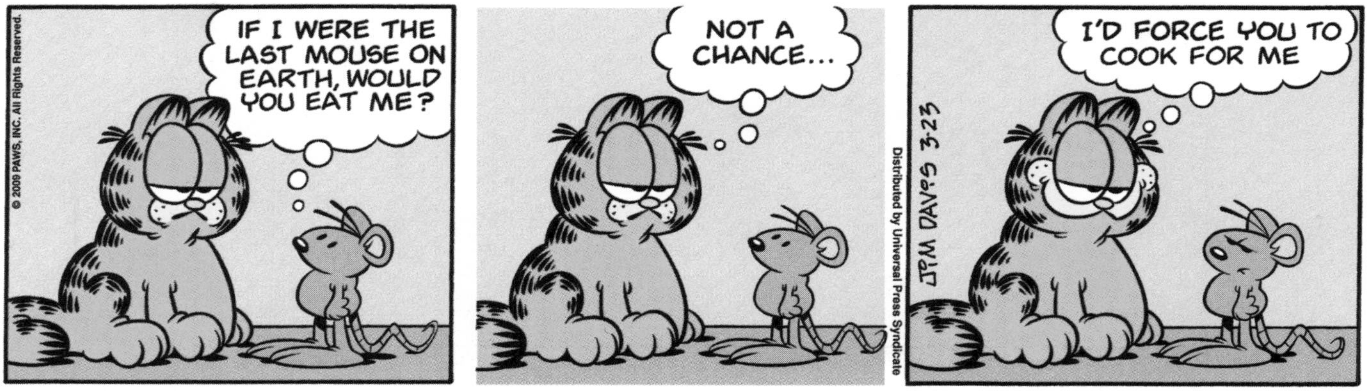
© 2009 PAWS, INC. All Rights Reserved.
IF I WERE THE LAST MOUSE ON EARTH, WOULD YOU EAT ME?
NOT A CHANCE...
Distributed by Universal Press Syndicate
JIM DAVIS 3-23
I'D FORCE YOU TO COOK FOR ME

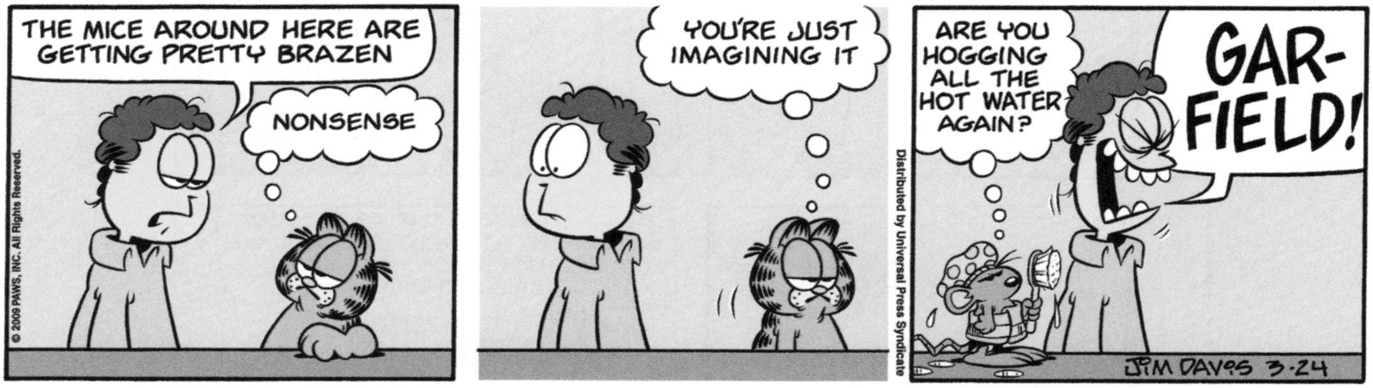
© 2009 PAWS, INC. All Rights Reserved.
THE MICE AROUND HERE ARE GETTING PRETTY BRAZEN
NONSENSE
YOU'RE JUST IMAGINING IT
Distributed by Universal Press Syndicate
ARE YOU HOGGING ALL THE HOT WATER AGAIN?
GAR-FIELD!
JIM DAVIS 3-24

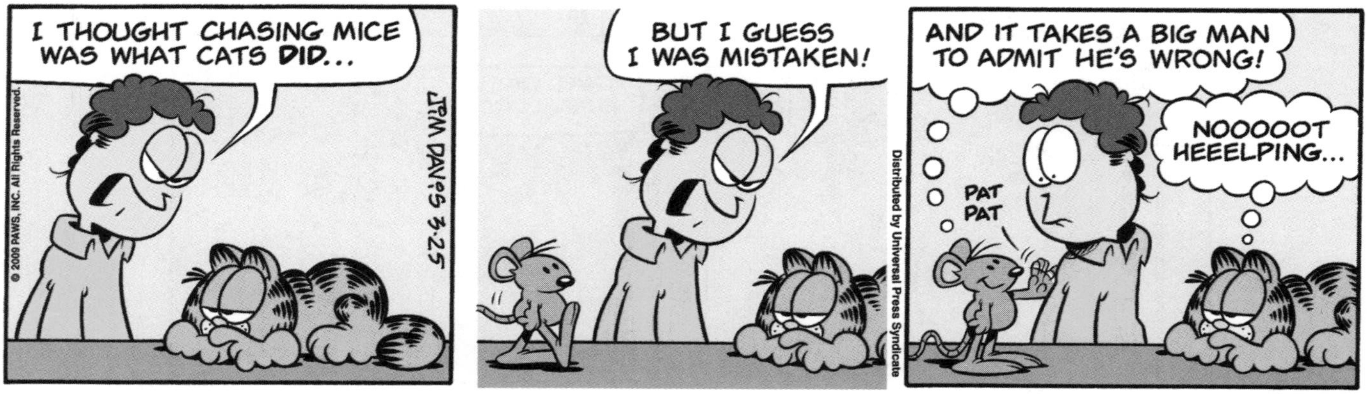
© 2009 PAWS, INC. All Rights Reserved.
I THOUGHT CHASING MICE WAS WHAT CATS DID...
JIM DAVIS 3-25
BUT I GUESS I WAS MISTAKEN!
Distributed by Universal Press Syndicate
AND IT TAKES A BIG MAN TO ADMIT HE'S WRONG!
NOOOOOT HEEELPING...
PAT PAT

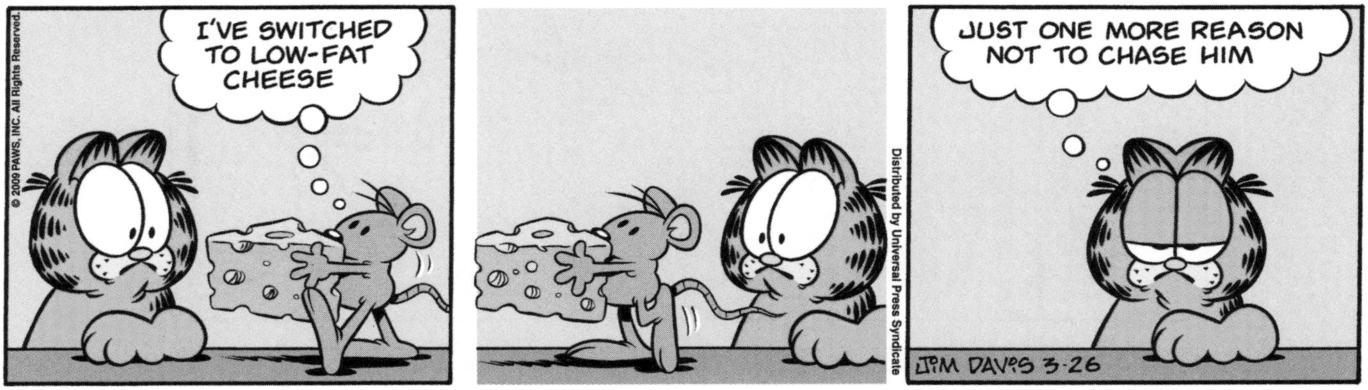
© 2009 PAWS, INC. All Rights Reserved.
I'VE SWITCHED TO LOW-FAT CHEESE
Distributed by Universal Press Syndicate
JUST ONE MORE REASON NOT TO CHASE HIM
JIM DAVIS 3-26

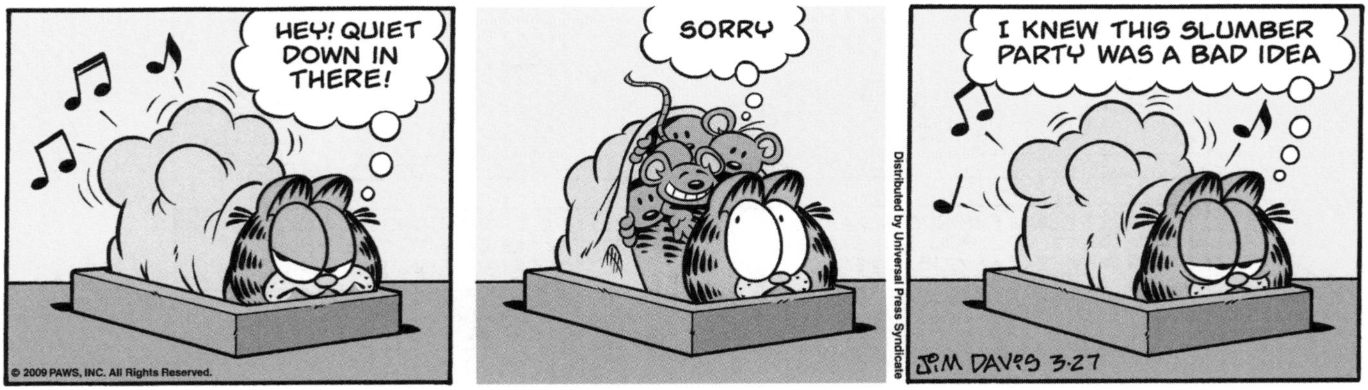
HEY! QUIET DOWN IN THERE!
© 2009 PAWS, INC. All Rights Reserved.
SORRY
Distributed by Universal Press Syndicate
I KNEW THIS SLUMBER PARTY WAS A BAD IDEA
JIM DAVIS 3-27

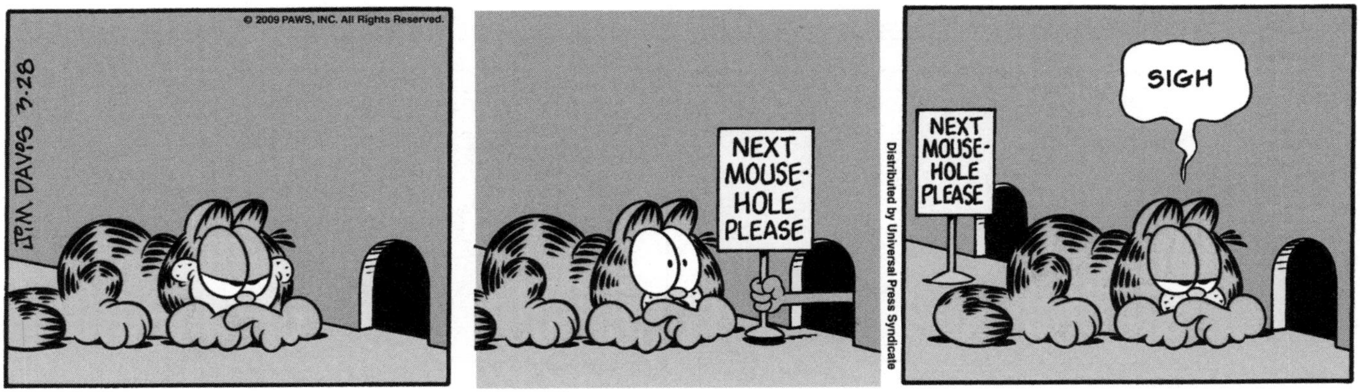
© 2009 PAWS, INC. All Rights Reserved.
JIM DAVIS 3-28
NEXT MOUSE-HOLE PLEASE
Distributed by Universal Press Syndicate
NEXT MOUSE-HOLE PLEASE
SIGH

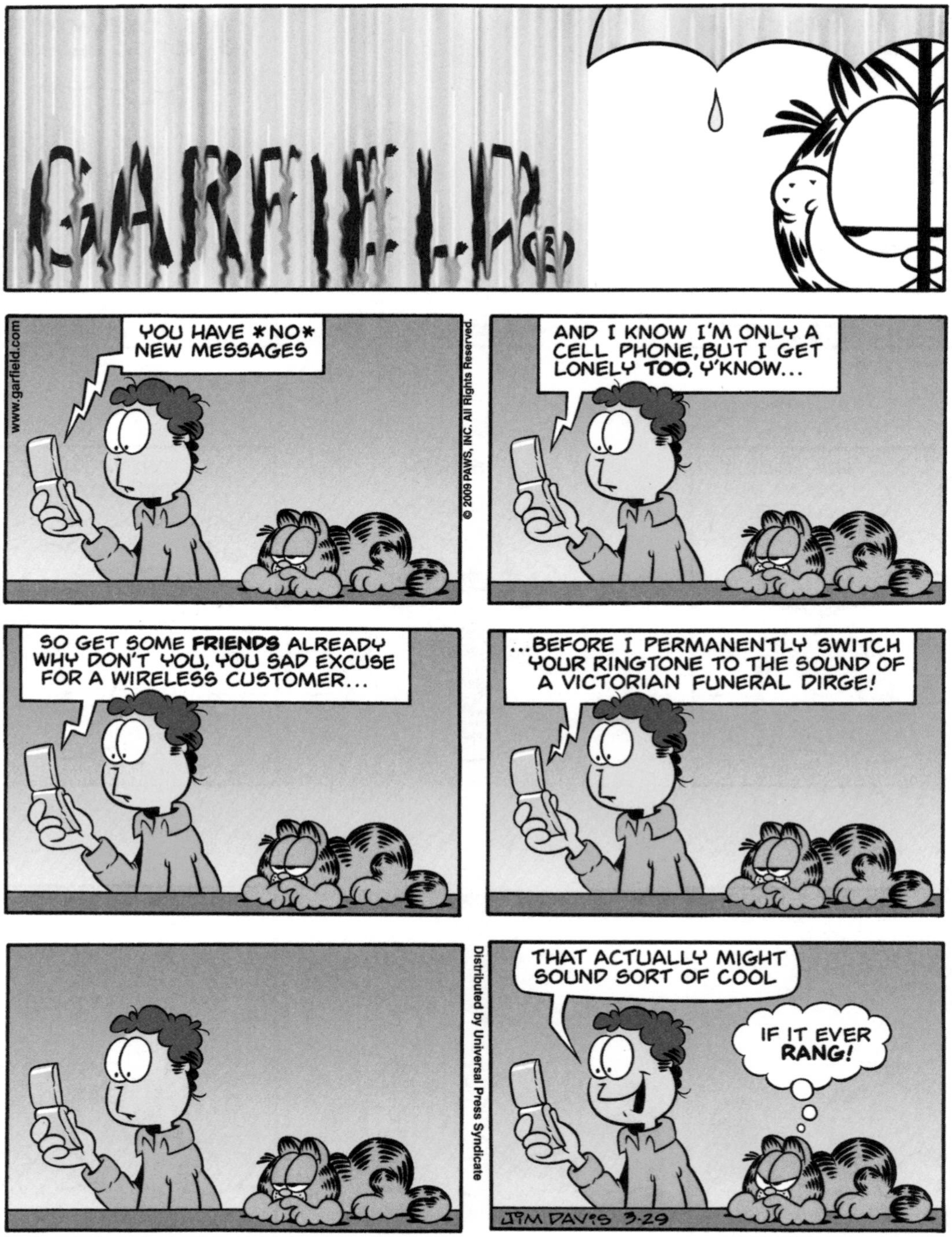
GARFIELD
www.garfield.com
YOU HAVE *NO* NEW MESSAGES
© 2009 PAWS, INC. All Rights Reserved.
AND I KNOW I'M ONLY A CELL PHONE, BUT I GET LONELY TOO, Y'KNOW...
SO GET SOME FRIENDS ALREADY WHY DON'T YOU, YOU SAD EXCUSE FOR A WIRELESS CUSTOMER...
...BEFORE I PERMANENTLY SWITCH YOUR RINGTONE TO THE SOUND OF A VICTORIAN FUNERAL DIRGE!
Distributed by Universal Press Syndicate
THAT ACTUALLY MIGHT SOUND SORT OF COOL
IF IT EVER RANG!
JIM DAVIS 3-29

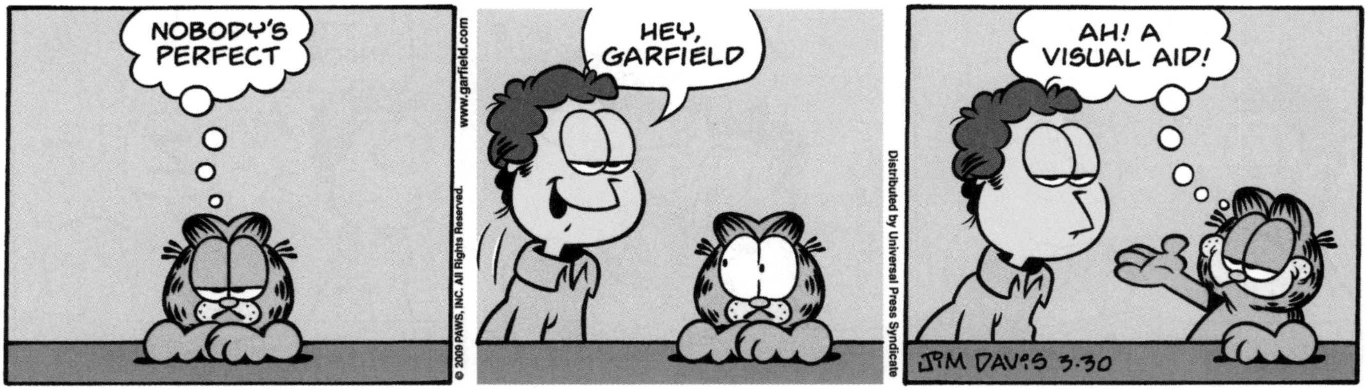
NOBODY'S PERFECT
© 2009 PAWS, INC. All Rights Reserved. www.garfield.com
HEY, GARFIELD
Distributed by Universal Press Syndicate
AH! A VISUAL AID!
JIM DAVIS 3-30

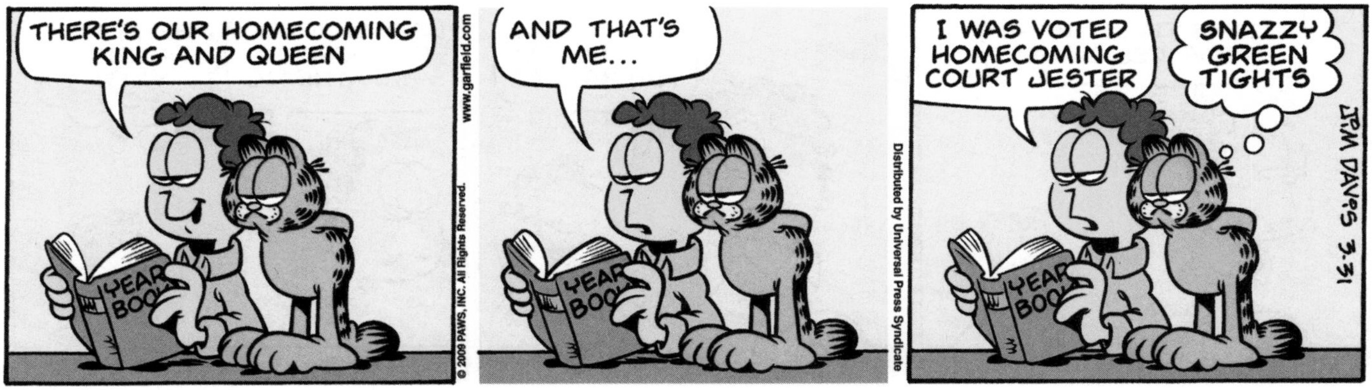
THERE'S OUR HOMECOMING KING AND QUEEN
YEAR BOOK
© 2009 PAWS, INC. All Rights Reserved. www.garfield.com
AND THAT'S ME...
Distributed by Universal Press Syndicate
I WAS VOTED HOMECOMING COURT JESTER
SNAZZY GREEN TIGHTS
JIM DAVIS 3-31

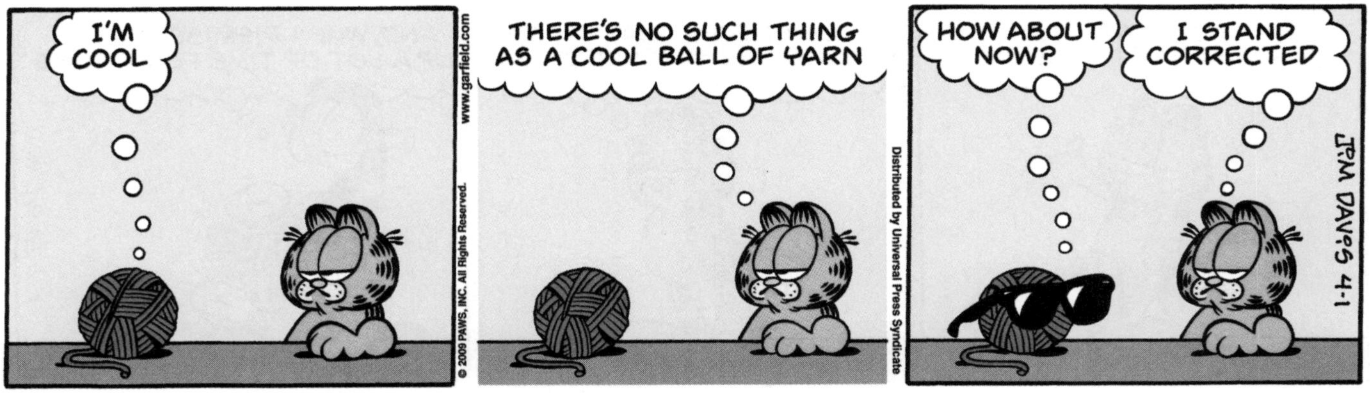
I'M COOL
© 2009 PAWS, INC. All Rights Reserved. www.garfield.com
THERE'S NO SUCH THING AS A COOL BALL OF YARN
Distributed by Universal Press Syndicate
HOW ABOUT NOW?
I STAND CORRECTED
JIM DAVIS 4-1

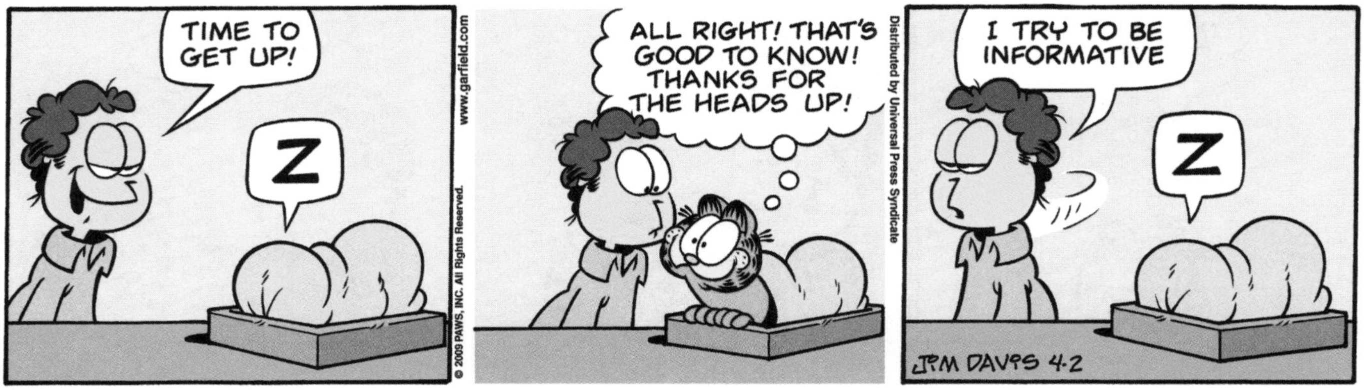
TIME TO GET UP!
Z
© 2009 PAWS, INC. All Rights Reserved. www.garfield.com
ALL RIGHT! THAT'S GOOD TO KNOW! THANKS FOR THE HEADS UP!
Distributed by Universal Press Syndicate
I TRY TO BE INFORMATIVE
Z
JIM DAVIS 4-2

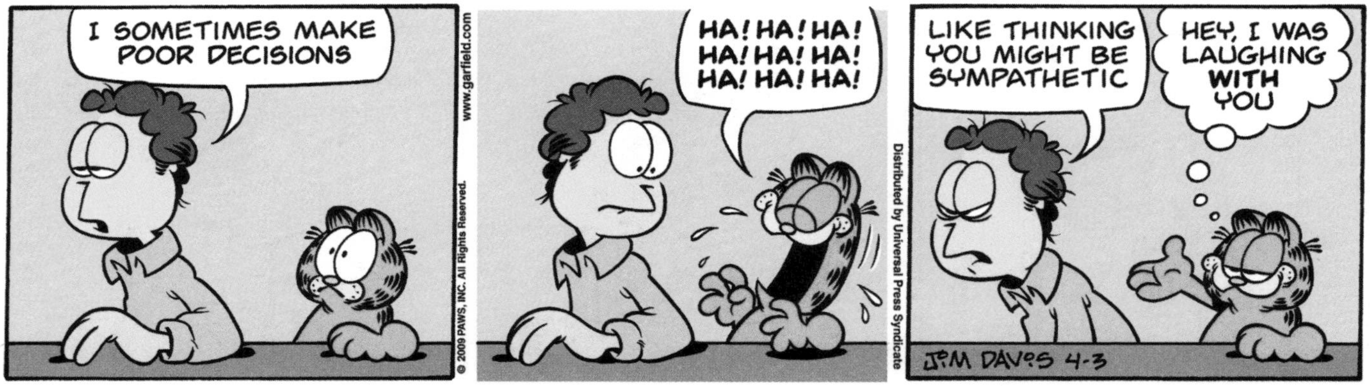
I SOMETIMES MAKE POOR DECISIONS
© 2009 PAWS, INC. All Rights Reserved. www.garfield.com
HA! HA! HA! HA! HA! HA! HA! HA! HA!
Distributed by Universal Press Syndicate
LIKE THINKING YOU MIGHT BE SYMPATHETIC
HEY, I WAS LAUGHING WITH YOU
JIM DAVIS 4-3

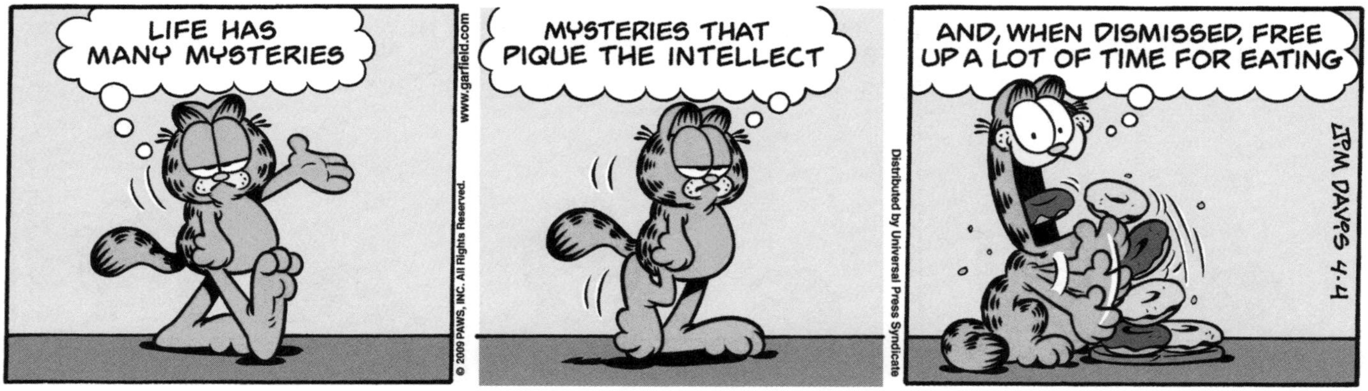
LIFE HAS MANY MYSTERIES
© 2009 PAWS, INC. All Rights Reserved. www.garfield.com
MYSTERIES THAT PIQUE THE INTELLECT
Distributed by Universal Press Syndicate
AND, WHEN DISMISSED, FREE UP A LOT OF TIME FOR EATING
JIM DAVIS 4-4

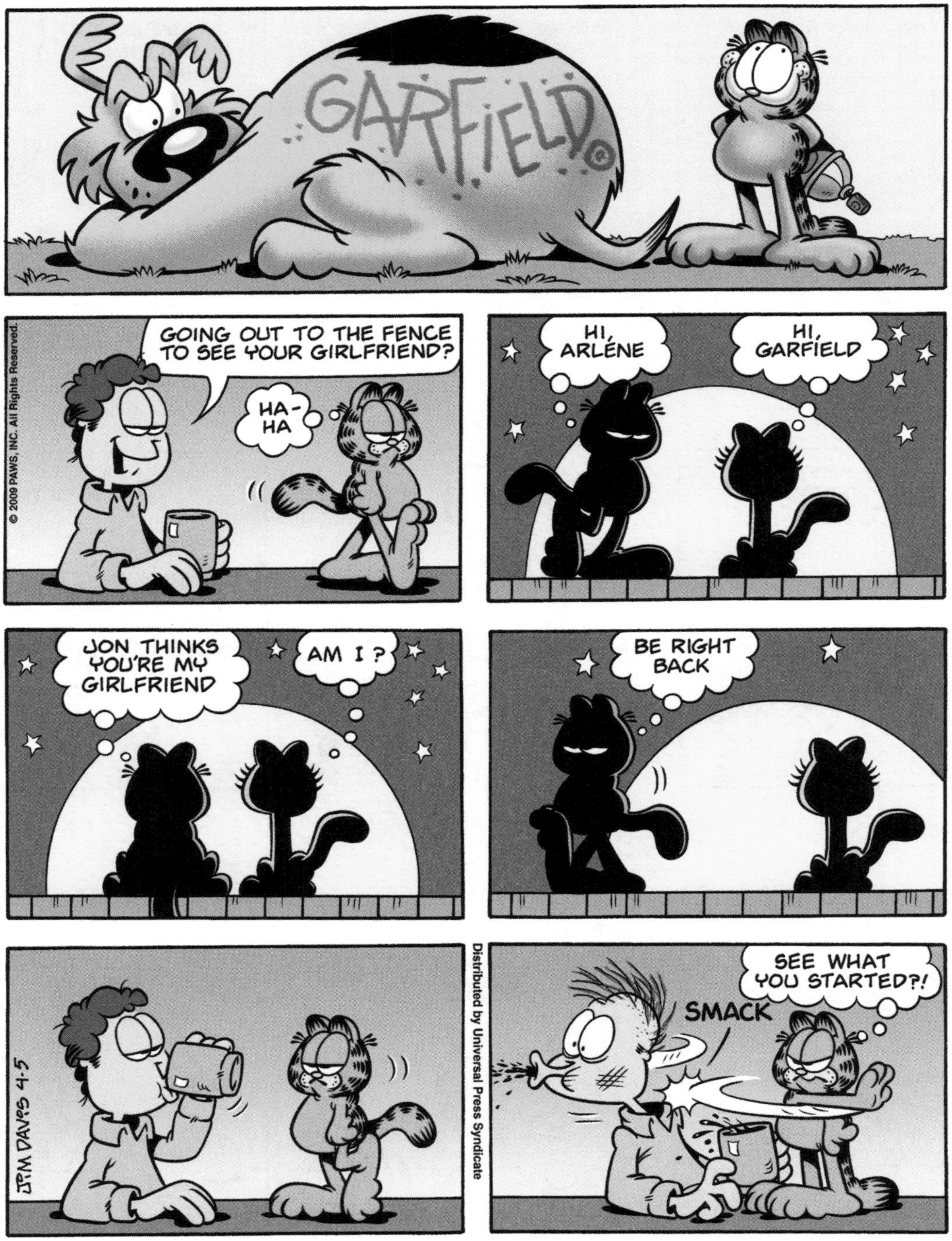
GARFIELD
GOING OUT TO THE FENCE TO SEE YOUR GIRLFRIEND?
HA-HA
HI, ARLÉNE
HI, GARFIELD
JON THINKS YOU'RE MY GIRLFRIEND
AM I ?
BE RIGHT BACK
SEE WHAT YOU STARTED?!
SMACK
JIM DAVIS 4-5

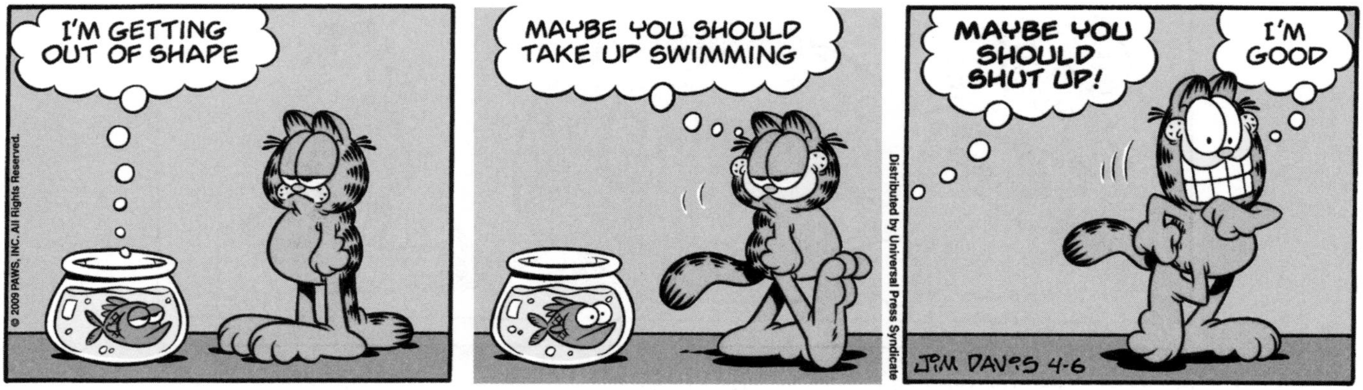
I'M GETTING OUT OF SHAPE
MAYBE YOU SHOULD TAKE UP SWIMMING
MAYBE YOU SHOULD SHUT UP!
I'M GOOD
JIM DAVIS 4-6
© 2009 PAWS, INC. All Rights Reserved.
Distributed by Universal Press Syndicate

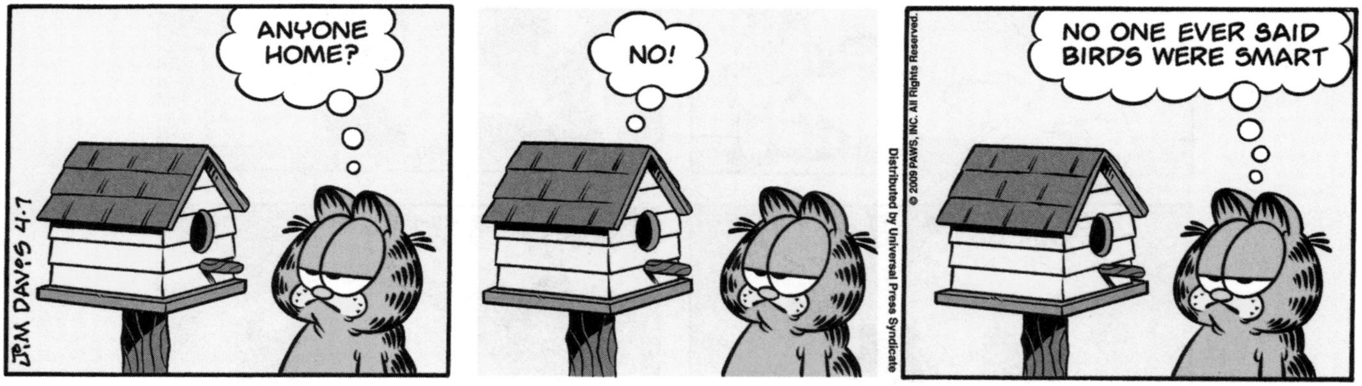
ANYONE HOME?
NO!
NO ONE EVER SAID BIRDS WERE SMART
JIM DAVIS 4-7
© 2009 PAWS, INC. All Rights Reserved.
Distributed by Universal Press Syndicate

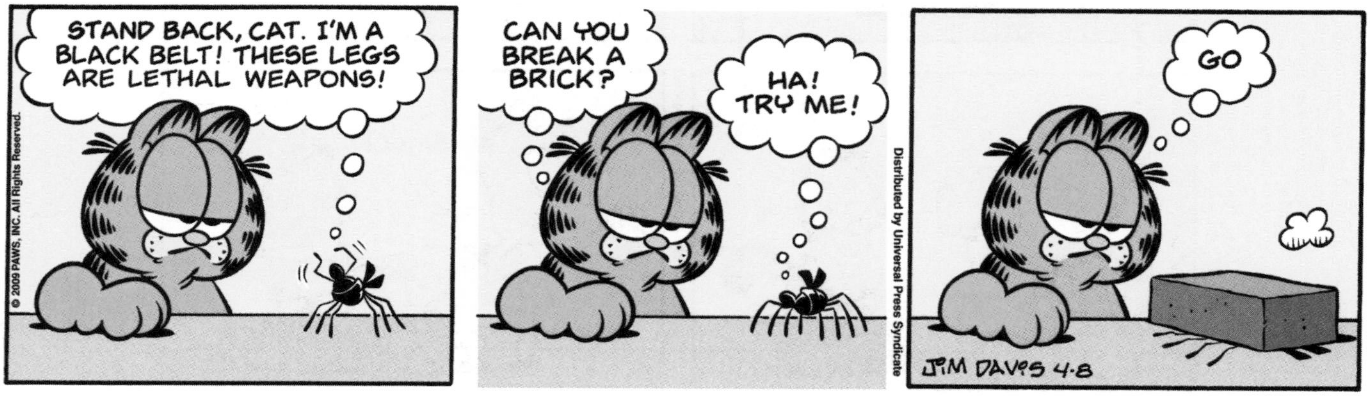
STAND BACK, CAT. I'M A BLACK BELT! THESE LEGS ARE LETHAL WEAPONS!
CAN YOU BREAK A BRICK?
HA! TRY ME!
GO
JIM DAVIS 4-8
© 2009 PAWS, INC. All Rights Reserved.
Distributed by Universal Press Syndicate

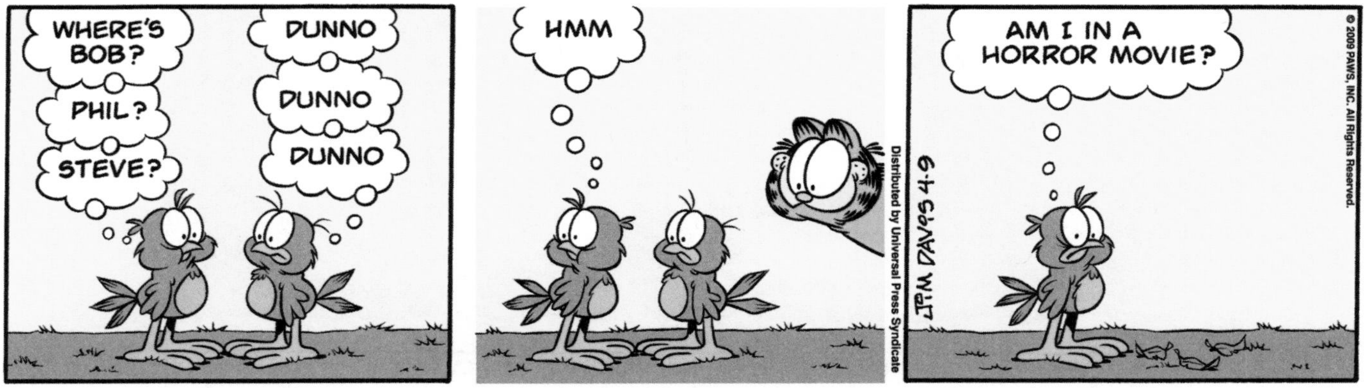
WHERE'S BOB?
DUNNO
PHIL?
DUNNO
STEVE?
DUNNO
HMM
JIM DAVIS 4-9
Distributed by Universal Press Syndicate
AM I IN A HORROR MOVIE?
© 2009 PAWS, INC. All Rights Reserved.

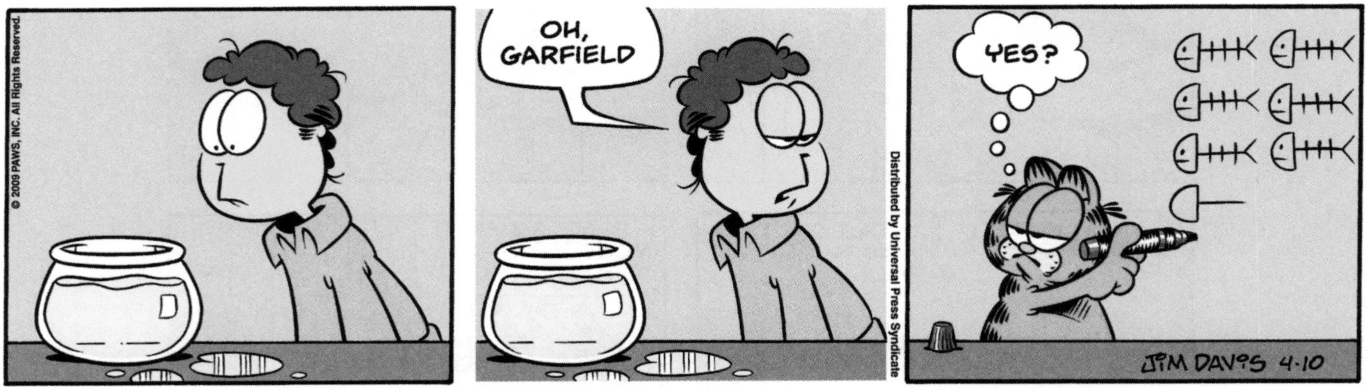
© 2009 PAWS, INC. All Rights Reserved.
OH, GARFIELD
Distributed by Universal Press Syndicate
YES?
JIM DAVIS 4-10

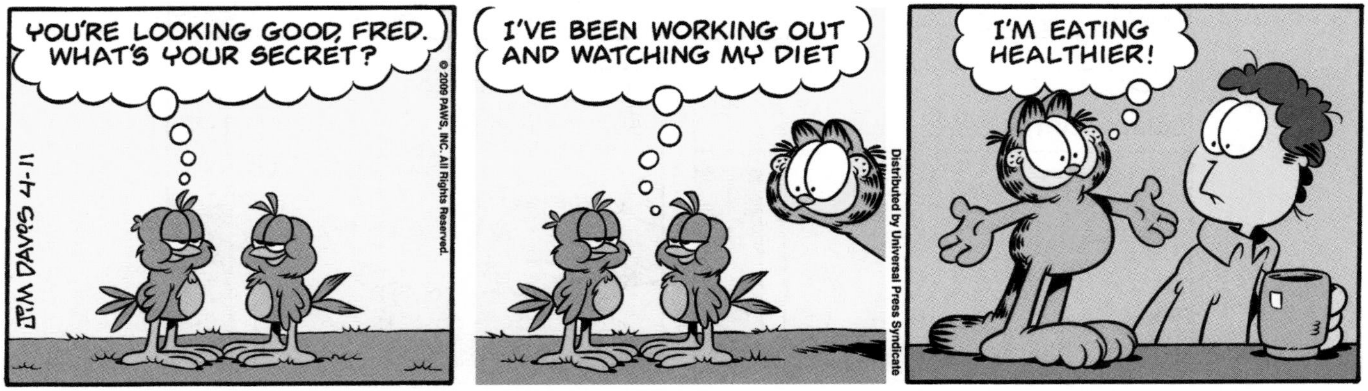
YOU'RE LOOKING GOOD, FRED. WHAT'S YOUR SECRET?
JIM DAVIS 4-11
© 2009 PAWS, INC. All Rights Reserved.
I'VE BEEN WORKING OUT AND WATCHING MY DIET
Distributed by Universal Press Syndicate
I'M EATING HEALTHIER!

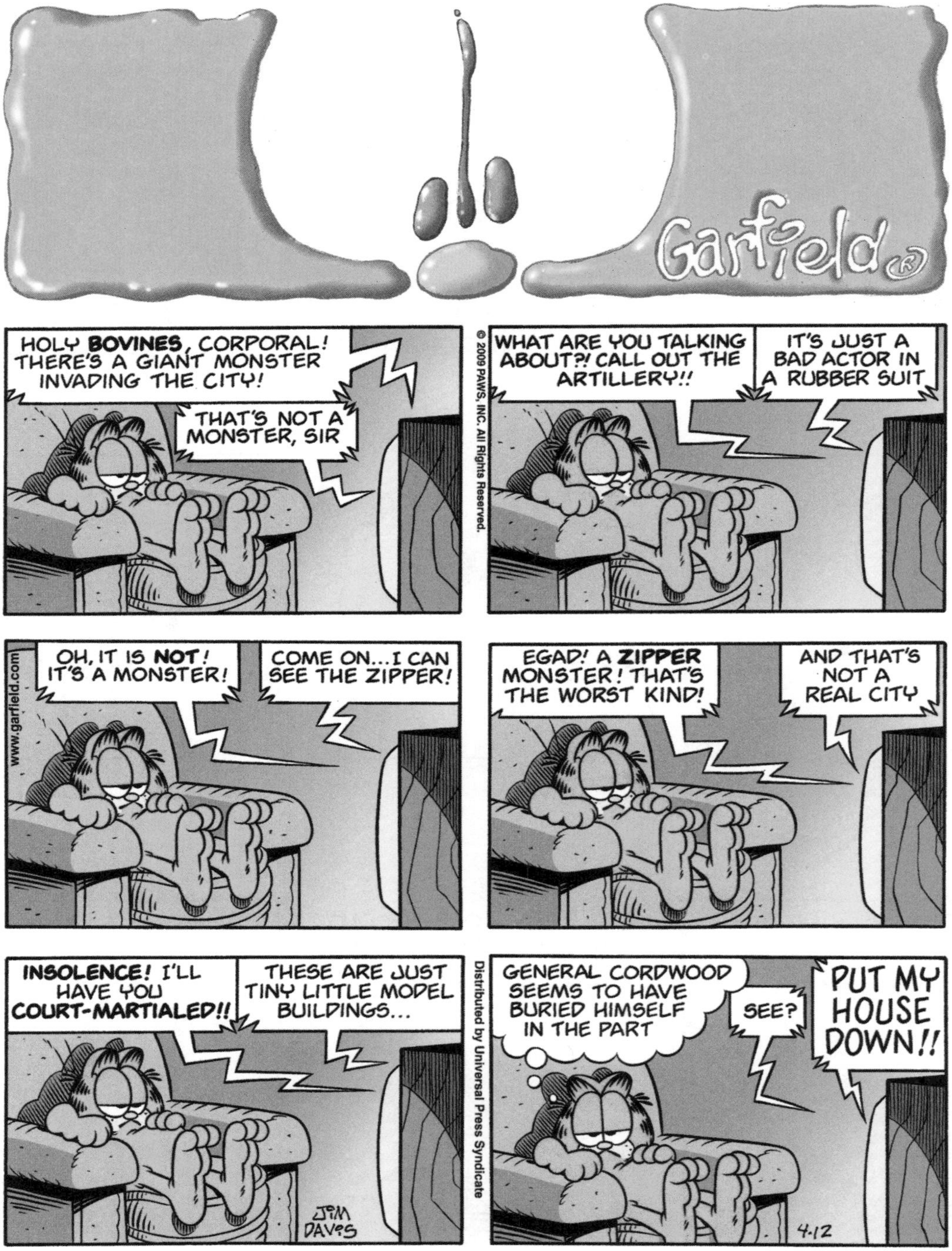
Garfield®
HOLY BOVINES, CORPORAL! THERE'S A GIANT MONSTER INVADING THE CITY!
THAT'S NOT A MONSTER, SIR
WHAT ARE YOU TALKING ABOUT?! CALL OUT THE ARTILLERY!!
IT'S JUST A BAD ACTOR IN A RUBBER SUIT
OH, IT IS NOT! IT'S A MONSTER!
COME ON...I CAN SEE THE ZIPPER!
EGAD! A ZIPPER MONSTER! THAT'S THE WORST KIND!
AND THAT'S NOT A REAL CITY
INSOLENCE! I'LL HAVE YOU COURT-MARTIALED!!
THESE ARE JUST TINY LITTLE MODEL BUILDINGS...
GENERAL CORDWOOD SEEMS TO HAVE BURIED HIMSELF IN THE PART
SEE?
PUT MY HOUSE DOWN!!
JIM DAVIS
4-12

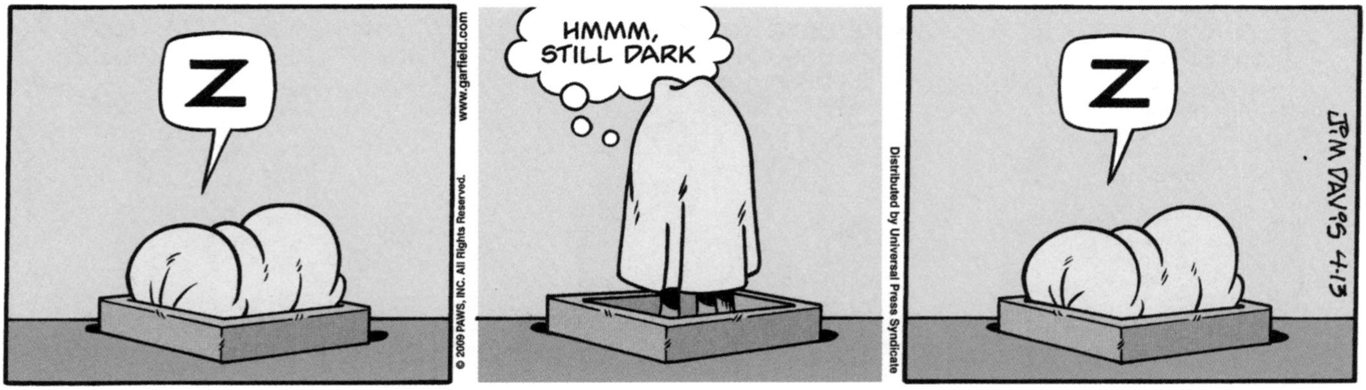
Z
HMMM, STILL DARK
Z
JIM DAVIS 4-13
© 2009 PAWS, INC. All Rights Reserved. www.garfield.com
Distributed by Universal Press Syndicate

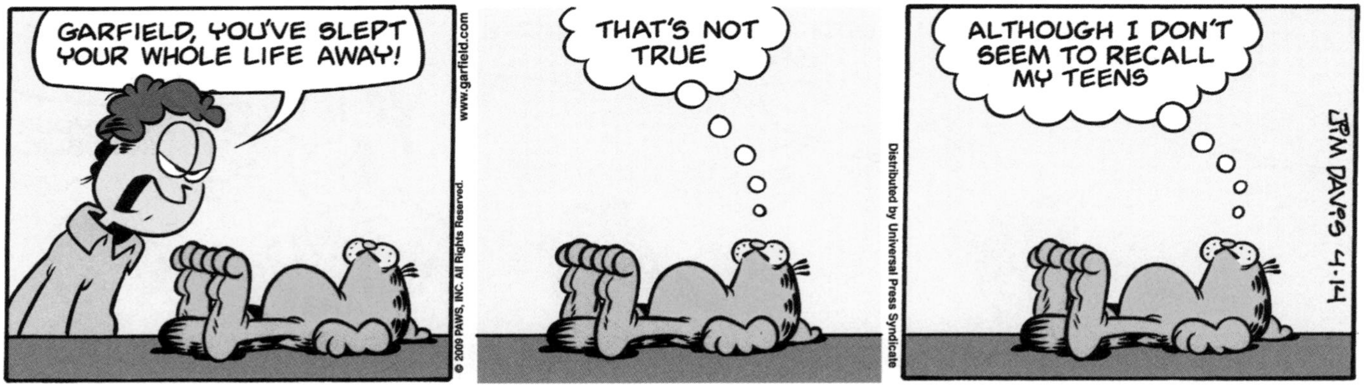
GARFIELD, YOU'VE SLEPT YOUR WHOLE LIFE AWAY!
THAT'S NOT TRUE
ALTHOUGH I DON'T SEEM TO RECALL MY TEENS
JIM DAVIS 4-14
© 2009 PAWS, INC. All Rights Reserved. www.garfield.com
Distributed by Universal Press Syndicate

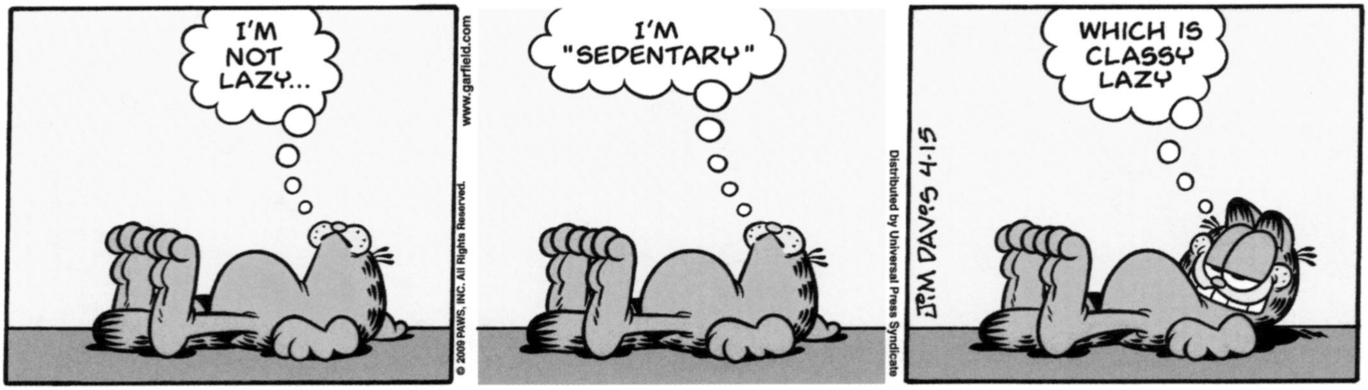
I'M NOT LAZY...
I'M "SEDENTARY"
WHICH IS CLASSY LAZY
JIM DAVIS 4-15
© 2009 PAWS, INC. All Rights Reserved. www.garfield.com
Distributed by Universal Press Syndicate

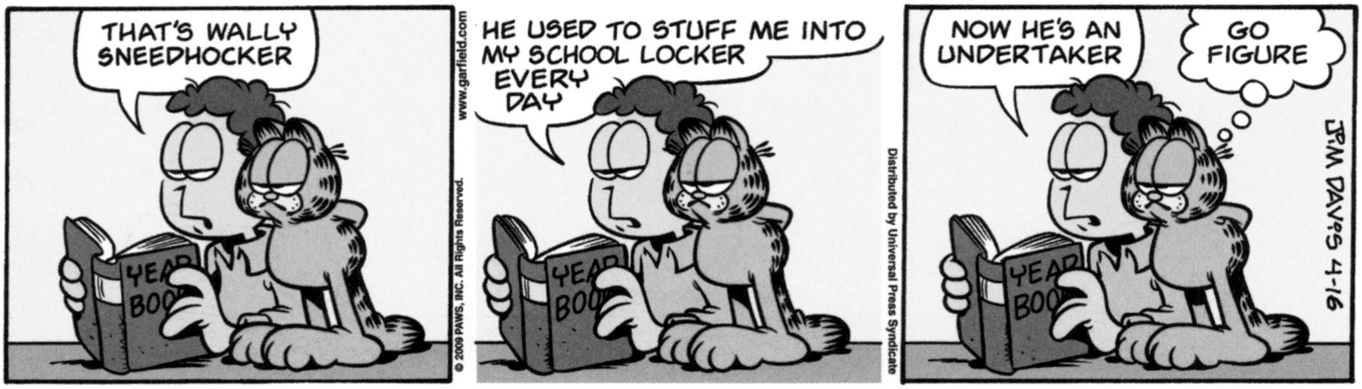
THAT'S WALLY SNEEDHOCKER
YEAR BOOK
© 2009 PAWS, INC. All Rights Reserved. www.garfield.com
HE USED TO STUFF ME INTO MY SCHOOL LOCKER EVERY DAY
Distributed by Universal Press Syndicate
NOW HE'S AN UNDERTAKER
GO FIGURE
JIM DAVIS 4-16

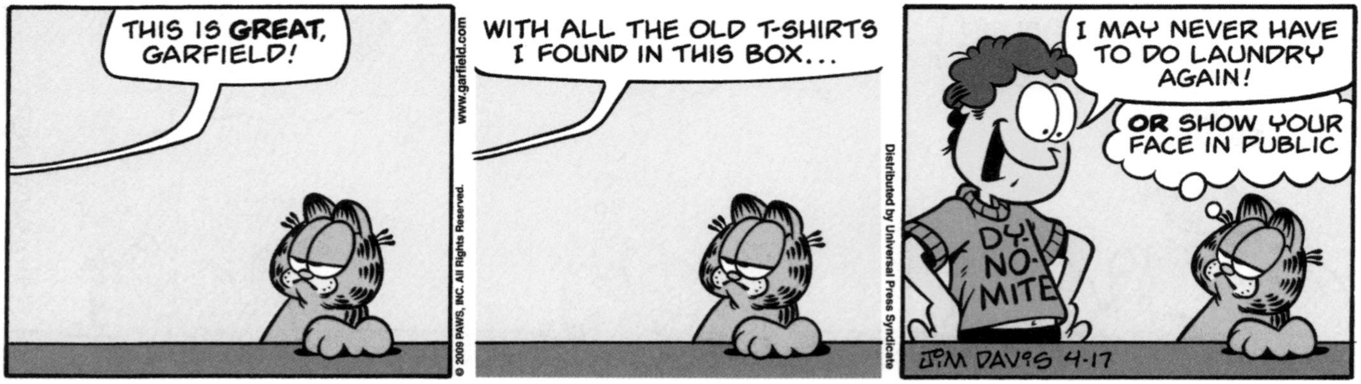
THIS IS **GREAT**, GARFIELD!
© 2009 PAWS, INC. All Rights Reserved. www.garfield.com
WITH ALL THE OLD T-SHIRTS I FOUND IN THIS BOX...
Distributed by Universal Press Syndicate
I MAY NEVER HAVE TO DO LAUNDRY AGAIN!
OR SHOW YOUR FACE IN PUBLIC
DY-NO-MITE
JIM DAVIS 4-17

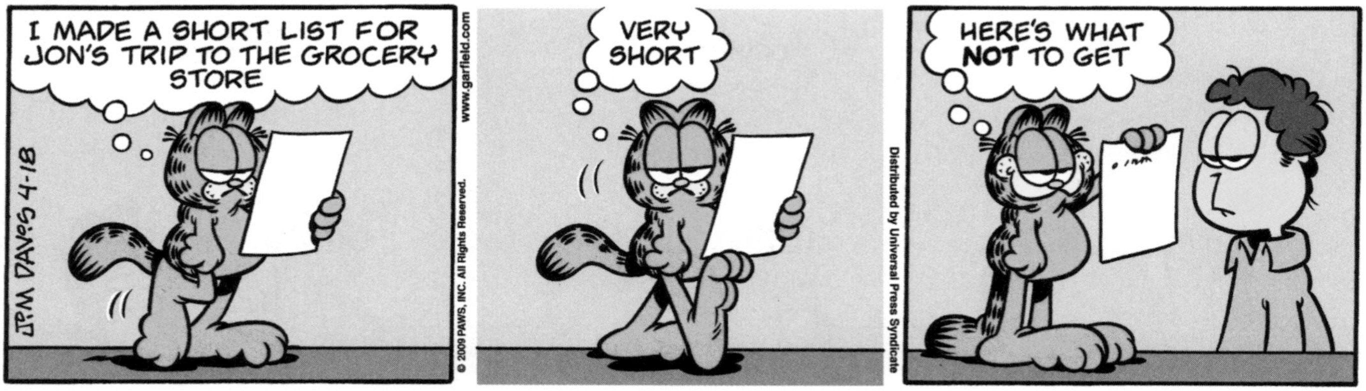
I MADE A SHORT LIST FOR JON'S TRIP TO THE GROCERY STORE
JIM DAVIS 4-18
© 2009 PAWS, INC. All Rights Reserved. www.garfield.com
VERY SHORT
Distributed by Universal Press Syndicate
HERE'S WHAT **NOT** TO GET

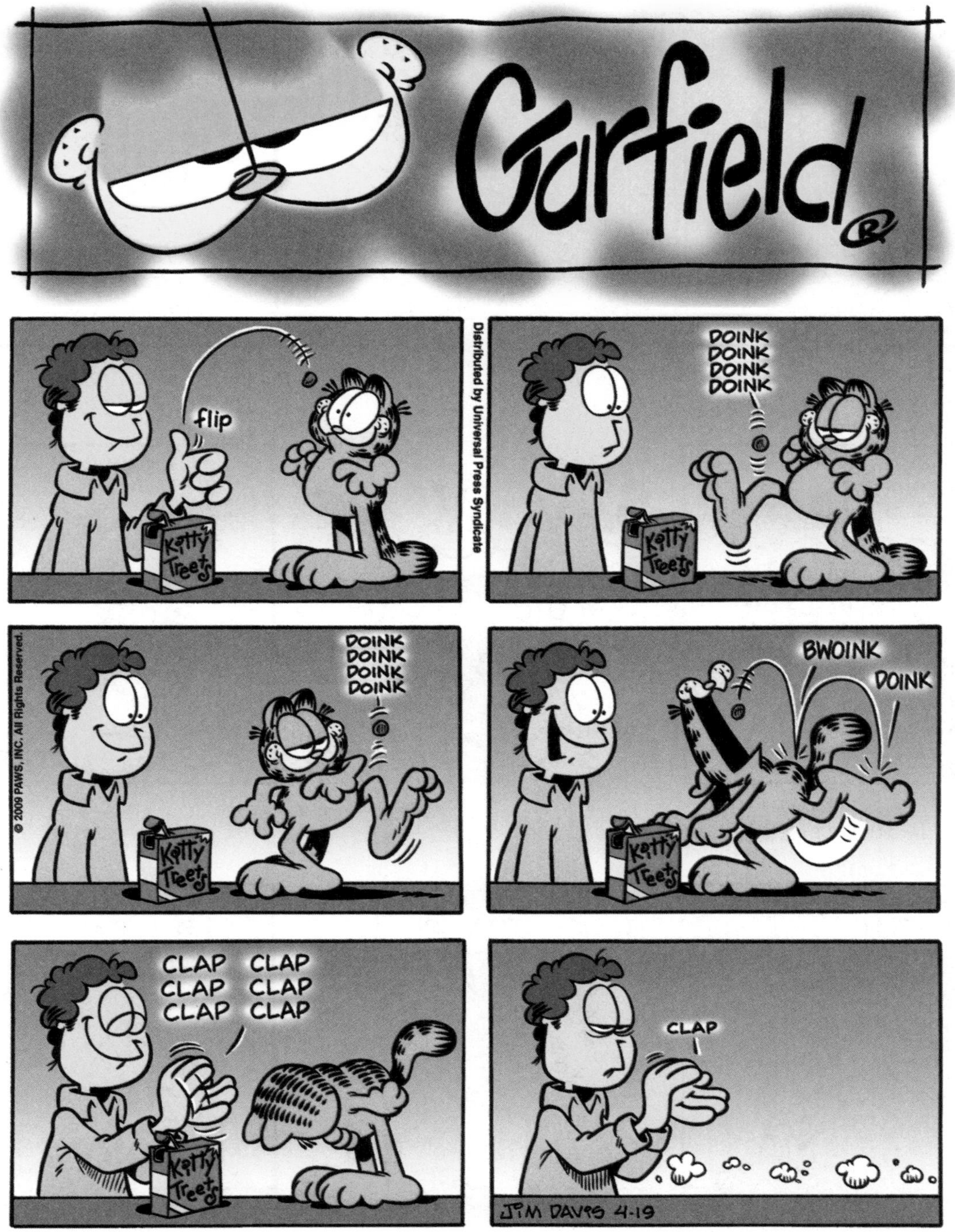
Garfield
flip
Distributed by Universal Press Syndicate
Katty Treets
DOINK DOINK DOINK DOINK
© 2009 PAWS, INC. All Rights Reserved.
DOINK DOINK DOINK DOINK
BWOINK
DOINK
CLAP CLAP CLAP
CLAP CLAP CLAP
CLAP
JIM DAVIS 4-19

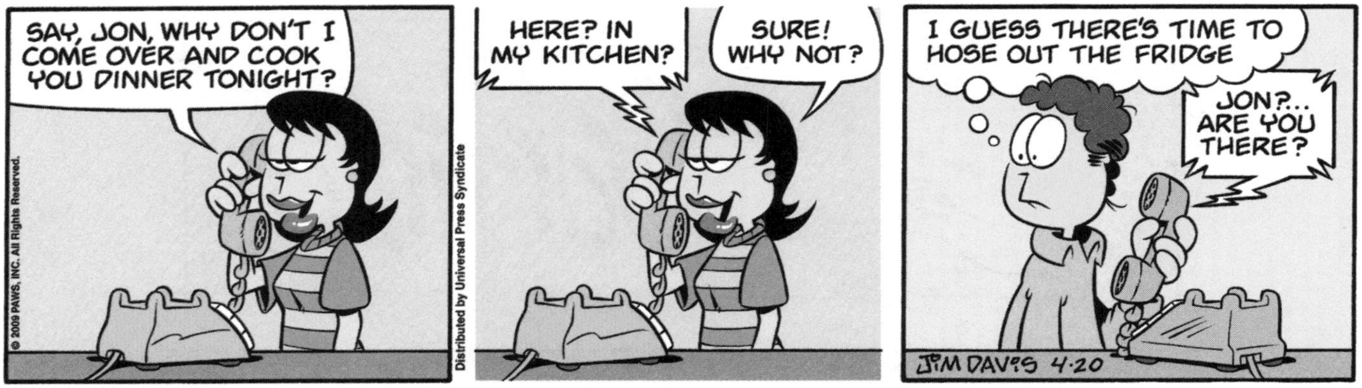
SAY, JON, WHY DON'T I COME OVER AND COOK YOU DINNER TONIGHT?
HERE? IN MY KITCHEN?
SURE! WHY NOT?
I GUESS THERE'S TIME TO HOSE OUT THE FRIDGE
JON?... ARE YOU THERE?
JIM DAVIS 4-20
© 2009 PAWS, INC. All Rights Reserved.
Distributed by Universal Press Syndicate

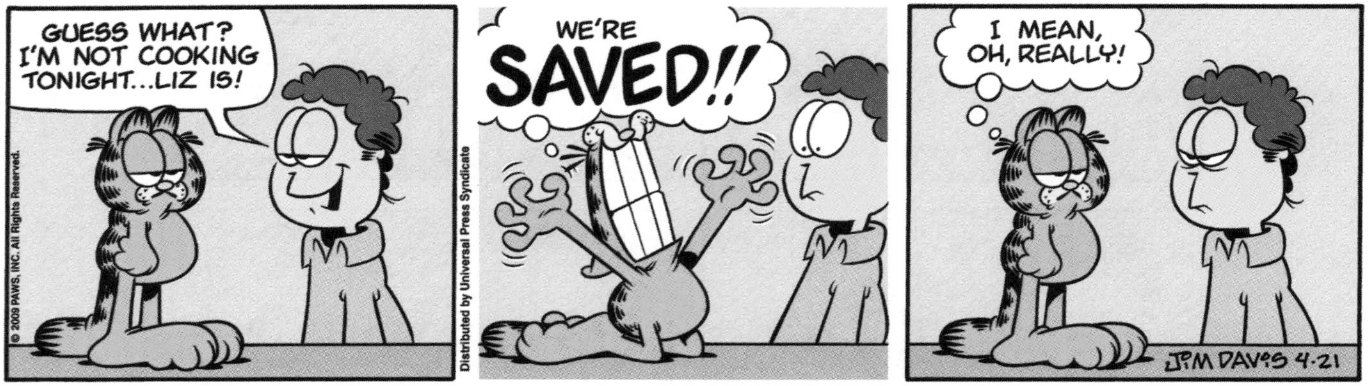
GUESS WHAT? I'M NOT COOKING TONIGHT...LIZ IS!
WE'RE SAVED!!
I MEAN, OH, REALLY!
JIM DAVIS 4-21
© 2009 PAWS, INC. All Rights Reserved.
Distributed by Universal Press Syndicate

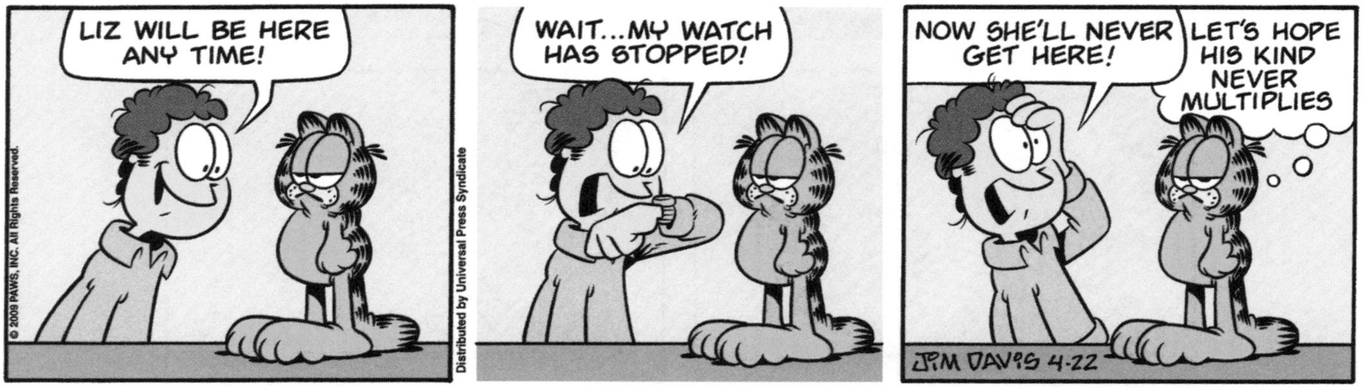
LIZ WILL BE HERE ANY TIME!
WAIT...MY WATCH HAS STOPPED!
NOW SHE'LL NEVER GET HERE!
LET'S HOPE HIS KIND NEVER MULTIPLIES
JIM DAVIS 4-22
© 2009 PAWS, INC. All Rights Reserved.
Distributed by Universal Press Syndicate

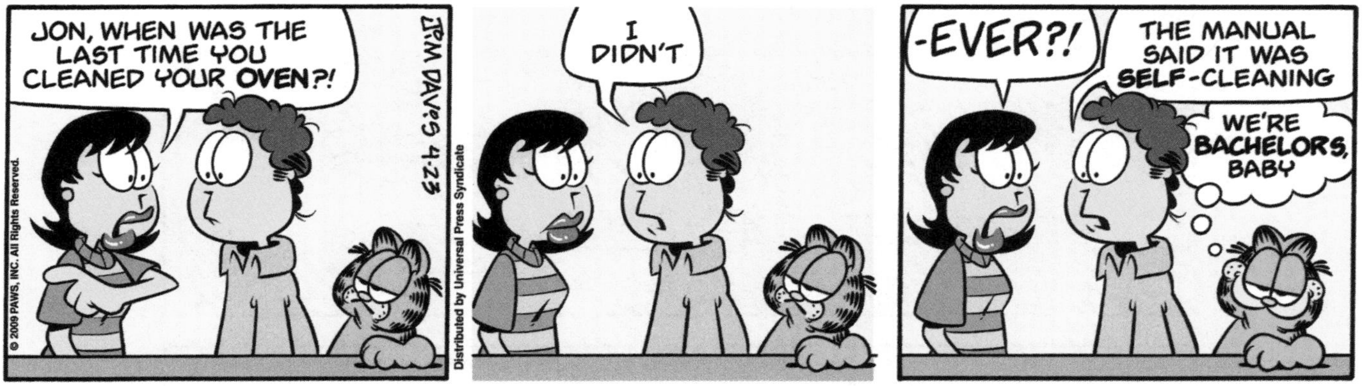
JON, WHEN WAS THE LAST TIME YOU CLEANED YOUR **OVEN**?!
JIM DAVIS 4-23
© 2009 PAWS, INC. All Rights Reserved.
Distributed by Universal Press Syndicate
I DIDN'T
-EVER?!
THE MANUAL SAID IT WAS **SELF**-CLEANING
WE'RE **BACHELORS**, BABY

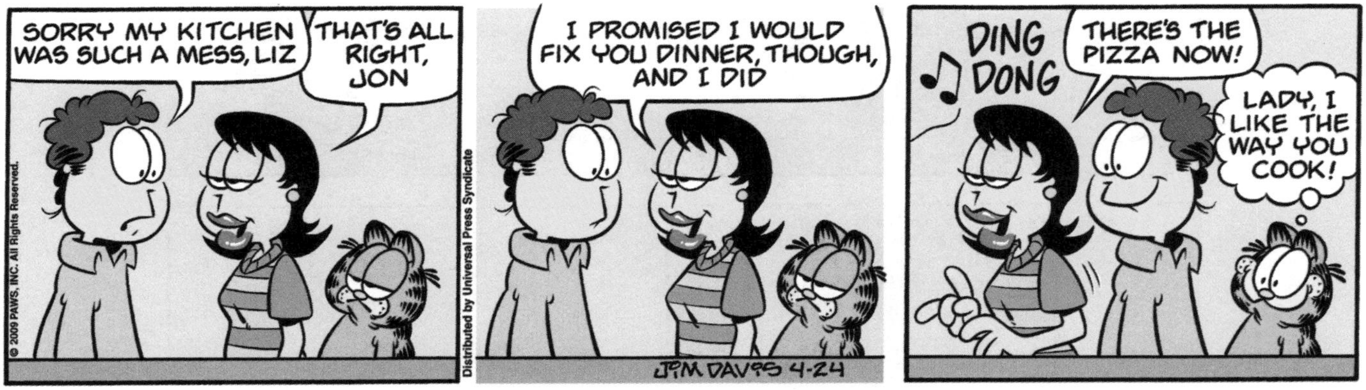
SORRY MY KITCHEN WAS SUCH A MESS, LIZ
THAT'S ALL RIGHT, JON
© 2009 PAWS, INC. All Rights Reserved.
Distributed by Universal Press Syndicate
I PROMISED I WOULD FIX YOU DINNER, THOUGH, AND I DID
JIM DAVIS 4-24
DING DONG
THERE'S THE PIZZA NOW!
LADY, I LIKE THE WAY YOU COOK!

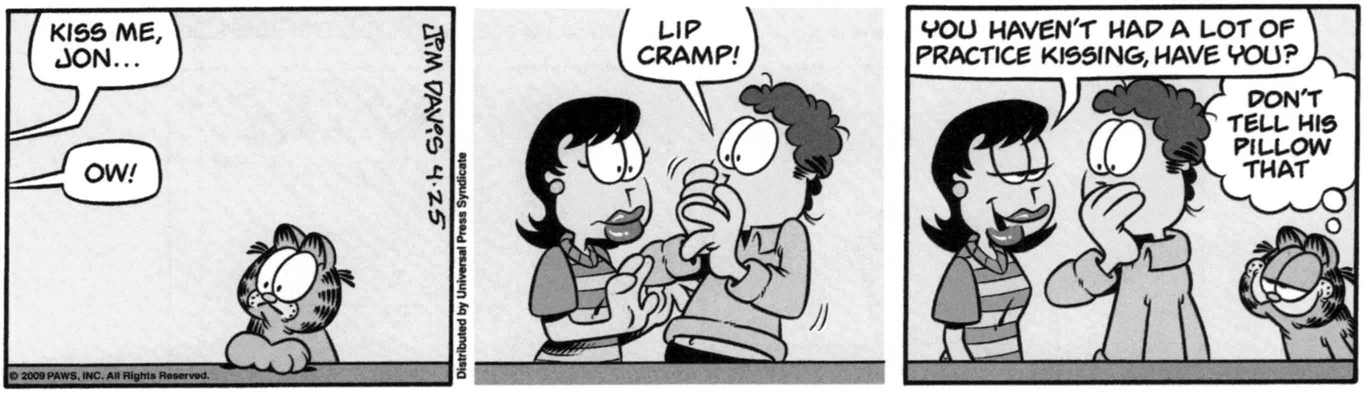
KISS ME, JON...
OW!
JIM DAVIS 4-25
© 2009 PAWS, INC. All Rights Reserved.
Distributed by Universal Press Syndicate
LIP CRAMP!
YOU HAVEN'T HAD A LOT OF PRACTICE KISSING, HAVE YOU?
DON'T TELL HIS PILLOW THAT

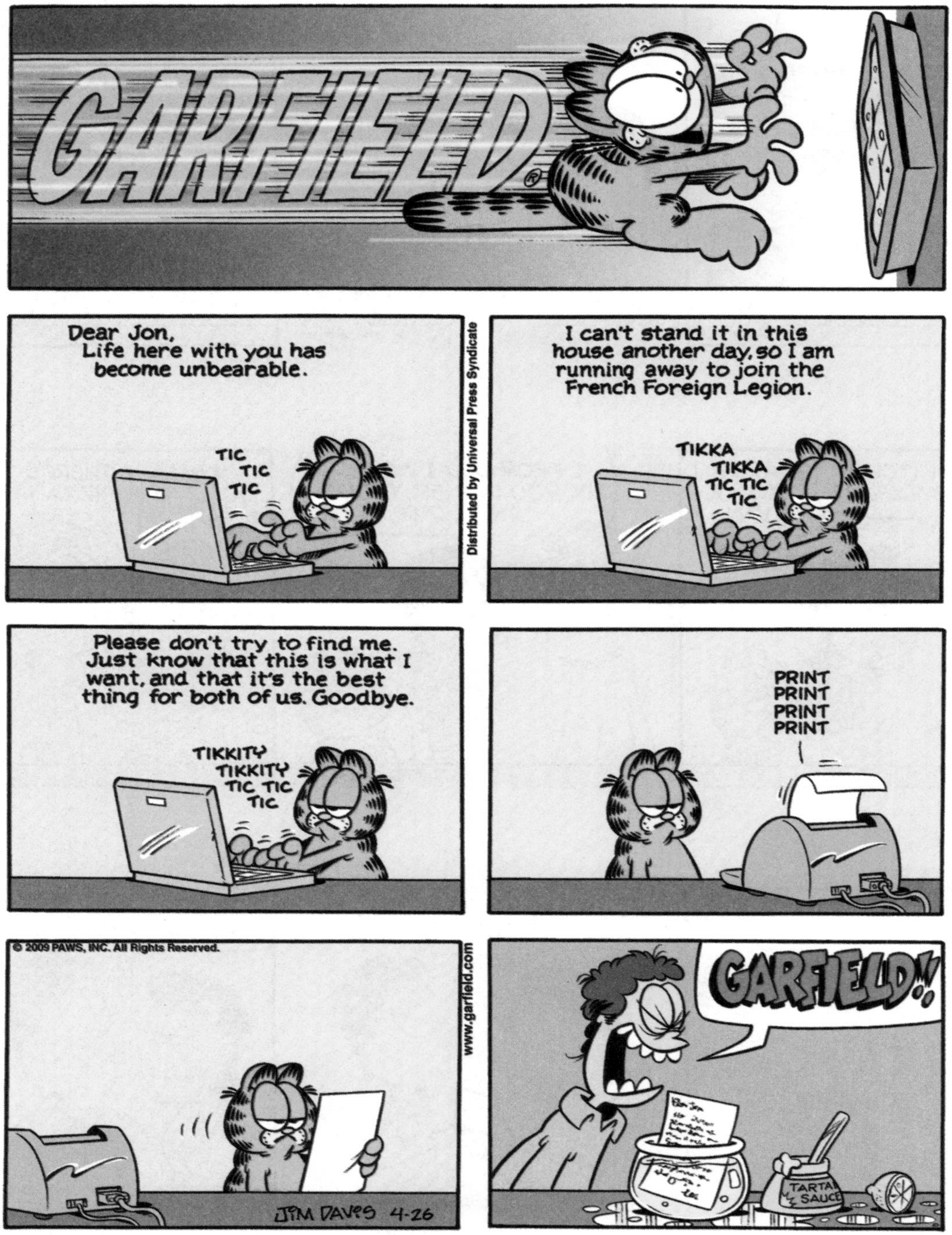
GARFIELD®
Dear Jon,
Life here with you has become unbearable.
TIC TIC TIC
Distributed by Universal Press Syndicate
I can't stand it in this house another day, so I am running away to join the French Foreign Legion.
TIKKA TIKKA TIC TIC TIC
Please don't try to find me. Just know that this is what I want, and that it's the best thing for both of us. Goodbye.
TIKKITY TIKKITY TIC TIC TIC
PRINT PRINT PRINT PRINT
© 2009 PAWS, INC. All Rights Reserved.
www.garfield.com
JIM DAVIS 4-26
GARFIELD!!
TARTAR SAUCE

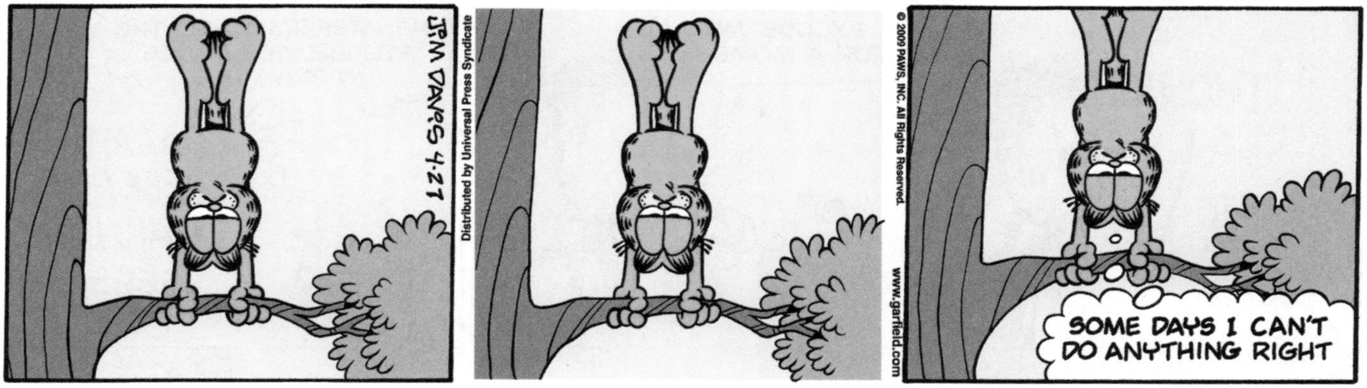

SOME DAYS I CAN'T DO ANYTHING RIGHT

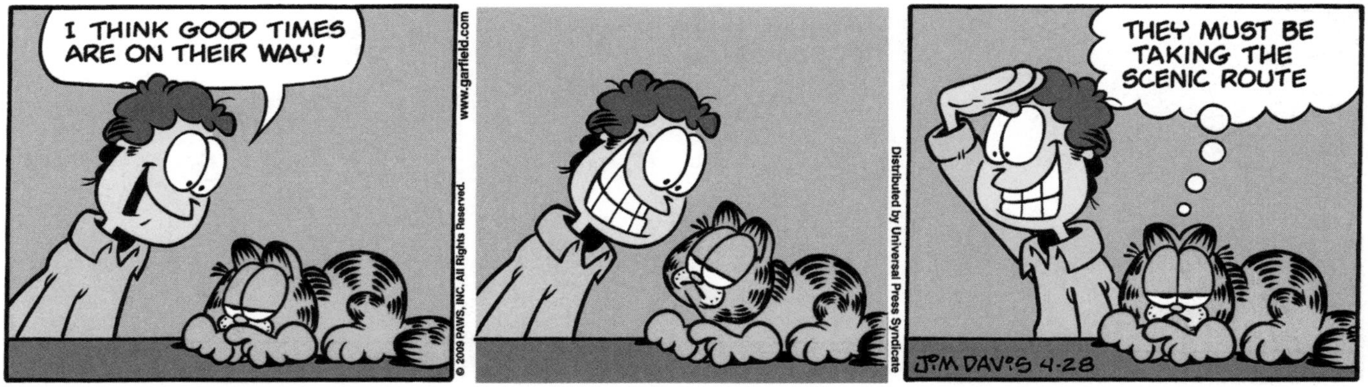

I THINK GOOD TIMES ARE ON THEIR WAY!
THEY MUST BE TAKING THE SCENIC ROUTE

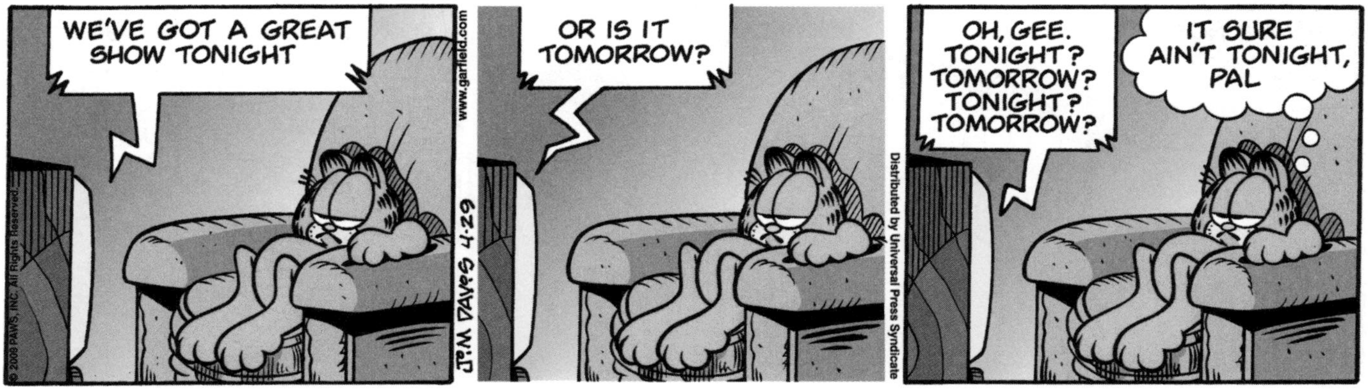

WE'VE GOT A GREAT SHOW TONIGHT
OR IS IT TOMORROW?
OH, GEE. TONIGHT? TOMORROW? TONIGHT? TOMORROW?
IT SURE AIN'T TONIGHT, PAL

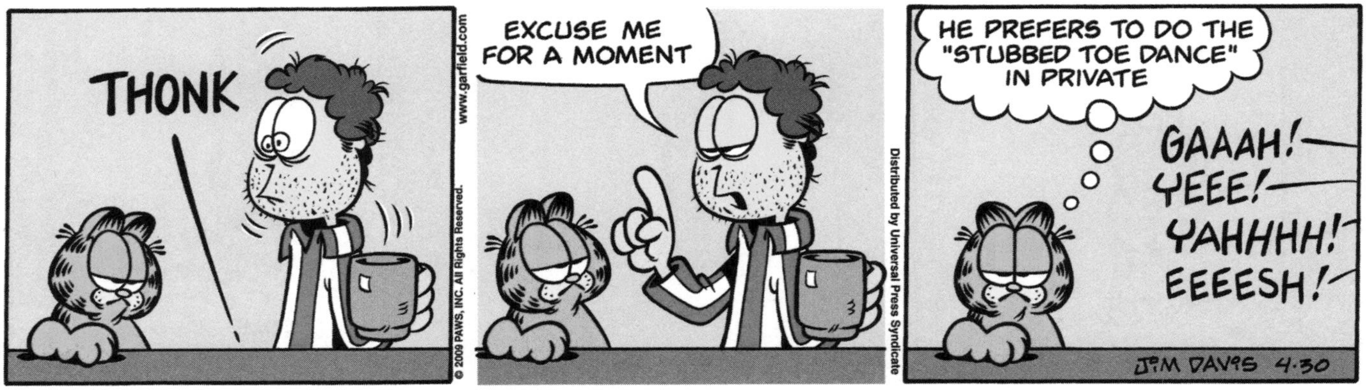
THONK
EXCUSE ME FOR A MOMENT
HE PREFERS TO DO THE "STUBBED TOE DANCE" IN PRIVATE
GAAAH! YEEE! YAHHHH! EEEESH!
JIM DAVIS 4·30
© 2009 PAWS, INC. All Rights Reserved. www.garfield.com
Distributed by Universal Press Syndicate

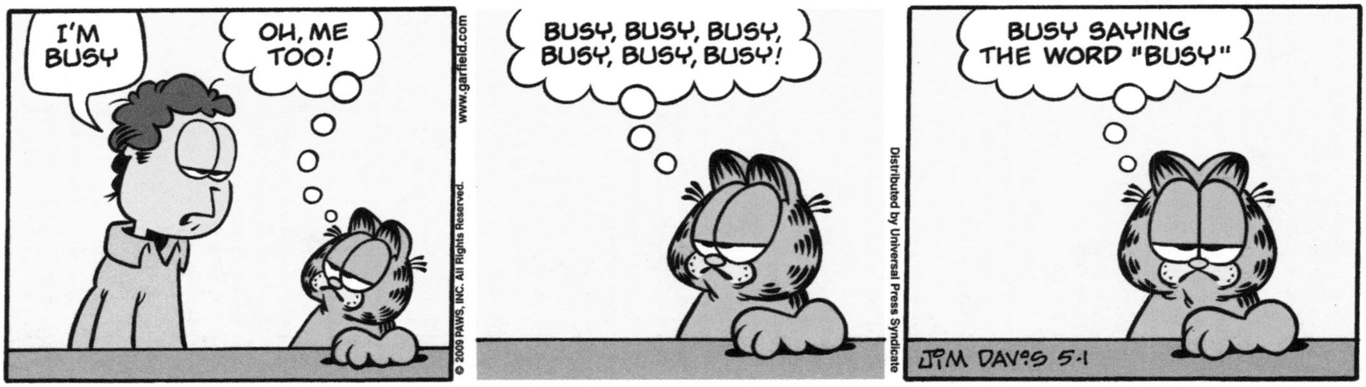
I'M BUSY
OH, ME TOO!
BUSY, BUSY, BUSY, BUSY, BUSY, BUSY!
BUSY SAYING THE WORD "BUSY"
JIM DAVIS 5·1
© 2009 PAWS, INC. All Rights Reserved. www.garfield.com
Distributed by Universal Press Syndicate

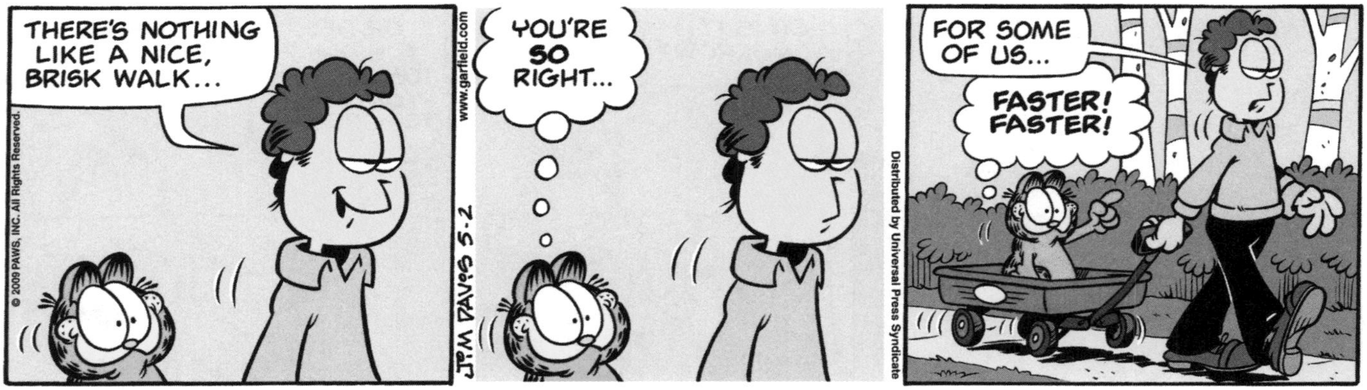
THERE'S NOTHING LIKE A NICE, BRISK WALK...
YOU'RE **SO** RIGHT...
FOR SOME OF US...
FASTER! FASTER!
JIM DAVIS 5·2
© 2009 PAWS, INC. All Rights Reserved. www.garfield.com
Distributed by Universal Press Syndicate

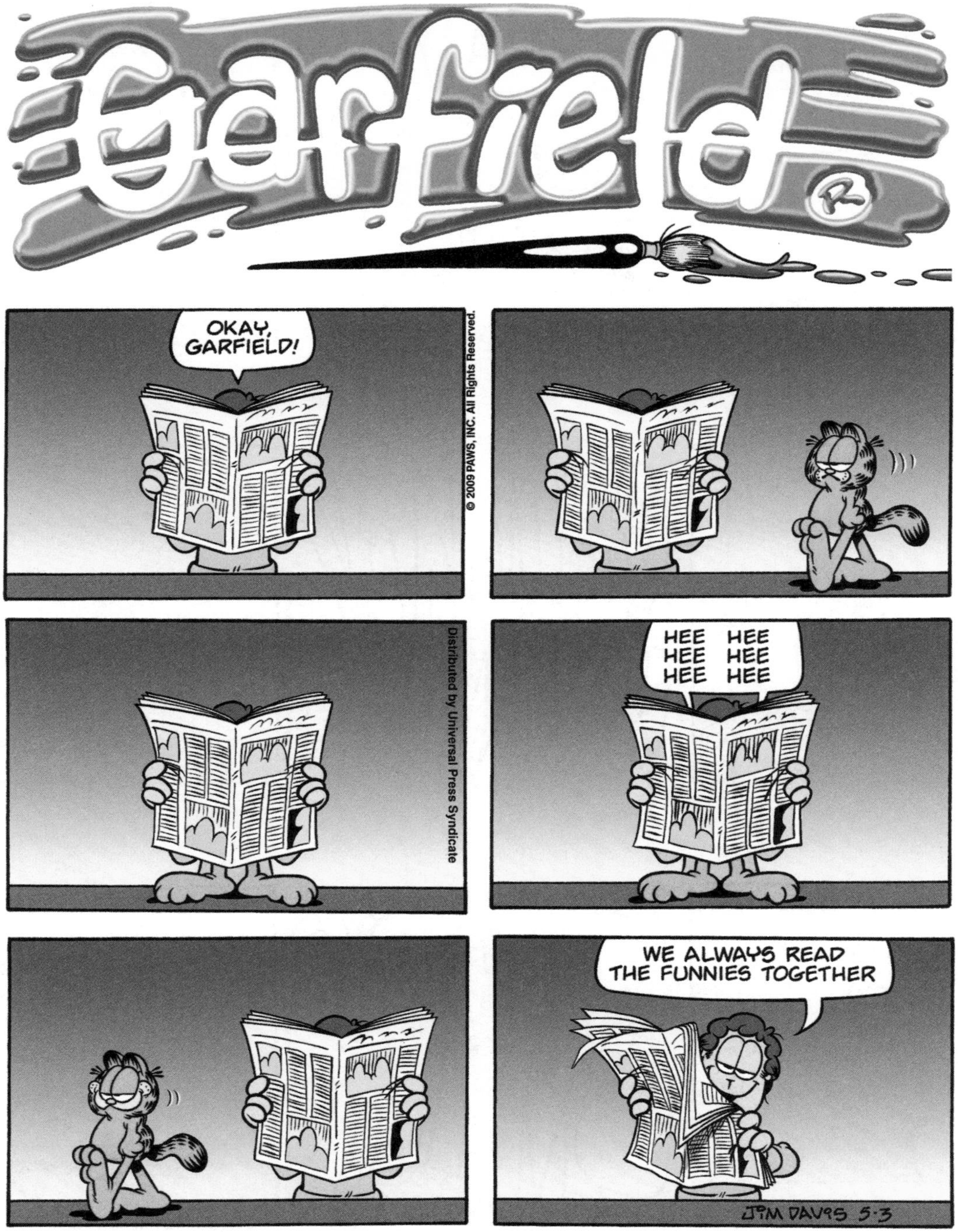
Garfield®
OKAY, GARFIELD!
© 2009 PAWS, INC. All Rights Reserved.
Distributed by Universal Press Syndicate
HEE HEE HEE HEE HEE HEE
WE ALWAYS READ THE FUNNIES TOGETHER
JIM DAVIS 5-3

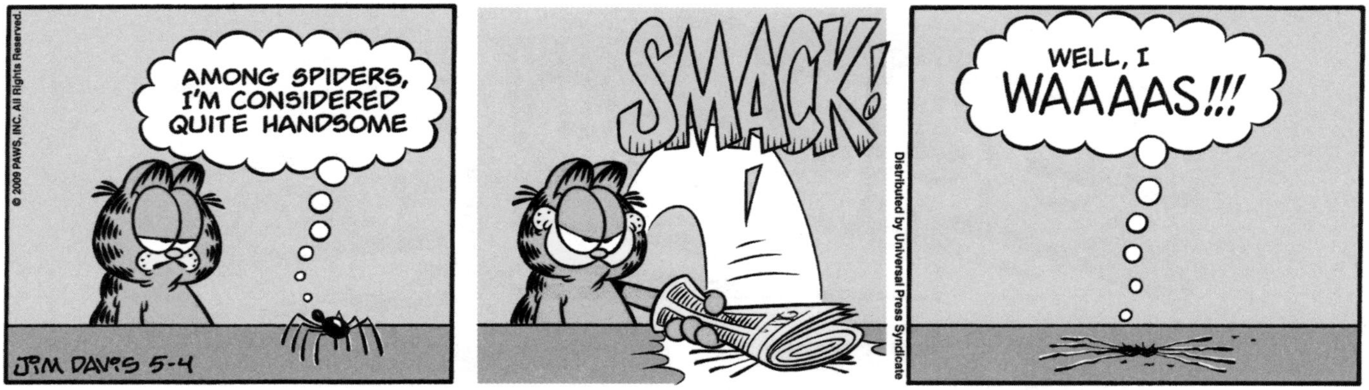
© 2009 PAWS, INC. All Rights Reserved.
AMONG SPIDERS, I'M CONSIDERED QUITE HANDSOME
JIM DAVIS 5-4
SMACK!
Distributed by Universal Press Syndicate
WELL, I WAAAAS!!!

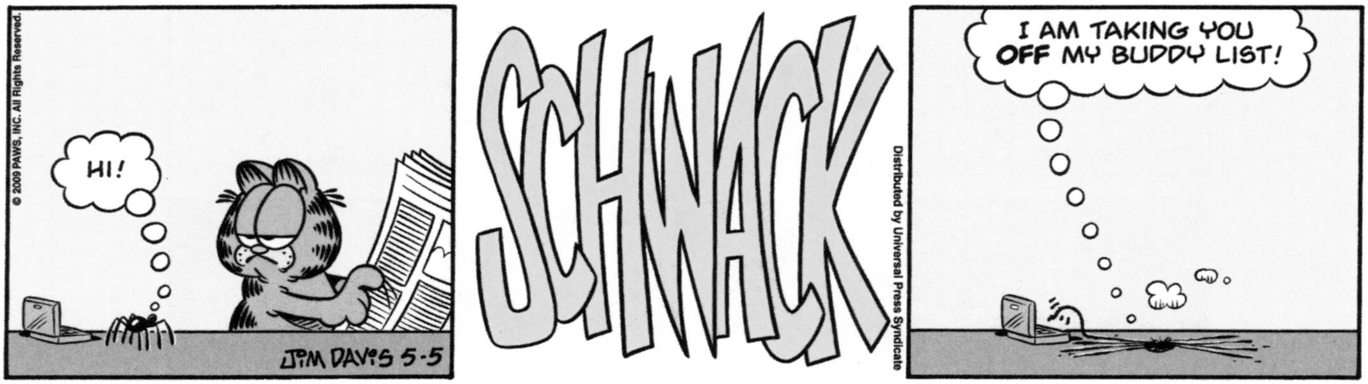
© 2009 PAWS, INC. All Rights Reserved.
HI!
JIM DAVIS 5-5
SCHWACK
Distributed by Universal Press Syndicate
I AM TAKING YOU **OFF** MY BUDDY LIST!

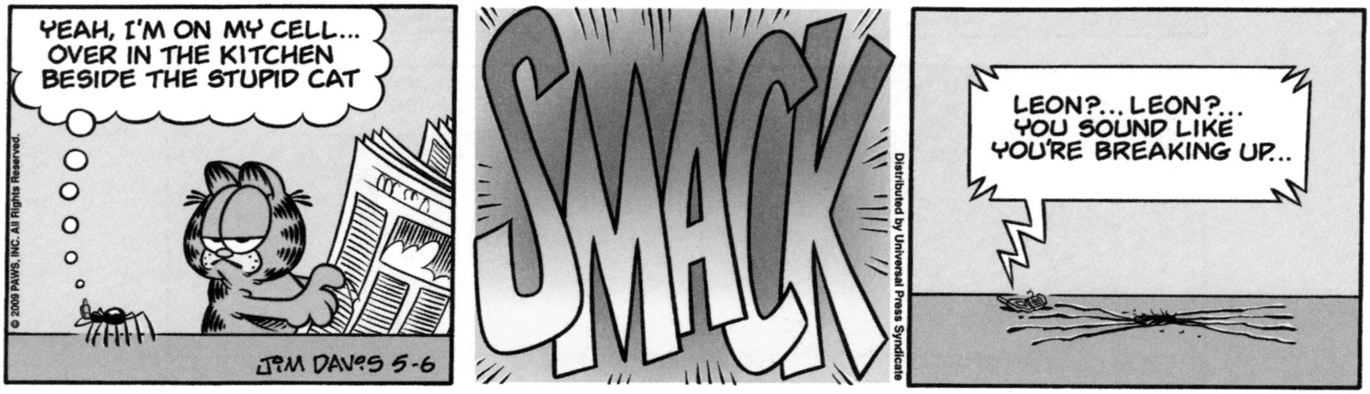
YEAH, I'M ON MY CELL... OVER IN THE KITCHEN BESIDE THE STUPID CAT
© 2009 PAWS, INC. All Rights Reserved.
JIM DAVIS 5-6
SMACK
Distributed by Universal Press Syndicate
LEON?... LEON?... YOU SOUND LIKE YOU'RE BREAKING UP...

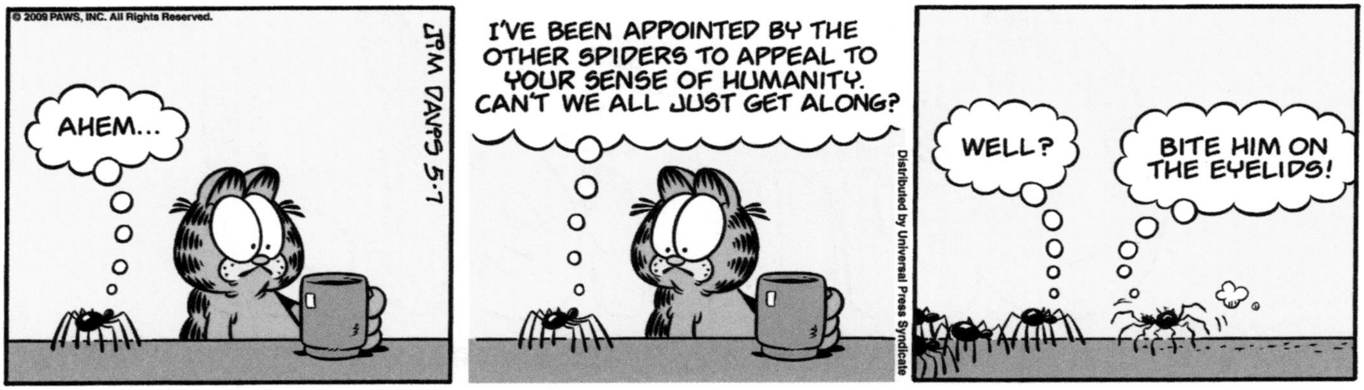
© 2009 PAWS, INC. All Rights Reserved.
JIM DAVIS 5-7
AHEM...
I'VE BEEN APPOINTED BY THE OTHER SPIDERS TO APPEAL TO YOUR SENSE OF HUMANITY. CAN'T WE ALL JUST GET ALONG?
Distributed by Universal Press Syndicate
WELL?
BITE HIM ON THE EYELIDS!

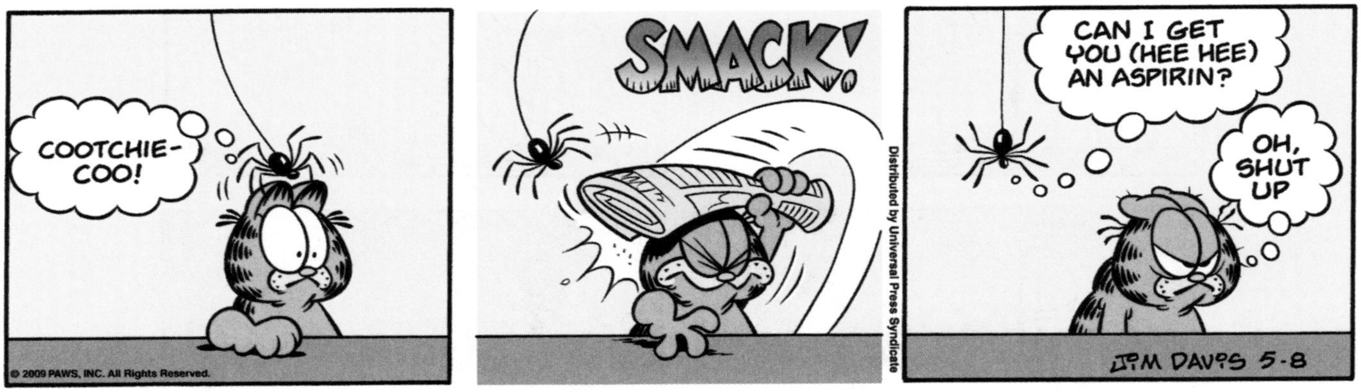
COOTCHIE-COO!
© 2009 PAWS, INC. All Rights Reserved.
SMACK!
Distributed by Universal Press Syndicate
CAN I GET YOU (HEE HEE) AN ASPIRIN?
OH, SHUT UP
JIM DAVIS 5-8

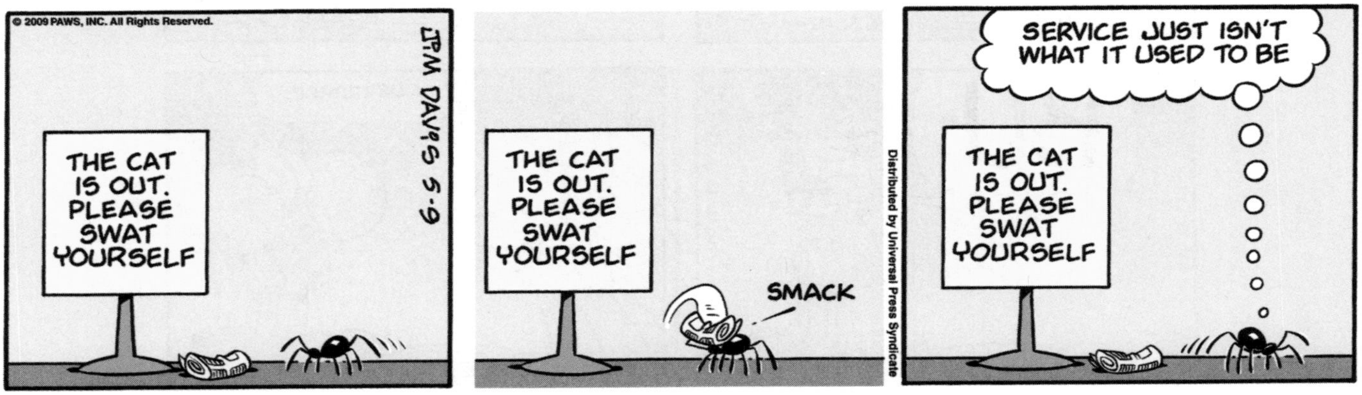
© 2009 PAWS, INC. All Rights Reserved.
JIM DAVIS 5-9
THE CAT IS OUT. PLEASE SWAT YOURSELF
THE CAT IS OUT. PLEASE SWAT YOURSELF
SMACK
Distributed by Universal Press Syndicate
SERVICE JUST ISN'T WHAT IT USED TO BE
THE CAT IS OUT. PLEASE SWAT YOURSELF

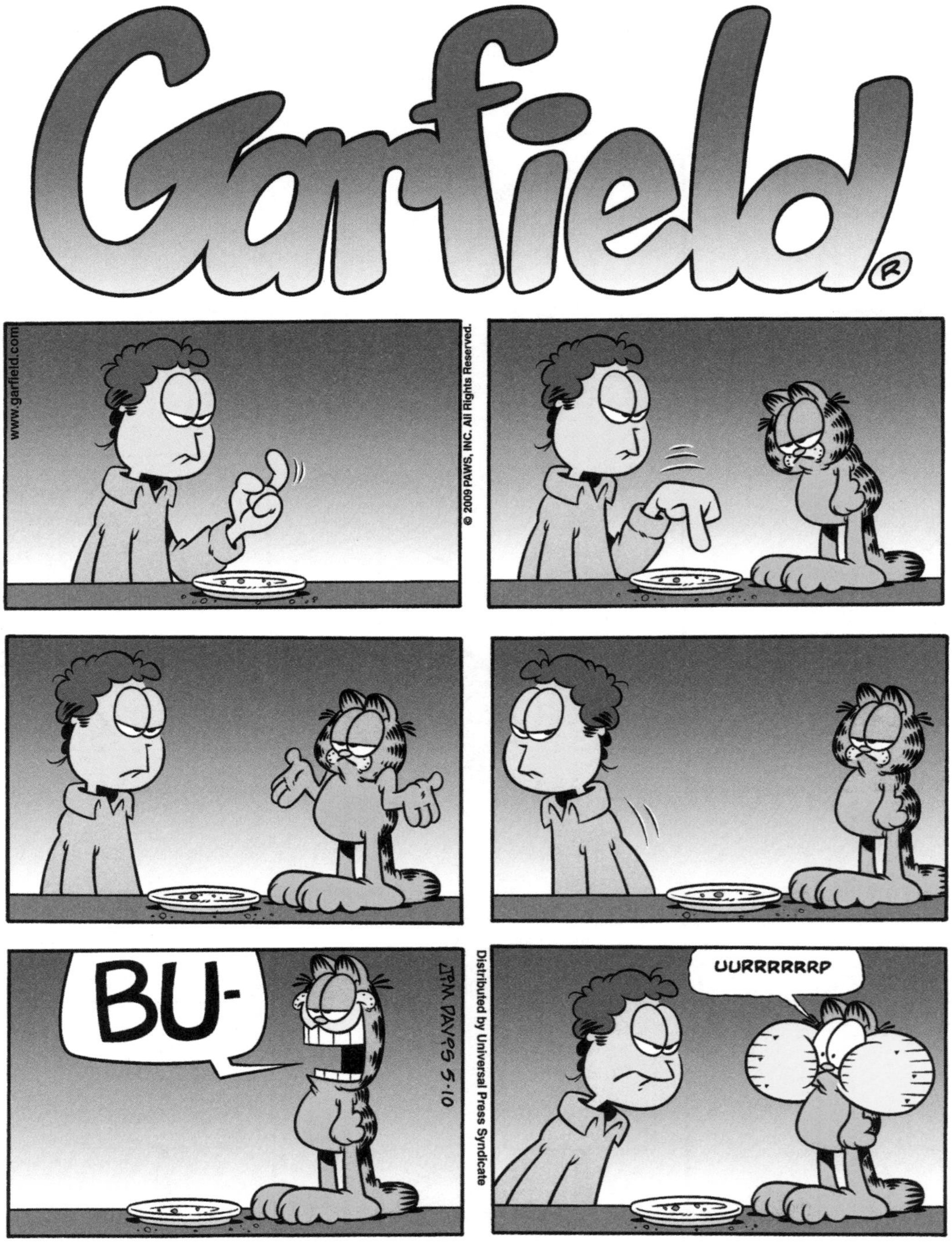
Garfield®
www.garfield.com
© 2009 PAWS, INC. All Rights Reserved.
BU-
JPM DAVIS 5-10
Distributed by Universal Press Syndicate
UURRRRRRP

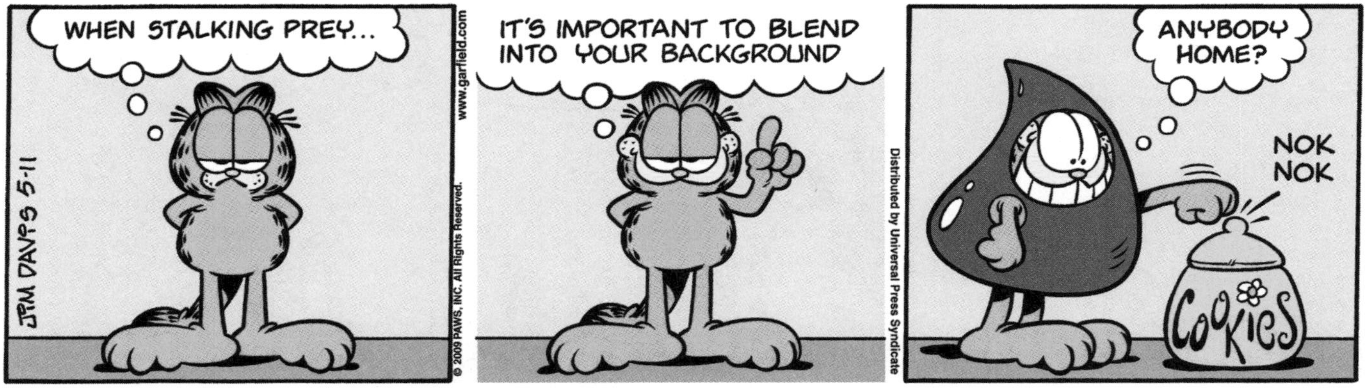
WHEN STALKING PREY...
JIM DAVIS 5-11
© 2009 PAWS, INC. All Rights Reserved.
www.garfield.com
IT'S IMPORTANT TO BLEND INTO YOUR BACKGROUND
Distributed by Universal Press Syndicate
ANYBODY HOME?
NOK NOK
COOKIES

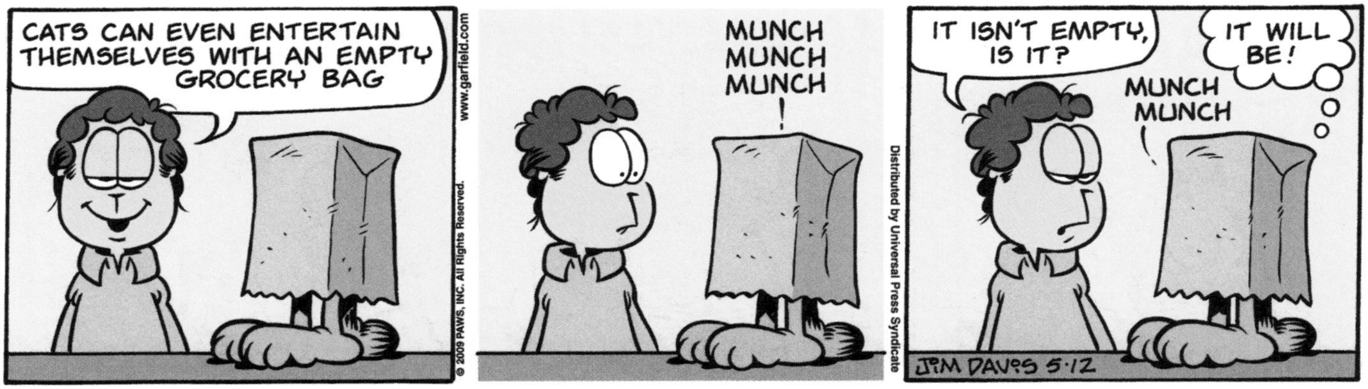
CATS CAN EVEN ENTERTAIN THEMSELVES WITH AN EMPTY GROCERY BAG
© 2009 PAWS, INC. All Rights Reserved.
www.garfield.com
MUNCH MUNCH MUNCH
Distributed by Universal Press Syndicate
IT ISN'T EMPTY, IS IT?
IT WILL BE!
MUNCH MUNCH
JIM DAVIS 5-12

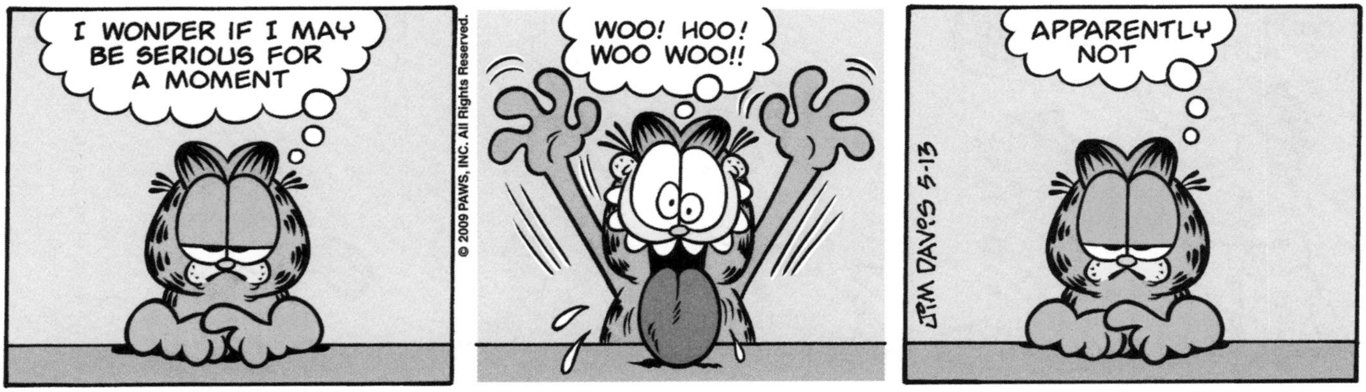
I WONDER IF I MAY BE SERIOUS FOR A MOMENT
© 2009 PAWS, INC. All Rights Reserved.
WOO! HOO! WOO WOO!!
JIM DAVIS 5-13
APPARENTLY NOT

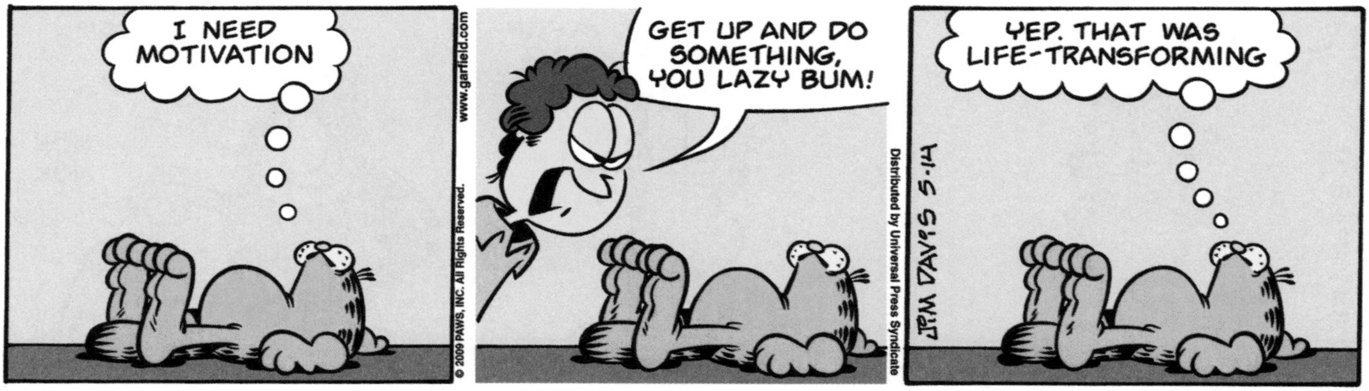
I NEED MOTIVATION
GET UP AND DO SOMETHING, YOU LAZY BUM!
YEP. THAT WAS LIFE-TRANSFORMING

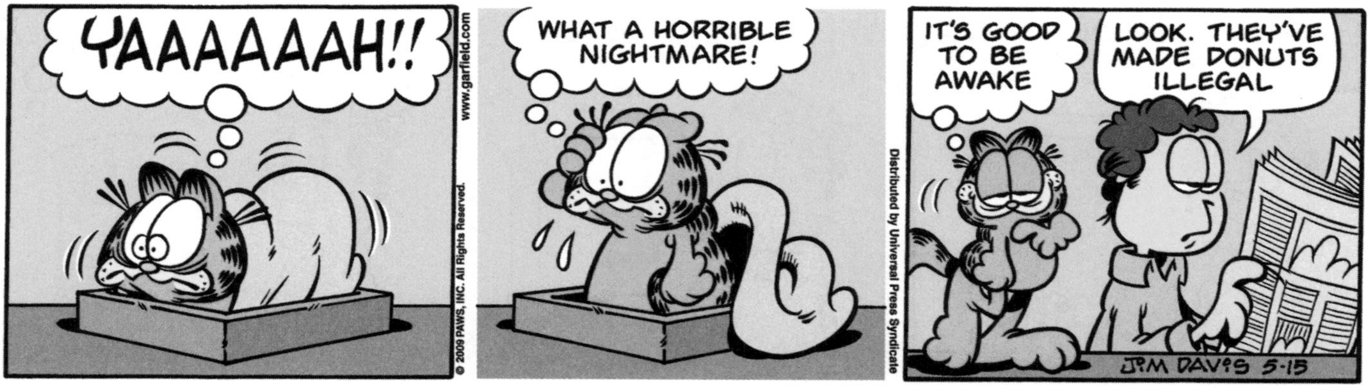
YAAAAAAH!!
WHAT A HORRIBLE NIGHTMARE!
IT'S GOOD TO BE AWAKE
LOOK. THEY'VE MADE DONUTS ILLEGAL

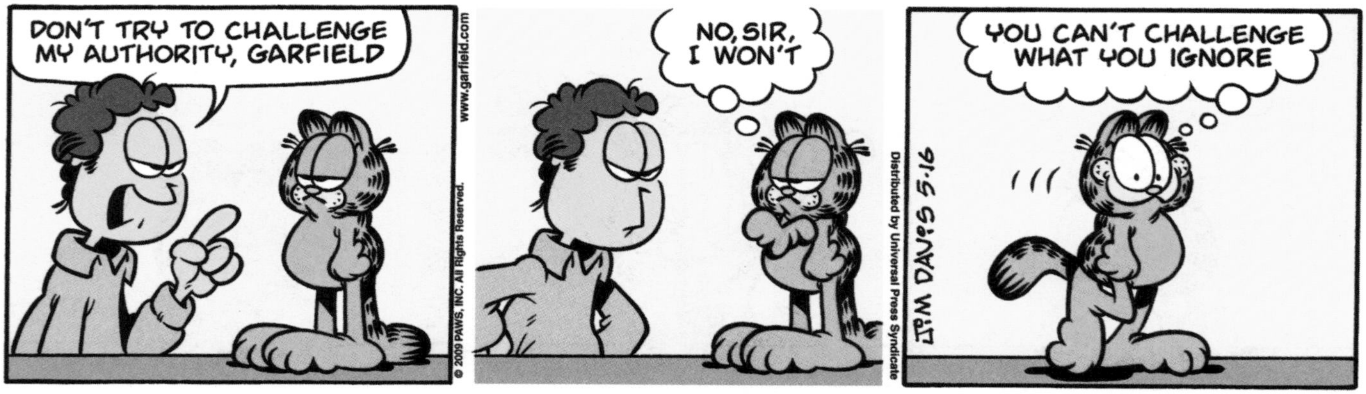
DON'T TRY TO CHALLENGE MY AUTHORITY, GARFIELD
NO, SIR, I WON'T
YOU CAN'T CHALLENGE WHAT YOU IGNORE

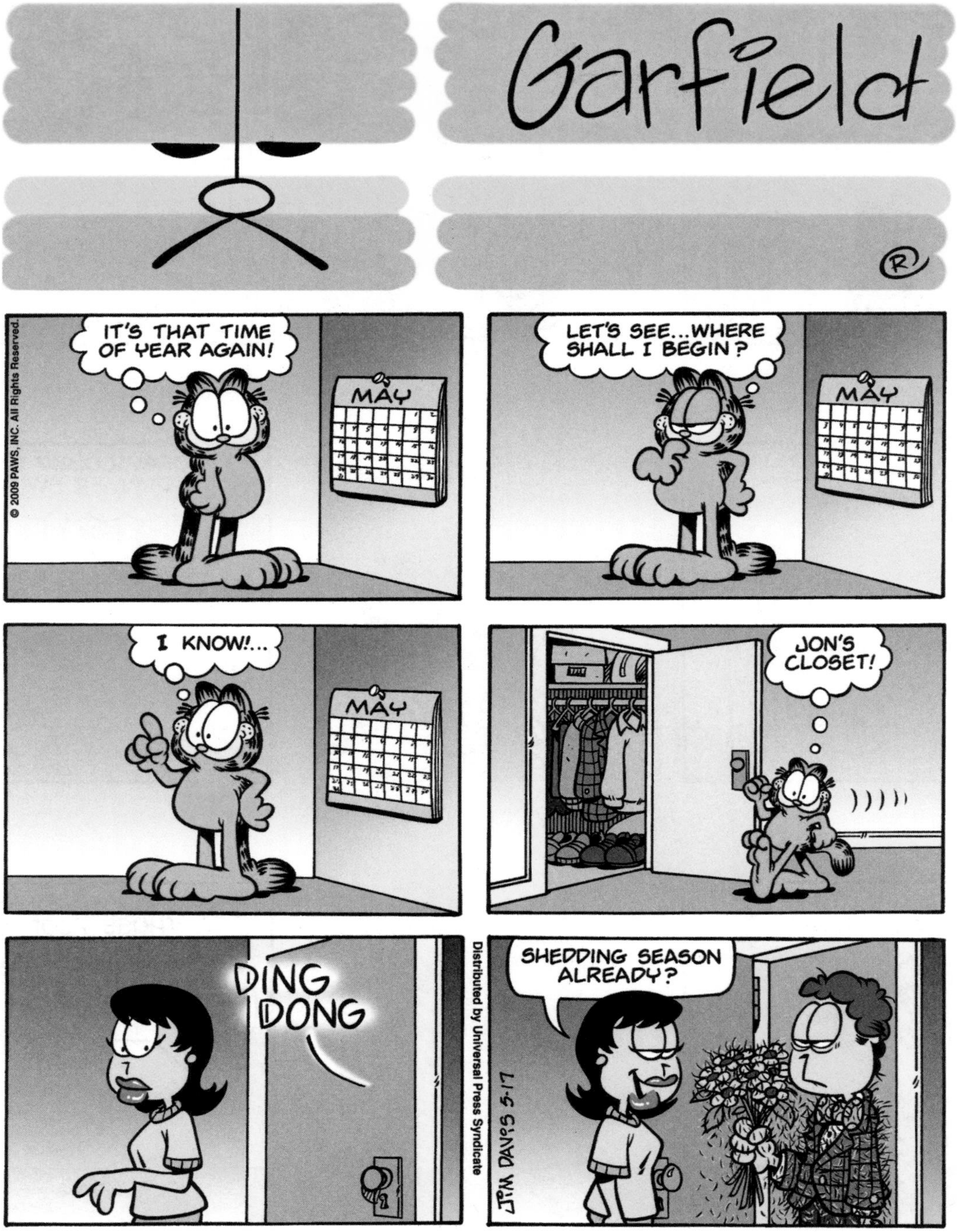
Garfield
© 2009 PAWS, INC. All Rights Reserved.
IT'S THAT TIME OF YEAR AGAIN!
MAY
LET'S SEE...WHERE SHALL I BEGIN?
MAY
I KNOW!...
MAY
JON'S CLOSET!
DING DONG
Distributed by Universal Press Syndicate
JIM DAVIS 5-17
SHEDDING SEASON ALREADY?

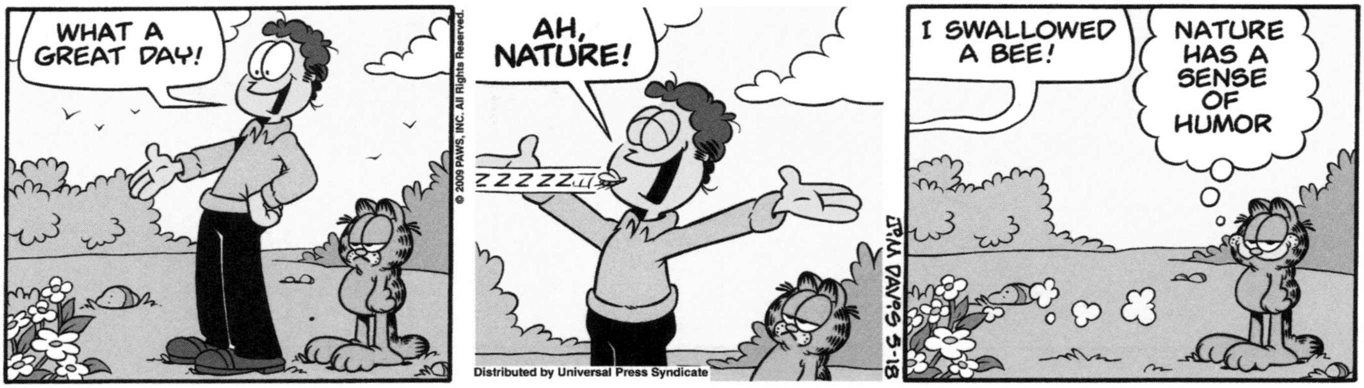
WHAT A GREAT DAY!
© 2009 PAWS, INC. All Rights Reserved.
AH, NATURE!
ZZZZZ
Distributed by Universal Press Syndicate
JIM DAVIS 5-18
I SWALLOWED A BEE!
NATURE HAS A SENSE OF HUMOR

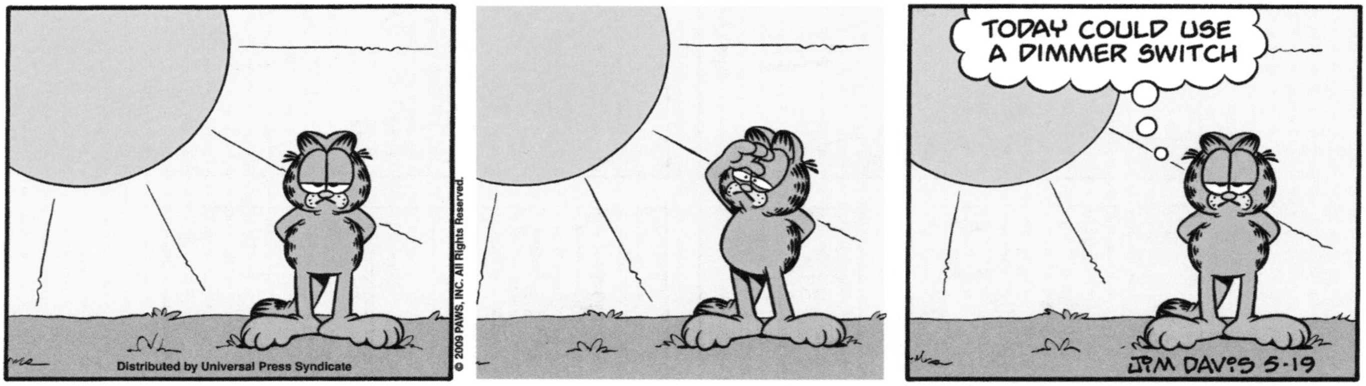
Distributed by Universal Press Syndicate
© 2009 PAWS, INC. All Rights Reserved.
TODAY COULD USE A DIMMER SWITCH
JIM DAVIS 5-19

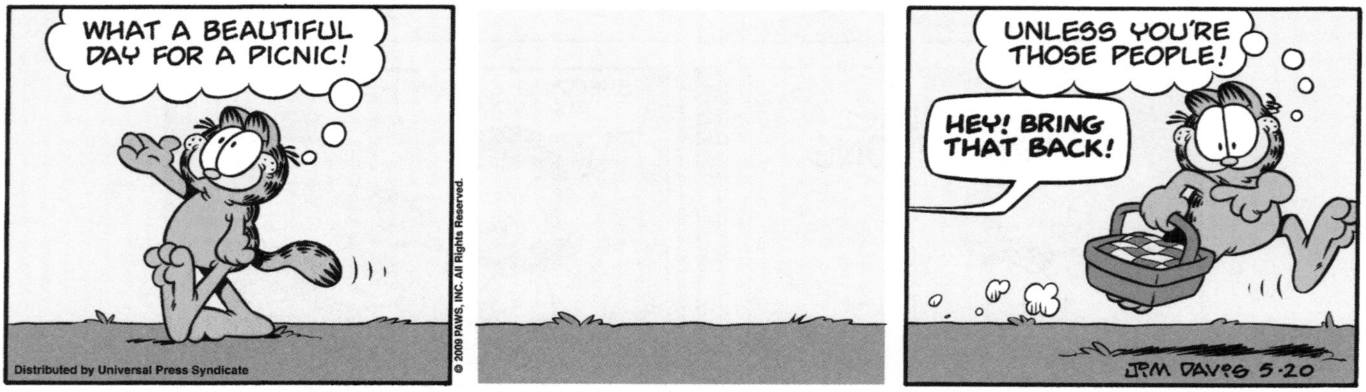
WHAT A BEAUTIFUL DAY FOR A PICNIC!
Distributed by Universal Press Syndicate
© 2009 PAWS, INC. All Rights Reserved.
UNLESS YOU'RE THOSE PEOPLE!
HEY! BRING THAT BACK!
JIM DAVIS 5-20

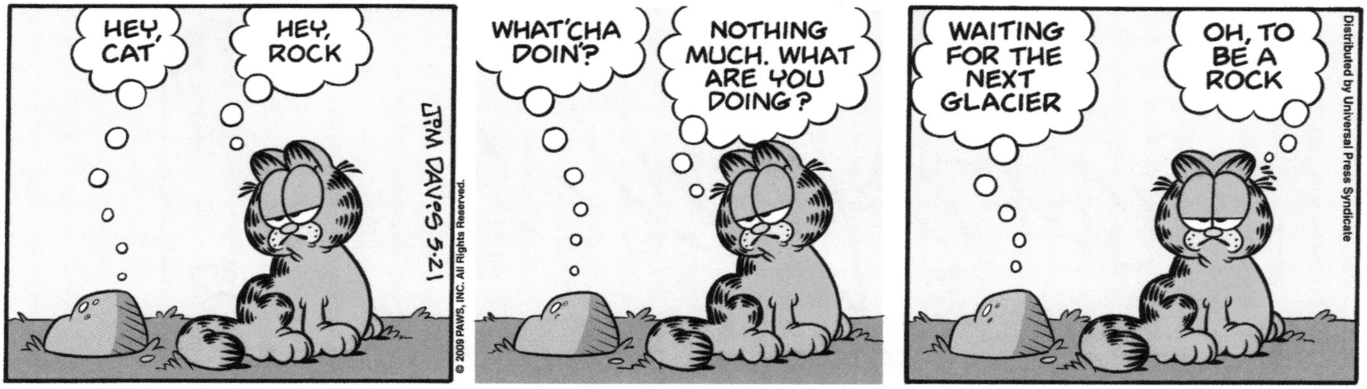
HEY, CAT
HEY, ROCK
JIM DAVIS 5-21
© 2009 PAWS, INC. All Rights Reserved.
WHAT'CHA DOIN'?
NOTHING MUCH. WHAT ARE YOU DOING?
WAITING FOR THE NEXT GLACIER
OH, TO BE A ROCK
Distributed by Universal Press Syndicate

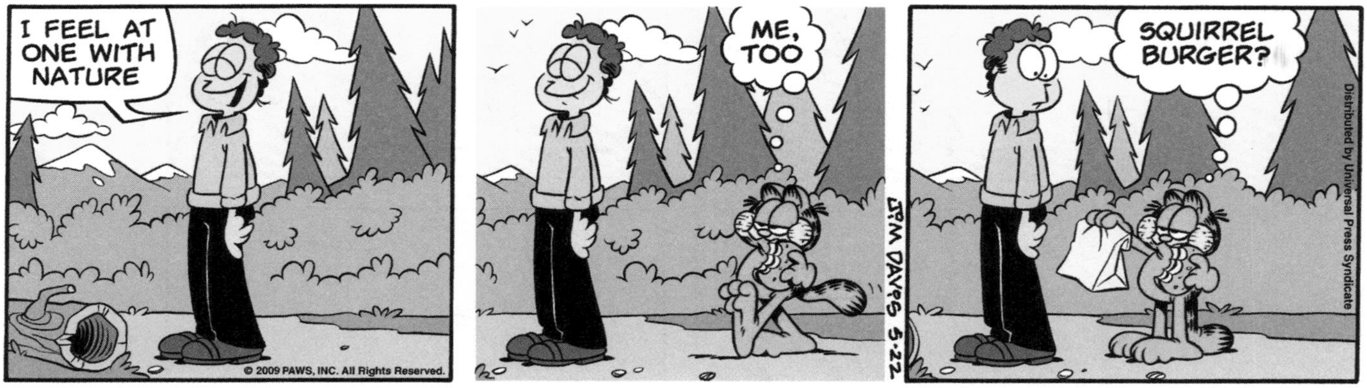
I FEEL AT ONE WITH NATURE
© 2009 PAWS, INC. All Rights Reserved.
ME, TOO
JIM DAVIS 5-22
SQUIRREL BURGER?
Distributed by Universal Press Syndicate

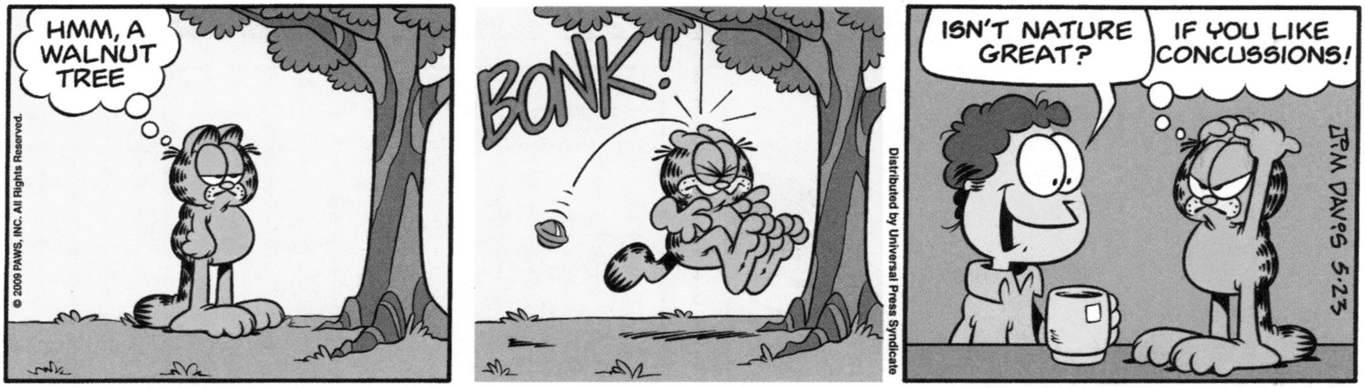
HMM, A WALNUT TREE
© 2009 PAWS, INC. All Rights Reserved.
BONK!
Distributed by Universal Press Syndicate
ISN'T NATURE GREAT?
IF YOU LIKE CONCUSSIONS!
JIM DAVIS 5-23

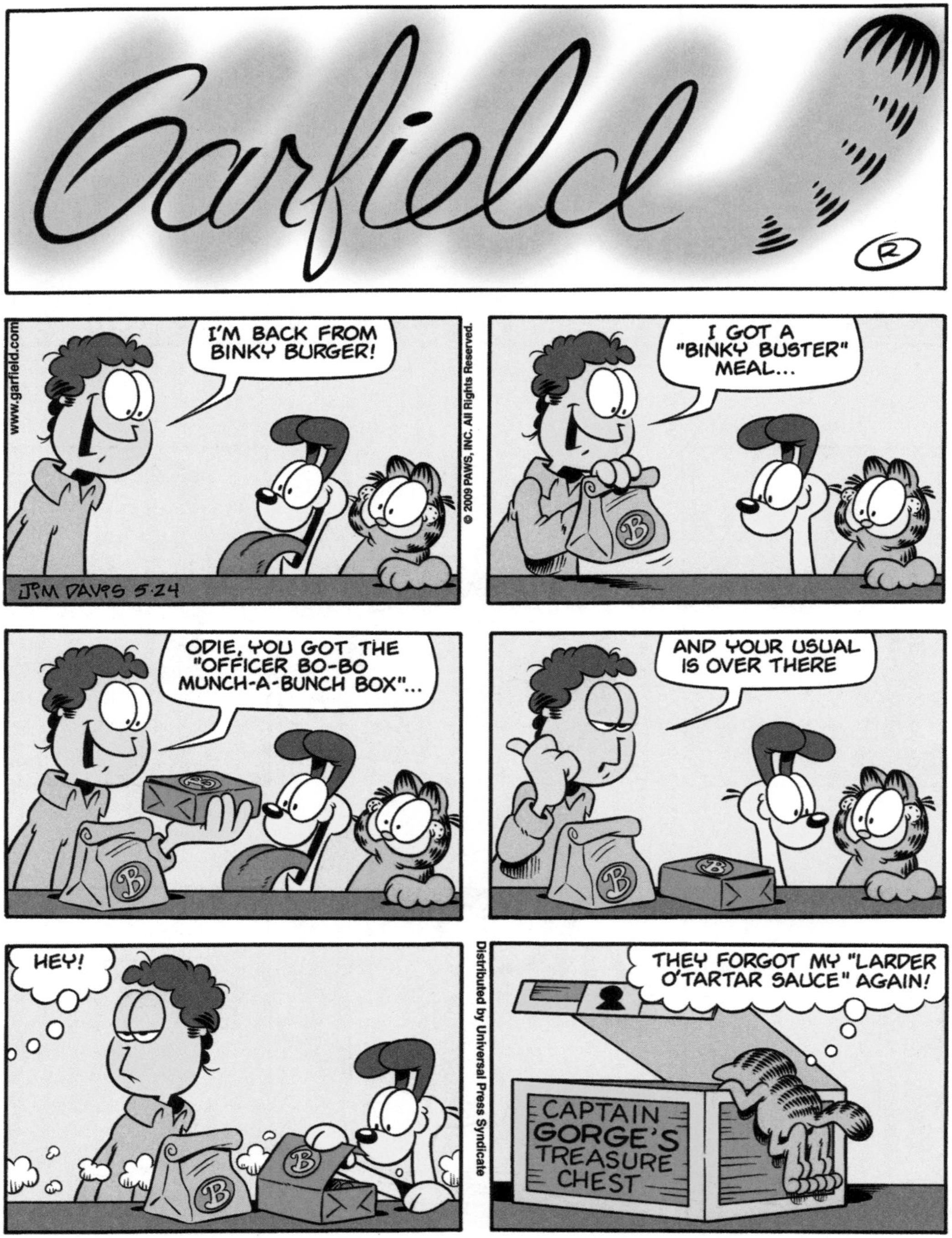

Garfield
www.garfield.com
JIM DAVIS 5·24
I'M BACK FROM BINKY BURGER!
© 2009 PAWS, INC. All Rights Reserved.
I GOT A "BINKY BUSTER" MEAL...
ODIE, YOU GOT THE "OFFICER BO-BO MUNCH-A-BUNCH BOX"...
AND YOUR USUAL IS OVER THERE
HEY!
Distributed by Universal Press Syndicate
THEY FORGOT MY "LARDER O'TARTAR SAUCE" AGAIN!
CAPTAIN GORGE'S TREASURE CHEST

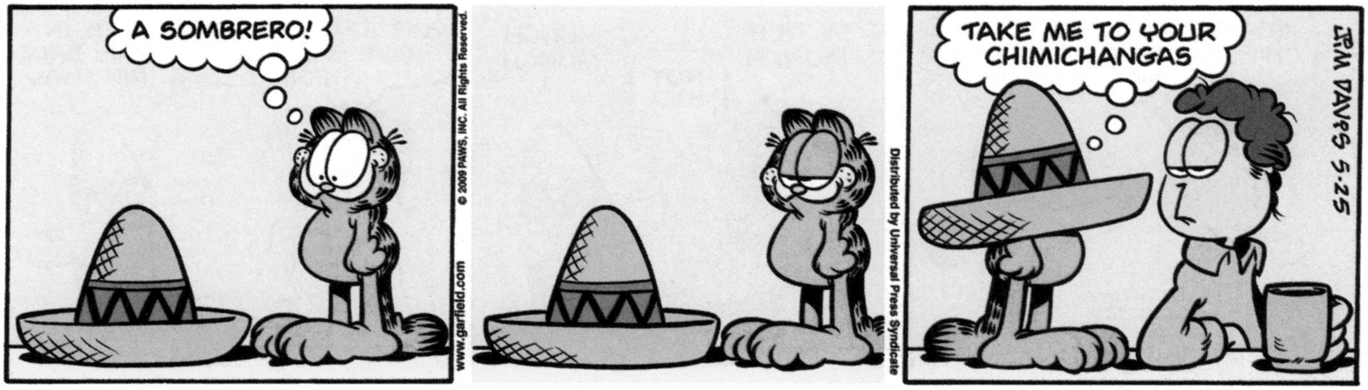
A SOMBRERO!
TAKE ME TO YOUR CHIMICHANGAS

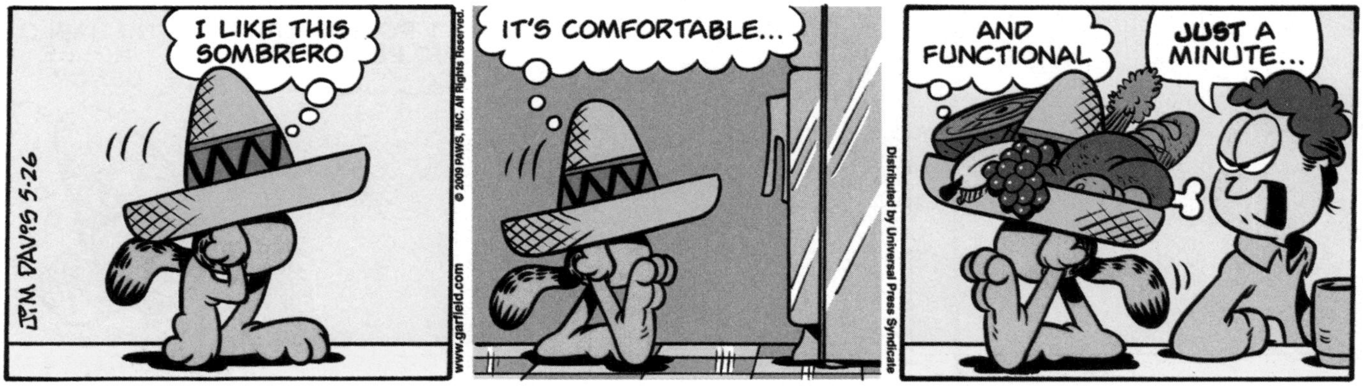
I LIKE THIS SOMBRERO
IT'S COMFORTABLE...
AND FUNCTIONAL
JUST A MINUTE...

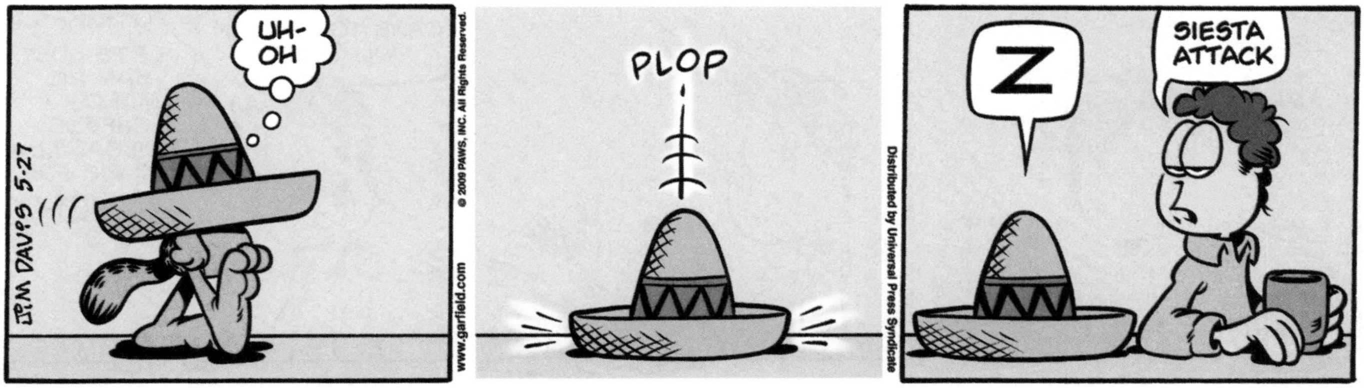
UH-OH
PLOP
Z
SIESTA ATTACK

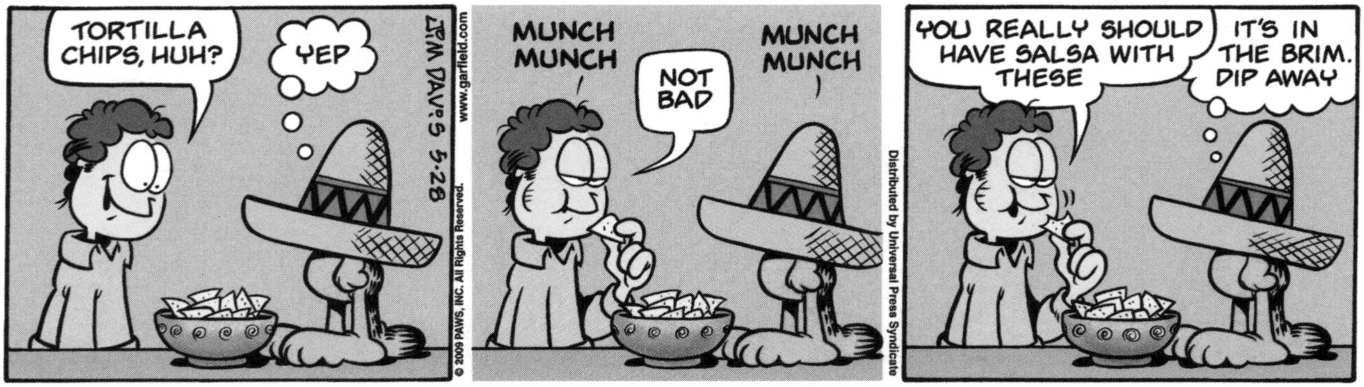
TORTILLA CHIPS, HUH?
YEP
JIM DAVIS 5-28
www.garfield.com
© 2009 PAWS, INC. All Rights Reserved.
MUNCH MUNCH
NOT BAD
MUNCH MUNCH
Distributed by Universal Press Syndicate
YOU REALLY SHOULD HAVE SALSA WITH THESE
IT'S IN THE BRIM. DIP AWAY

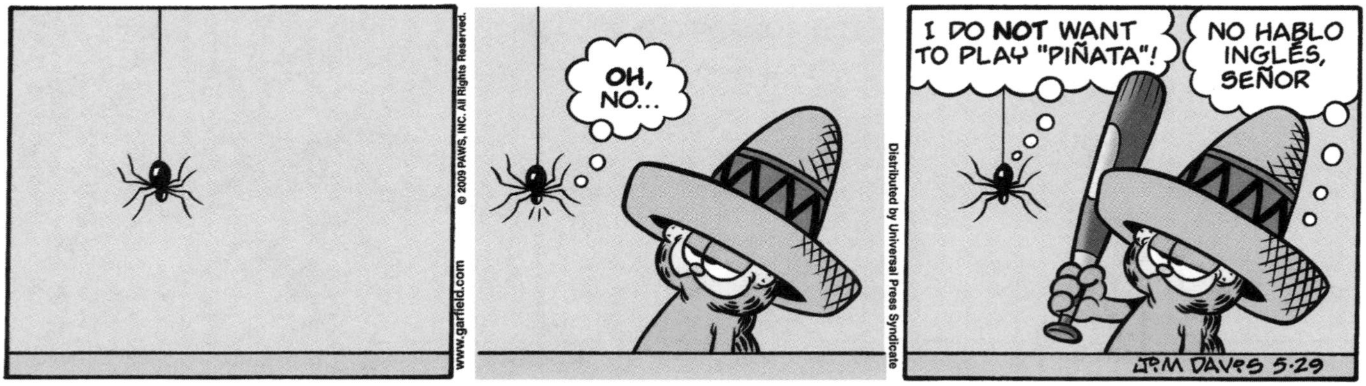
www.garfield.com
© 2009 PAWS, INC. All Rights Reserved.
OH, NO...
Distributed by Universal Press Syndicate
I DO **NOT** WANT TO PLAY "PIÑATA"!
NO HABLO INGLÉS, SEÑOR
JIM DAVIS 5-29

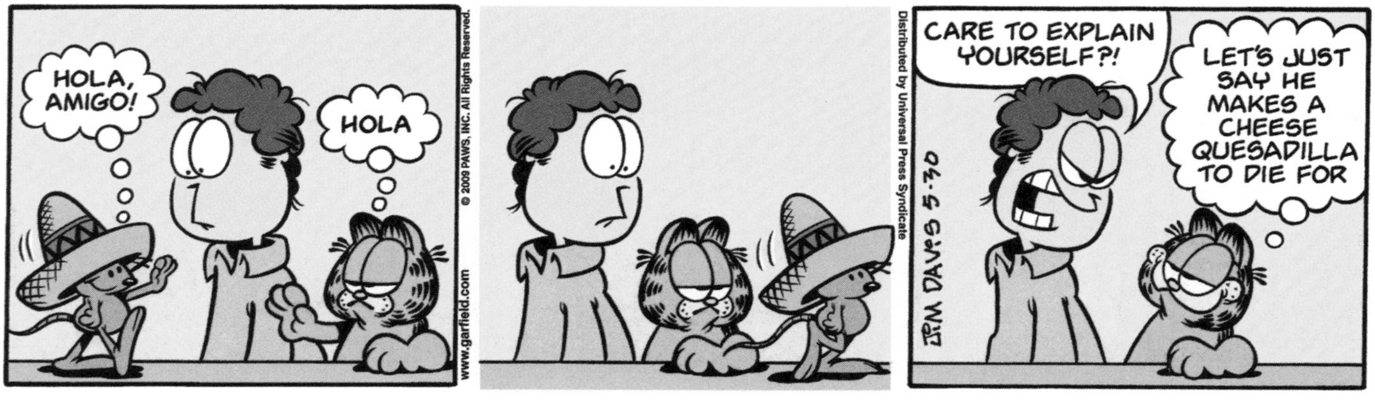
HOLA, AMIGO!
HOLA
www.garfield.com
© 2009 PAWS, INC. All Rights Reserved.
Distributed by Universal Press Syndicate
JIM DAVIS 5-30
CARE TO EXPLAIN YOURSELF?!
LET'S JUST SAY HE MAKES A CHEESE QUESADILLA TO DIE FOR

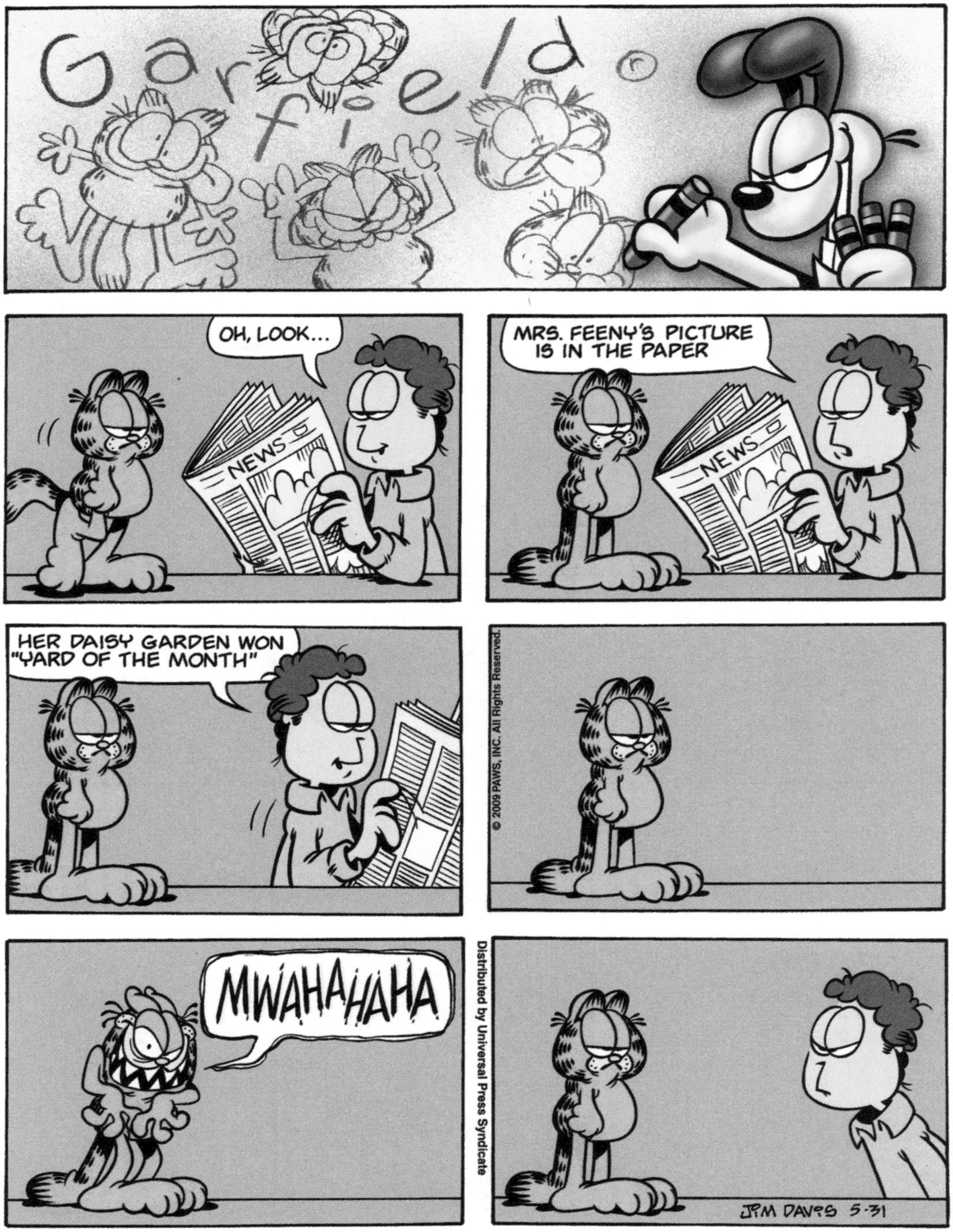
Garfield ©
OH, LOOK...
MRS. FEENY'S PICTURE IS IN THE PAPER
NEWS
HER DAISY GARDEN WON "YARD OF THE MONTH"
© 2009 PAWS, INC. All Rights Reserved.
MWAHAHAHA
Distributed by Universal Press Syndicate
JIM DAVIS 5-31

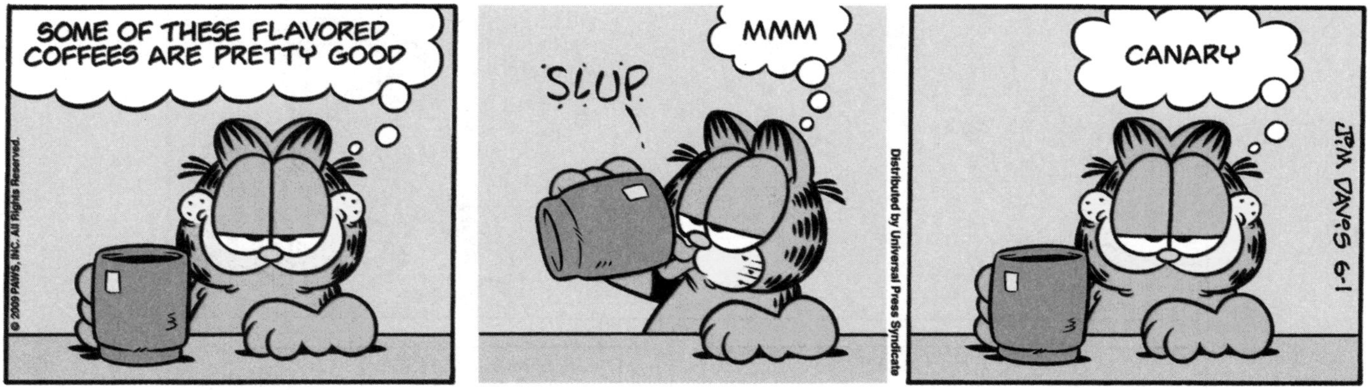
SOME OF THESE FLAVORED COFFEES ARE PRETTY GOOD
SLUP
MMM
CANARY
JIM DAVIS 6-1
© 2009 PAWS, INC. All Rights Reserved.
Distributed by Universal Press Syndicate

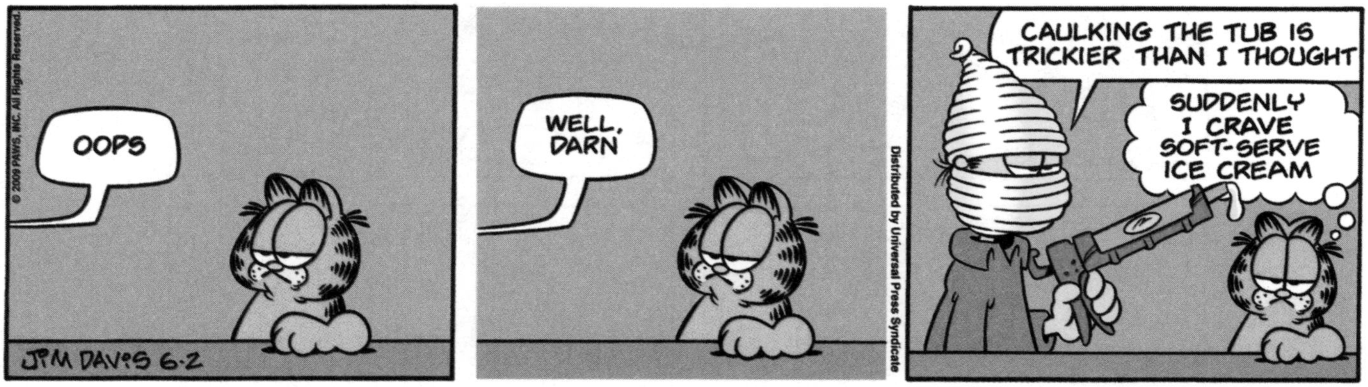
OOPS
WELL, DARN
CAULKING THE TUB IS TRICKIER THAN I THOUGHT
SUDDENLY I CRAVE SOFT-SERVE ICE CREAM
JIM DAVIS 6-2
© 2009 PAWS, INC. All Rights Reserved.
Distributed by Universal Press Syndicate

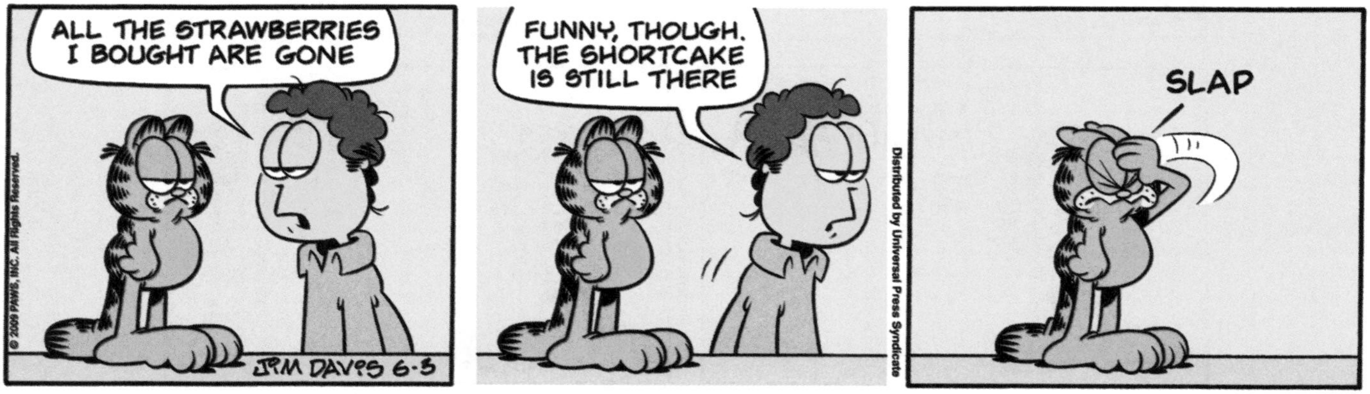
ALL THE STRAWBERRIES I BOUGHT ARE GONE
FUNNY, THOUGH. THE SHORTCAKE IS STILL THERE
SLAP
JIM DAVIS 6-3
© 2009 PAWS, INC. All Rights Reserved.
Distributed by Universal Press Syndicate

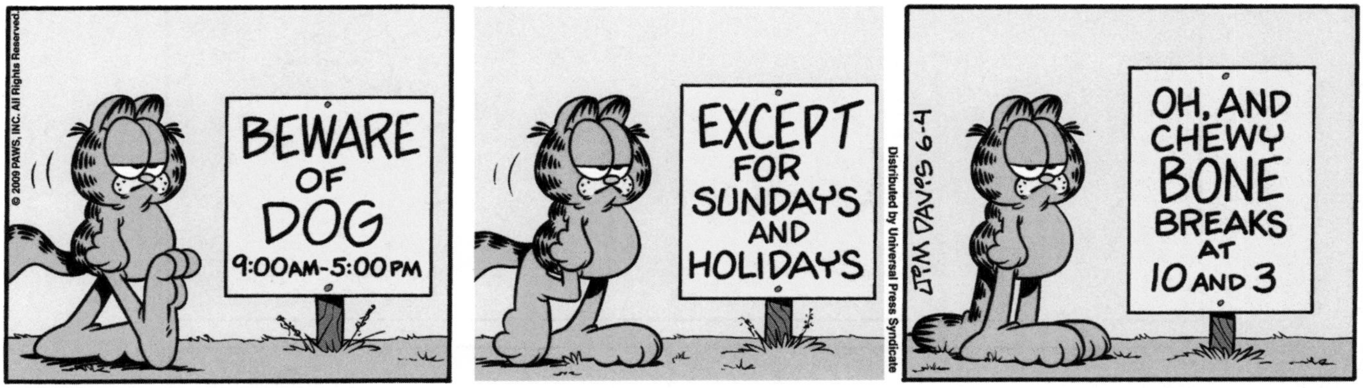
© 2009 PAWS, INC. All Rights Reserved.
BEWARE OF DOG 9:00AM-5:00PM
EXCEPT FOR SUNDAYS AND HOLIDAYS
Distributed by Universal Press Syndicate
JIM DAVIS 6-4
OH, AND CHEWY BONE BREAKS AT 10 AND 3

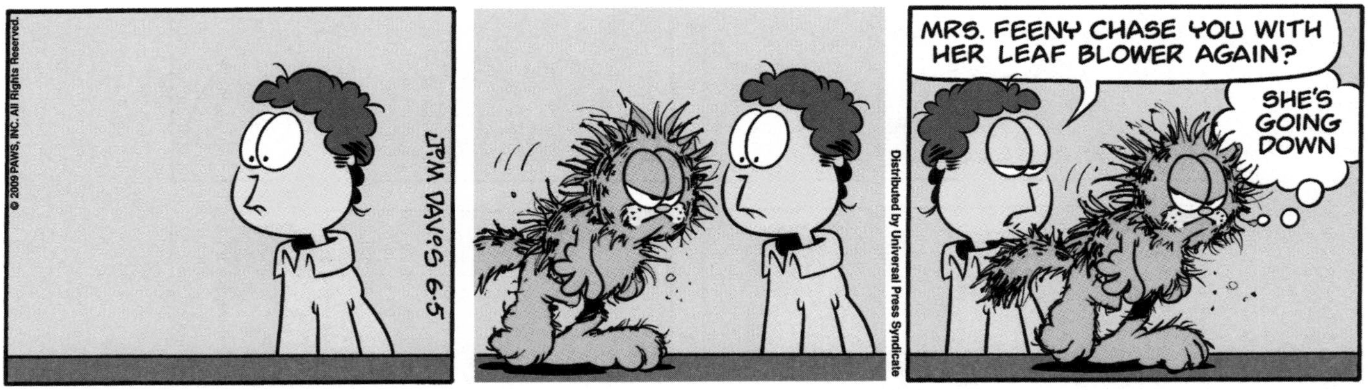
© 2009 PAWS, INC. All Rights Reserved.
JIM DAVIS 6-5
Distributed by Universal Press Syndicate
MRS. FEENY CHASE YOU WITH HER LEAF BLOWER AGAIN?
SHE'S GOING DOWN

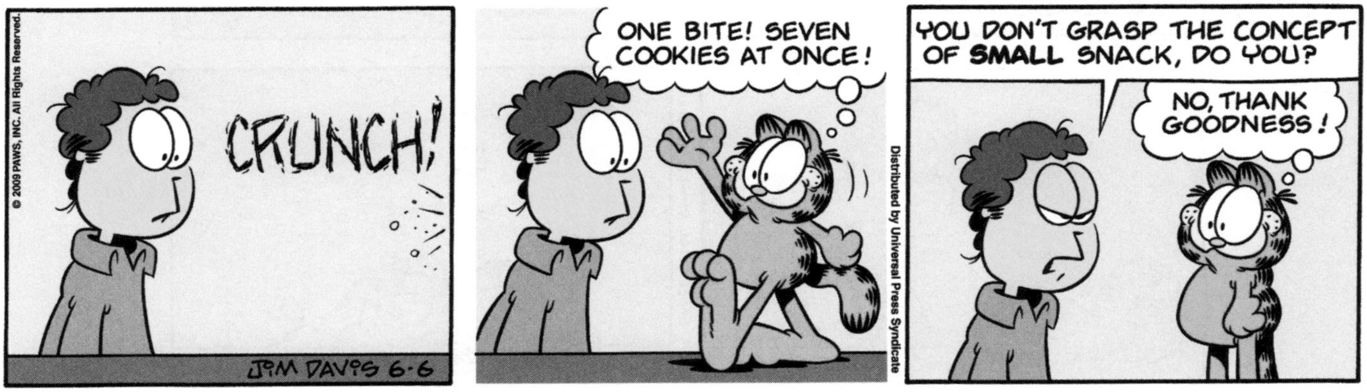
© 2009 PAWS, INC. All Rights Reserved.
CRUNCH!
JIM DAVIS 6-6
ONE BITE! SEVEN COOKIES AT ONCE!
Distributed by Universal Press Syndicate
YOU DON'T GRASP THE CONCEPT OF **SMALL** SNACK, DO YOU?
NO, THANK GOODNESS!

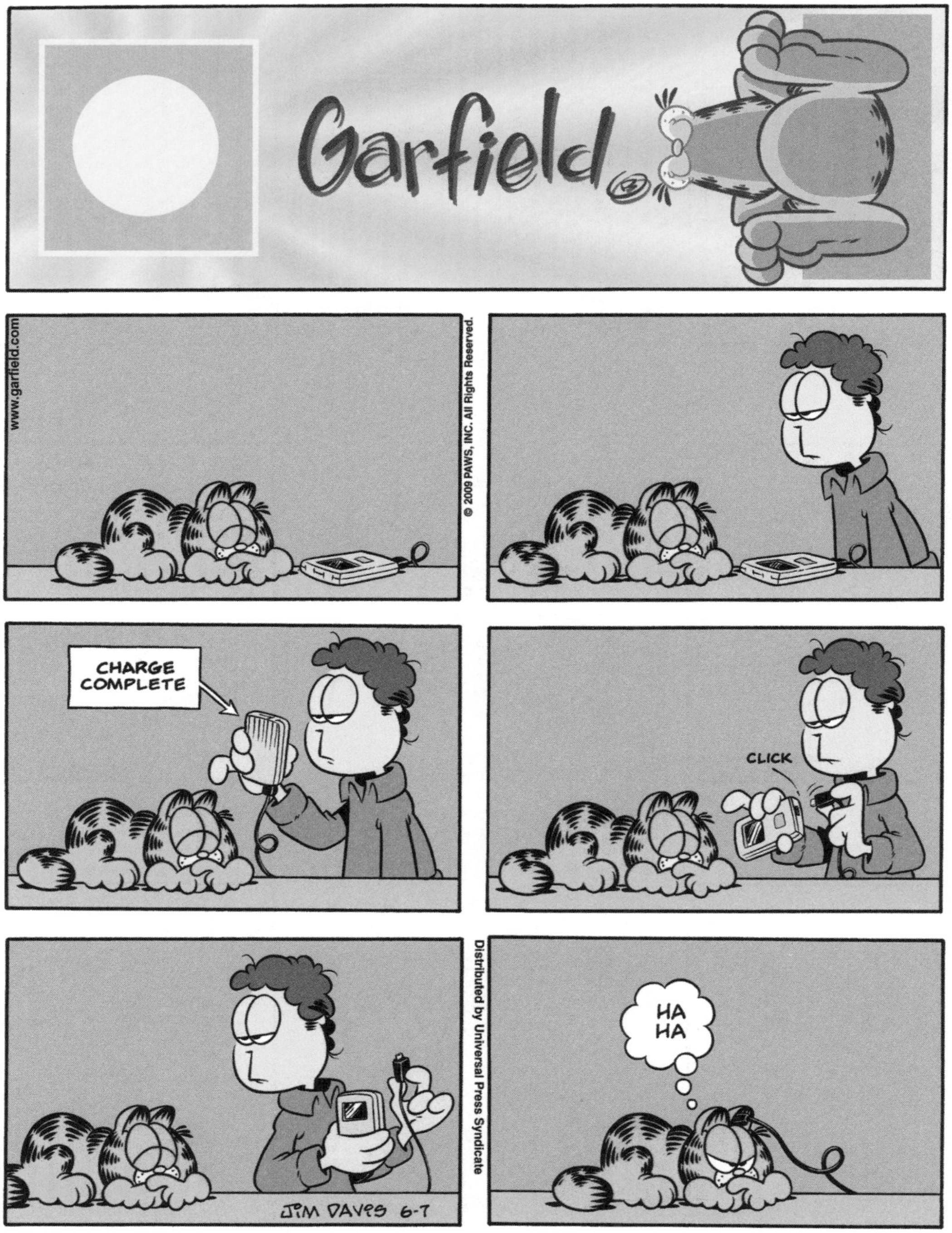
Garfield
www.garfield.com
© 2009 PAWS, INC. All Rights Reserved.
CHARGE COMPLETE
CLICK
Distributed by Universal Press Syndicate
JIM DAVIS 6-7
HA HA

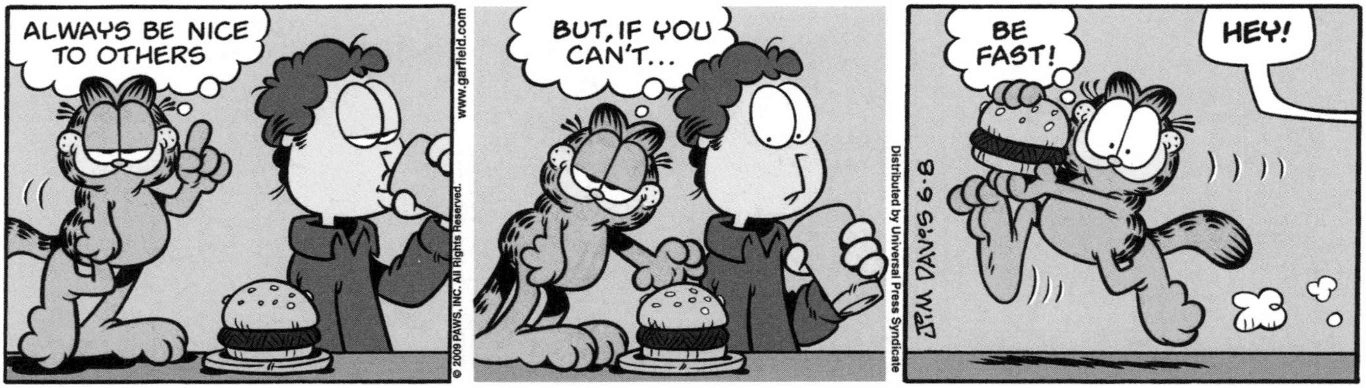
ALWAYS BE NICE TO OTHERS
© 2009 PAWS, INC. All Rights Reserved. www.garfield.com
BUT, IF YOU CAN'T...
Distributed by Universal Press Syndicate
JIM DAVIS 6-8
BE FAST!
HEY!

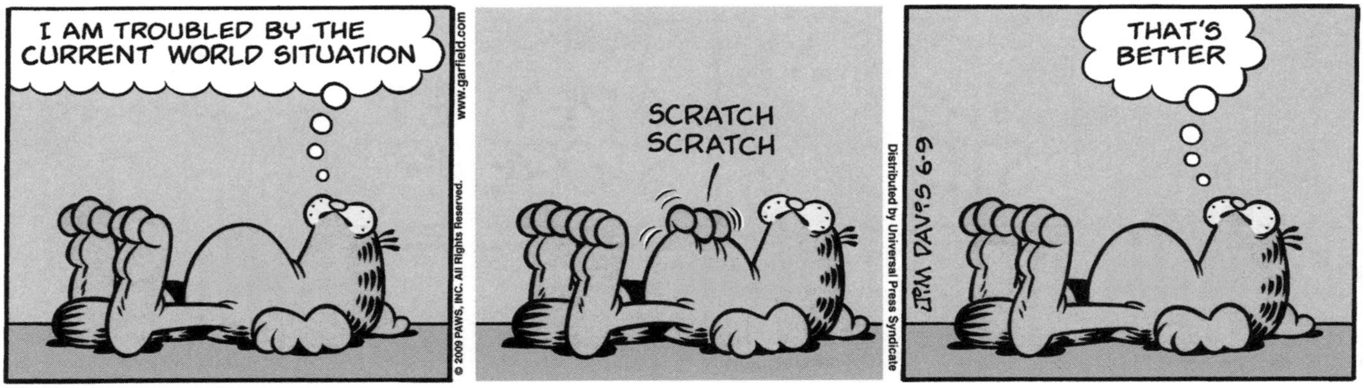
I AM TROUBLED BY THE CURRENT WORLD SITUATION
© 2009 PAWS, INC. All Rights Reserved. www.garfield.com
SCRATCH SCRATCH
Distributed by Universal Press Syndicate
JIM DAVIS 6-9
THAT'S BETTER

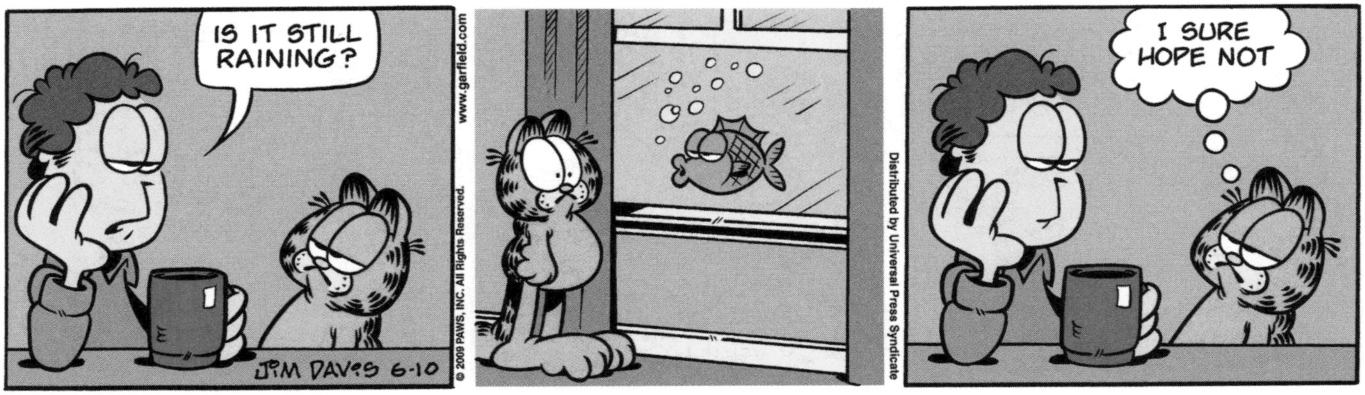
IS IT STILL RAINING?
JIM DAVIS 6-10
© 2009 PAWS, INC. All Rights Reserved. www.garfield.com
Distributed by Universal Press Syndicate
I SURE HOPE NOT

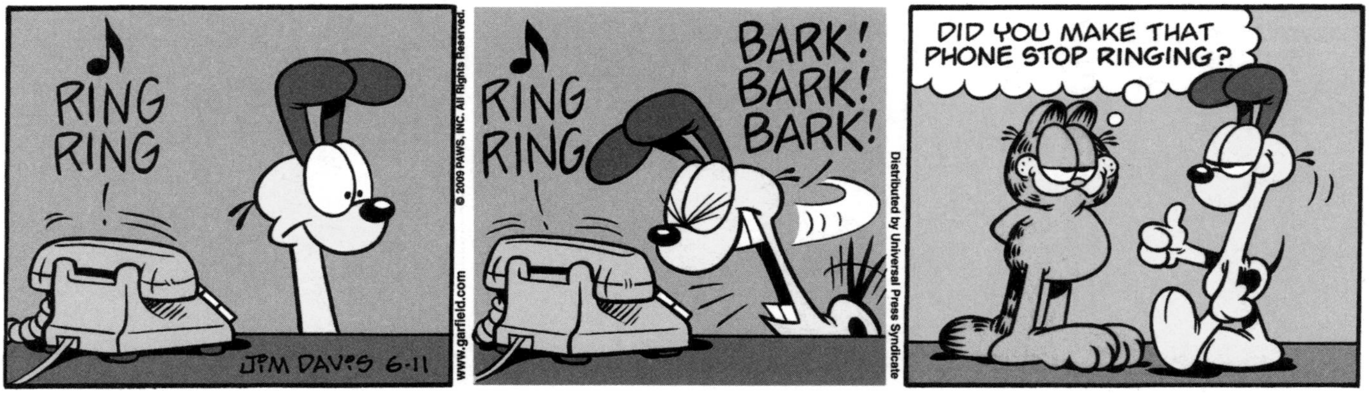
RING RING
RING RING
BARK! BARK! BARK!
DID YOU MAKE THAT PHONE STOP RINGING?
JIM DAVIS 6-11
© 2009 PAWS, INC. All Rights Reserved.
www.garfield.com
Distributed by Universal Press Syndicate

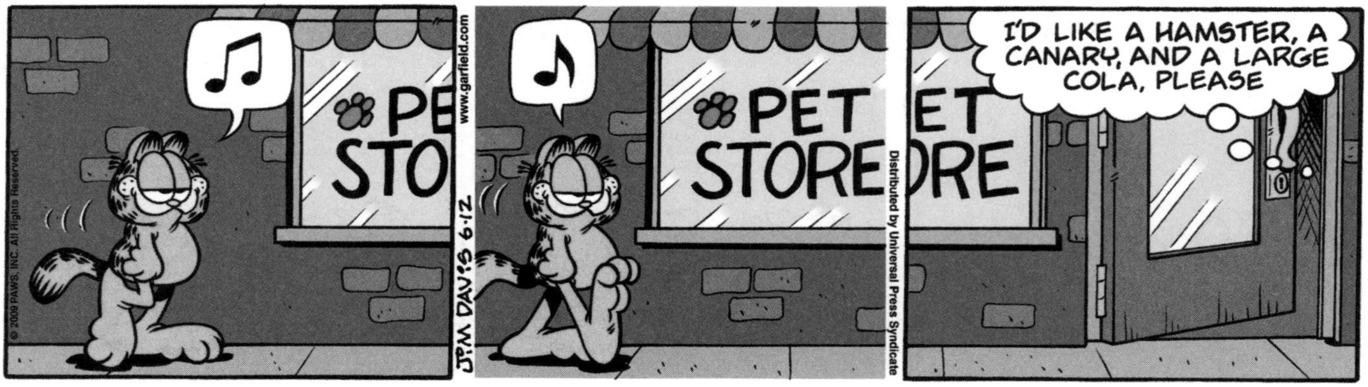
PET STORE
I'D LIKE A HAMSTER, A CANARY, AND A LARGE COLA, PLEASE
JIM DAVIS 6-12
© 2009 PAWS, INC. All Rights Reserved.
www.garfield.com
Distributed by Universal Press Syndicate

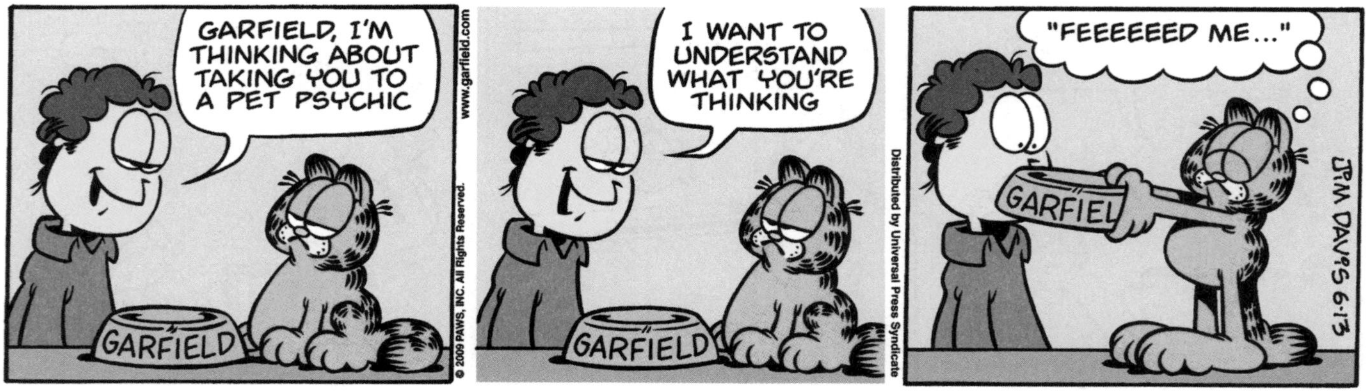
GARFIELD, I'M THINKING ABOUT TAKING YOU TO A PET PSYCHIC
GARFIELD
I WANT TO UNDERSTAND WHAT YOU'RE THINKING
GARFIELD
"FEEEEEED ME..."
GARFIEL
JIM DAVIS 6-13
© 2009 PAWS, INC. All Rights Reserved.
www.garfield.com
Distributed by Universal Press Syndicate

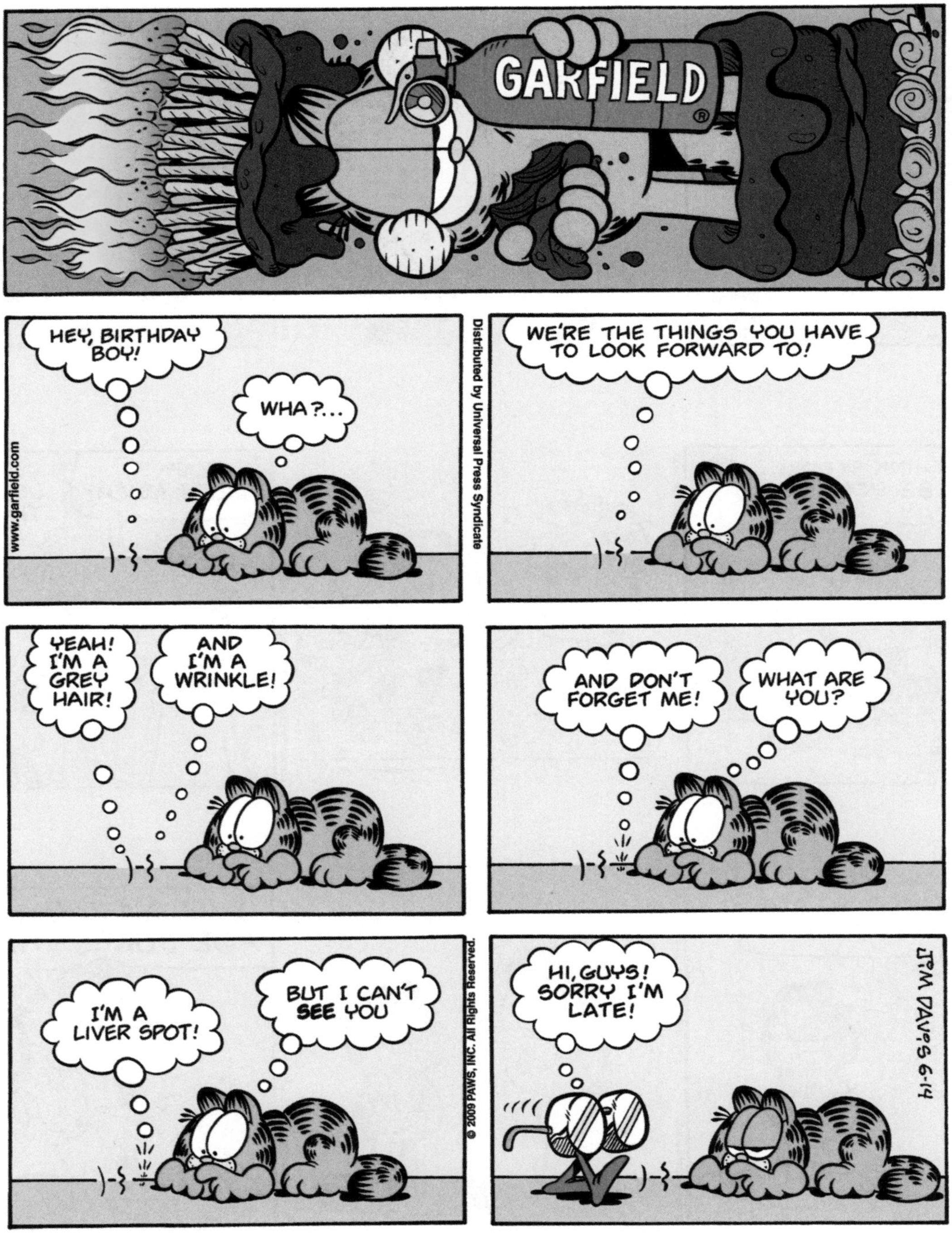

GARFIELD
HEY, BIRTHDAY BOY!
WHA?...
www.garfield.com
Distributed by Universal Press Syndicate
WE'RE THE THINGS YOU HAVE TO LOOK FORWARD TO!
YEAH! I'M A GREY HAIR!
AND I'M A WRINKLE!
AND DON'T FORGET ME!
WHAT ARE YOU?
I'M A LIVER SPOT!
BUT I CAN'T SEE YOU
© 2009 PAWS, INC. All Rights Reserved.
HI, GUYS! SORRY I'M LATE!
JIM DAVIS 6-14

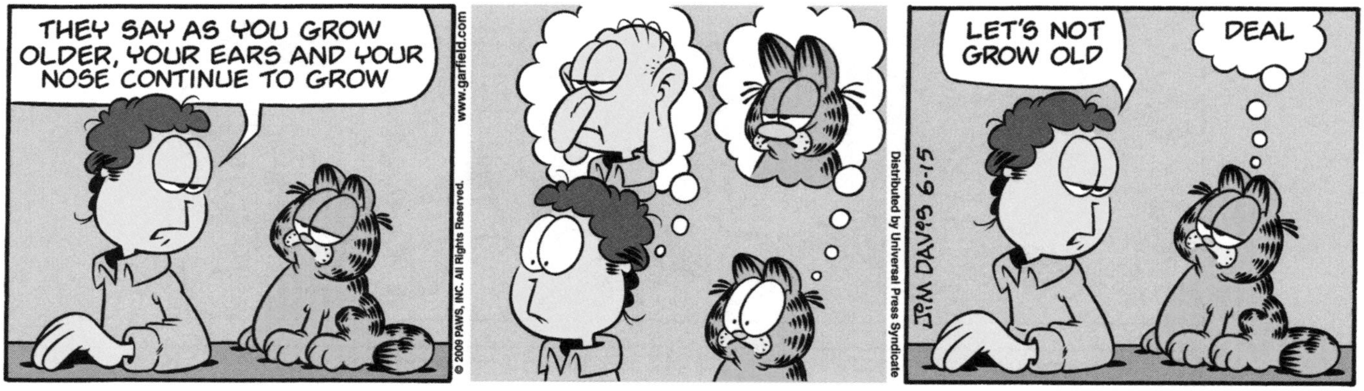
THEY SAY AS YOU GROW OLDER, YOUR EARS AND YOUR NOSE CONTINUE TO GROW
LET'S NOT GROW OLD
DEAL
JIM DAVIS 6-15
© 2009 PAWS, INC. All Rights Reserved.
www.garfield.com
Distributed by Universal Press Syndicate

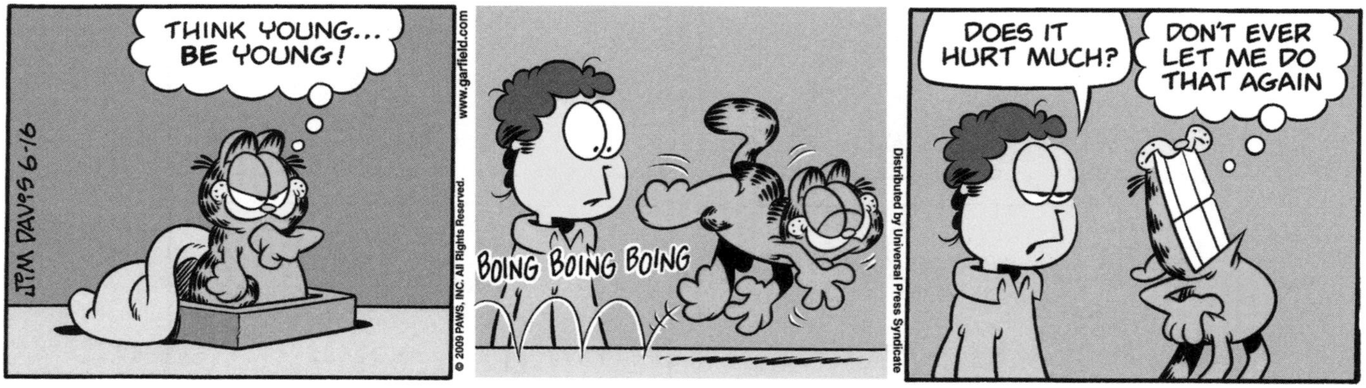
THINK YOUNG... BE YOUNG!
BOING BOING BOING
DOES IT HURT MUCH?
DON'T EVER LET ME DO THAT AGAIN
JIM DAVIS 6-16
© 2009 PAWS, INC. All Rights Reserved.
www.garfield.com
Distributed by Universal Press Syndicate

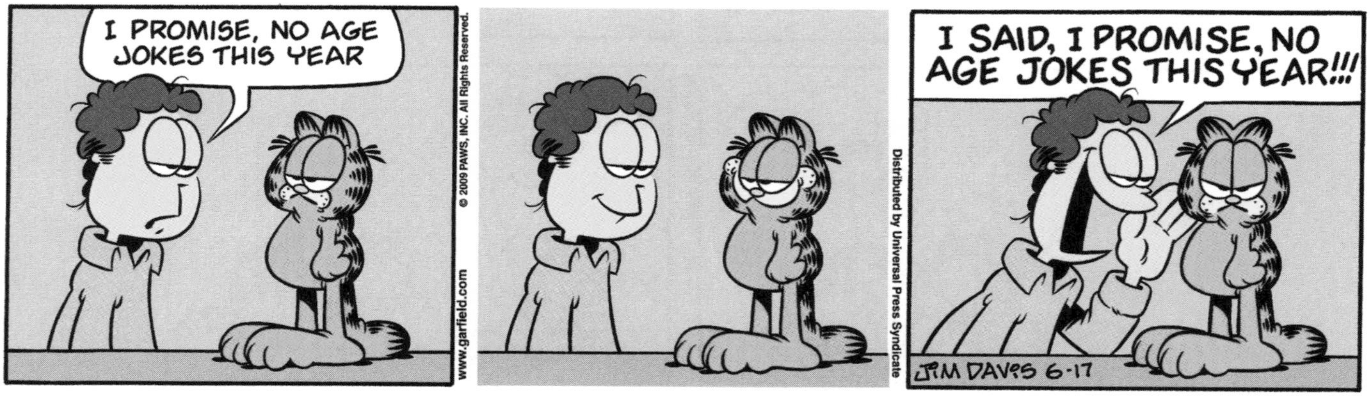
I PROMISE, NO AGE JOKES THIS YEAR
I SAID, I PROMISE, NO AGE JOKES THIS YEAR!!!
JIM DAVIS 6-17
© 2009 PAWS, INC. All Rights Reserved.
www.garfield.com
Distributed by Universal Press Syndicate

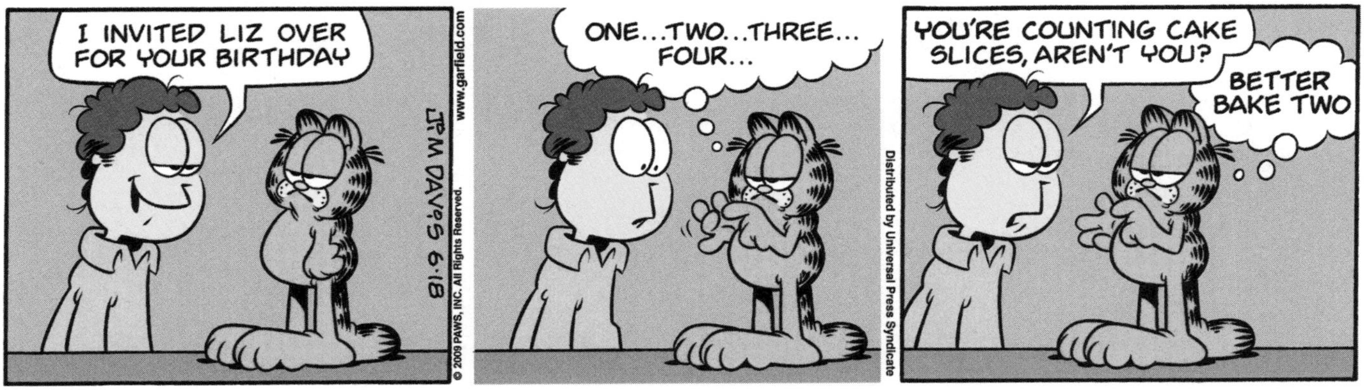
I INVITED LIZ OVER FOR YOUR BIRTHDAY
JIM DAVIS 6·18
www.garfield.com
© 2009 PAWS, INC. All Rights Reserved.
ONE...TWO...THREE... FOUR...
Distributed by Universal Press Syndicate
YOU'RE COUNTING CAKE SLICES, AREN'T YOU?
BETTER BAKE TWO

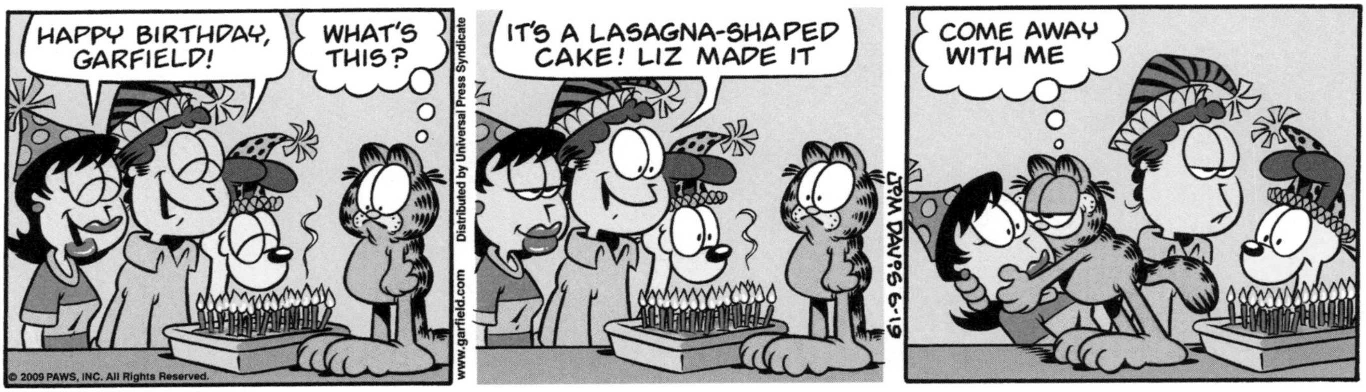
HAPPY BIRTHDAY, GARFIELD!
WHAT'S THIS?
© 2009 PAWS, INC. All Rights Reserved.
Distributed by Universal Press Syndicate
www.garfield.com
IT'S A LASAGNA-SHAPED CAKE! LIZ MADE IT
JIM DAVIS 6·19
COME AWAY WITH ME

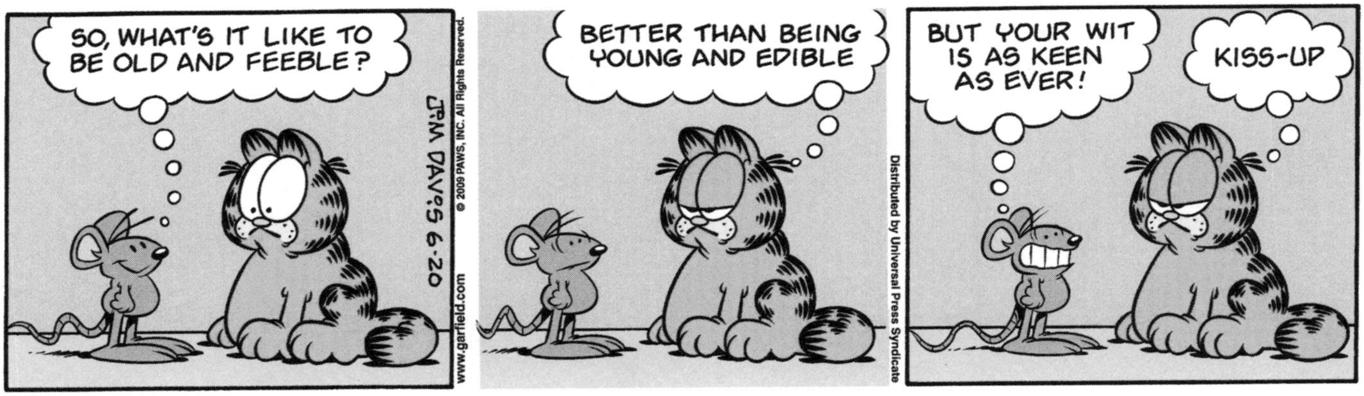
SO, WHAT'S IT LIKE TO BE OLD AND FEEBLE?
JIM DAVIS 6·20
© 2009 PAWS, INC. All Rights Reserved.
www.garfield.com
BETTER THAN BEING YOUNG AND EDIBLE
Distributed by Universal Press Syndicate
BUT YOUR WIT IS AS KEEN AS EVER!
KISS-UP

WORK ISN'T WORKING

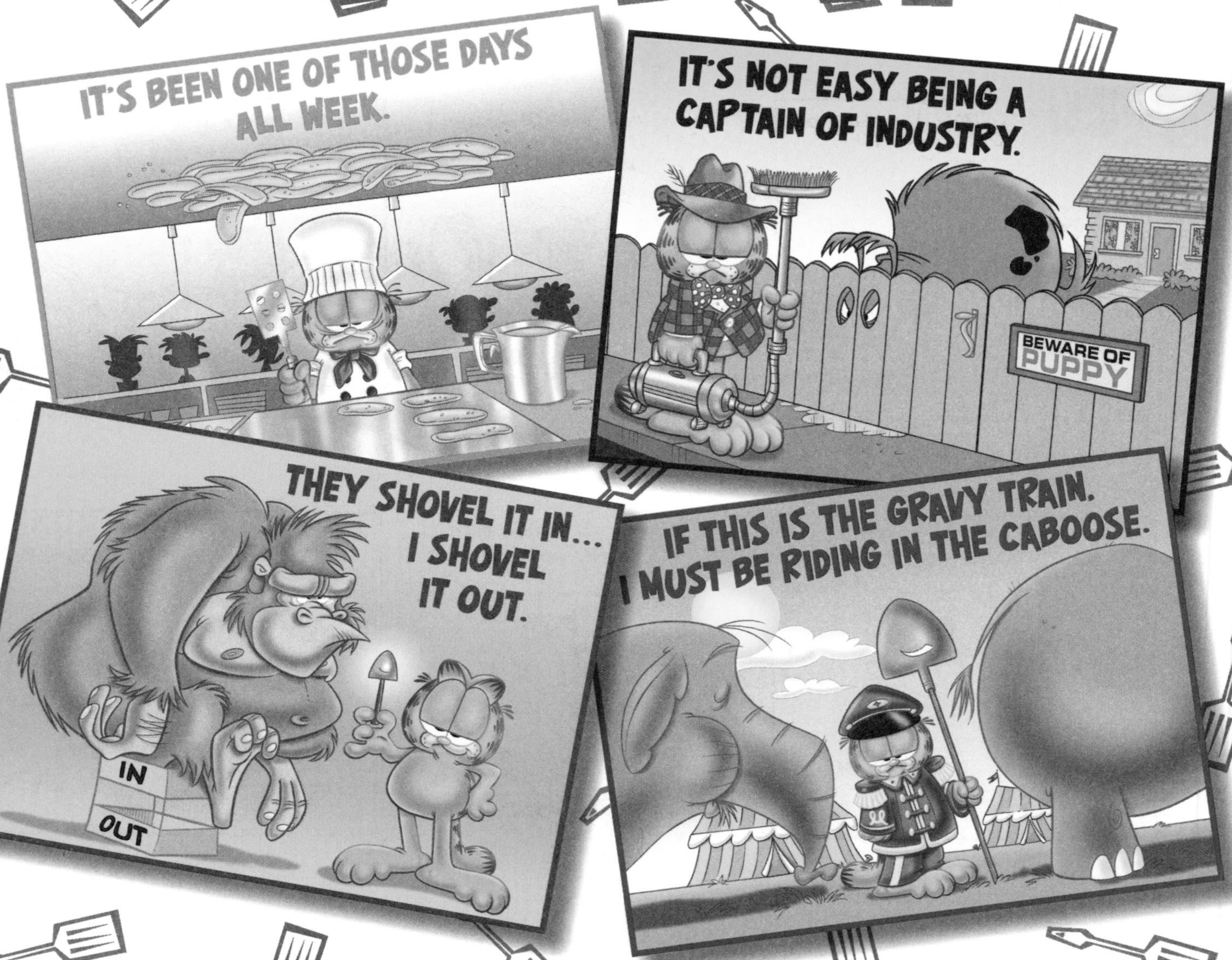
IT'S BEEN ONE OF THOSE DAYS ALL WEEK.
IT'S NOT EASY BEING A CAPTAIN OF INDUSTRY.
BEWARE OF PUPPY
THEY SHOVEL IT IN... I SHOVEL IT OUT.
IN
OUT
IF THIS IS THE GRAVY TRAIN, I MUST BE RIDING IN THE CABOOSE.

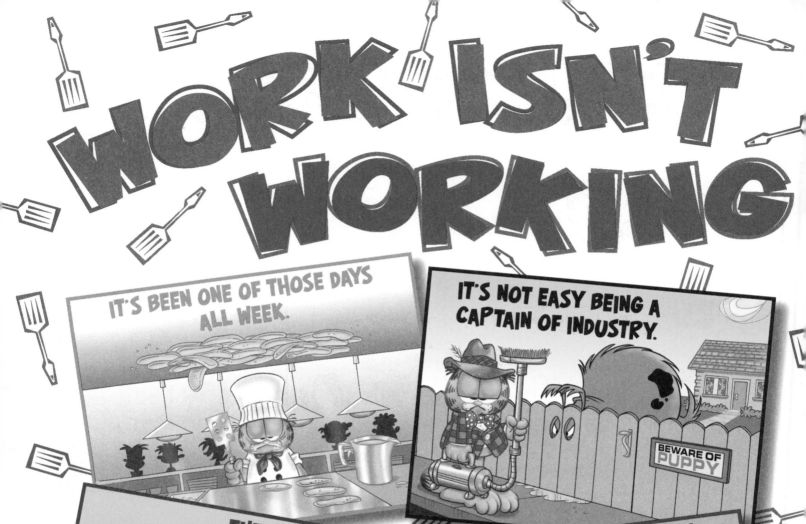

Watch. Read. Shop. Play.

DON'T FORGET THE SNACKS!

garfield.com

* **The Garfield Show**
  An all-new animated TV show on Cartoon Network!
  Watch FREE episodes online!

* **The Comic Strip**
  Search & read thousands of GARFIELD® comic strips!

* **Garfield on Facebook & Twitter**
  Read daily posts from Garfield. Share photos
  and connect with other Garfield fans!

* **Shop all the Garfield stores!**
  Original art & comic strips, books, apparel, personalized products, & more!

* **Play FREE Garfield games!**
  Plus, buy Garfield apps & games for your iPhone or iPod touch.

STRIPS, SPECIALS, OR BESTSELLING BOOKS . . .
GARFIELD'S ON EVERYONE'S MENU.

Don't miss even one episode in the Tubby Tabby's hilarious series!

DVD TIE-INS

AND DON'T MISS . . .

New larger, full-color format!